Praises for
BY THE WAY

Elgin is a man of great integrity. He is an artist and his work is unmatched by anyone. I'm honored to have him as one of my closest friends.

— Verdine White,
Bassist, Music Producer, Songwriter,
Founding Member of Earth, Wind & Fire

I have known Elgin for over 20 years and his talent, ingenuity and creativity is only surpassed by his heart and his faith. The "Emperor Of Hair" deserves all the accolades he's receiving for this book!

— Star Jones
Attorney, Best Selling Author,
Television Personality

I admire Elgin's work ethic and his integrity. He is so kind to all of his clients, always finding creative solutions to help us look and feel our best. He does all of this with a smile, and most times has us laughing our cares away. It is a passion of his and we are all the better for it.

— Chaz Ebert, Attorney, Philanthropist,
and CEO of Ebert Digital, LLC.

I had the privilege of performing with Elgin in a theatrical production. Aside from being a good hairdresser, he is an amazing actor.

— Legendary Actress, Director,
Producer, and Talk Show Host

Elgin Charles uses Southern Charm and West Coast, Beverly Hills style to creatively fashion an atmosphere of love, warmth, wonderful conversation, and fabulous hair.

— Dr. Gail Elizabeth Wyatt Ph.D,
Psychologist and Client

BY THE WAY

ELGIN CHARLES

WWW.13THANDJOAN.COM

The names and identifying characters of the individuals in this book have been changed to protect their interests and privacy. In some cases, composite characters have been created to preserve the integrity of the story. The ultimate goal is to navigate the reader through the series of events without inflicting harm or ill will towards the privacy of others, while maintaining the integrity and factual account of the story.

13th & Joan books may be purchased for educational, business or sales promotional use. For information, please email the Sales Department at sales@13thandjoan.com.

Printed in the U.S. A.
First Printing, April 2018
Library of Congress Cataloging-in-Publication Data has been applied for.
ISBN 978-0-9989702-2-6

DEDICATION

DEDICATED TO MY brilliant business manager, creative consultant, and most importantly, one of my dearest friends, Christopher J. Broughton. Were it not for your tireless efforts, words of encouragement, and years of unwavering friendship and support, this book would not have been possible, as I likely would have never mustered up the courage to write it.

You can wait your whole life for what could have been, or you could simply live life right now, in this moment, with your hair blowing in the wind.

—Elgin Charles

FOREWORD

THE FIRST WORD that comes to mind when I think of my friend Elgin Charles is legend. Over the more than thirty years that I have known him, I have watched him ascend from an African American hair stylist, working hard to establish himself in Los Angeles, to the Emperor of Hair. He is beloved by top Hollywood celebrities and society doyennes, revered by hair stylists across the country, has starred in his own reality television series, and was ensconced for many years in his fashionable and pioneering namesake salon in Beverly Hills. But while these accomplishments certainly make Elgin a great success, they do not, in and of themselves, give him legendary status. For me, the latter is derived from the true essence of the person.

It has been my privilege to know and work with many legends during my career as a film and television producer in Hollywood. I do not use the term legend lightly because I believe that such individuals are truly special. They are people who have great talent, who inspire others, and from whom we all can learn life lessons. While their accomplishments span the spectrum of human endeavors, they all share some very basic and beautiful qualities—Elgin is no exception.

Legends have vision. They are able to truly understand themselves and their gifts and abilities and thereby see themselves realizing their full potential. They are not constrained or deterred by external limitations that circumstances, other people, or society may seek to place upon the realization of that potential. In other words, they dream big.

Legends have faith. To realize the true vision of yourself, you have to believe in yourself. Such confidence is almost always supported by a belief—whether derived from a specific religion or the recognition of a universal spirit—that there is a power greater than you that will guide and protect you on your journey to accomplishment.

Legends have courage. Great success does not happen without taking great risk, and you must have courage to take such risks. You have to often face seemingly insurmountable mountains, armed with only the strength of your convictions and have the courage to undertake the climb, knowing that you may fail. And perhaps most importantly, on those occasions when you do fail, which are an inevitable part of success and life, you have to possess the determination to not only pick yourself up and try again, but to allow yourself to learn the valuable lessons to be gleaned from your mistakes.

Finally, legends have humility. They understand that great achievement does not happen without the support and encouragement of others. Therefore, they know that it is their duty to be generous with their spirit and wisdom, to have respect for all people who are of good intent, to be an inspiration to other people to dare to dream big, and to nurture and help other talented individuals on their journeys to realize those dreams.

As you read further and learn about the remarkable life journey of Elgin Charles, you will come to understand why I believe that by definition he is truly a legend and why I am so very happy to have him as a friend.

—Debra Martin Chase

PREFACE

Bound, Broken, and Wrapped in Chains

"To be honest in your deed, is to be righteous."
— Elgin Charles

To LIVE A RIGHTEOUS life is among my heart's greatest desires. There was a time when I longed for the days that I could present myself to the world and show thyself approved. A proclamation such as this is the ultimate submission to vulnerability. Over the years, I have learned that the unfiltered truth can lead to disapproval and rejection from the world around you. And while he who has discovered that to walk in their truth unapologetically, discovers power—the essence of who we are and who we become is forever bound in notions of acceptance. Like many, the threat of not being accepted, forced me to wear an invisible mask for much of my life.

It is my belief that we all wear an invisible mask that the world knows nothing of. I call it "Power." If it were not for this mask, we would run the risk of being exposed to the masses. The mask that I speak of shields, covers, hides, and shelters us from dangers seen and unseen. Power is the face that we decide to show the world. It is that of who we desire to be and the fullness of what we believe matters most to others. The face of power has the ability to allow us to fly under the radar and to blend in with the elements that remove the danger of scrutiny. Power gives us permission to be pleasing in the eyes of others, shielding our greatest pain. The mask of power does not allow for transparency; it cannot thrive there and it is not worthy there.

Lo and behold, just beneath the surface, lies the mask of truth. I call it "Weakness." The mask of weakness shields the true and purest versions of ourselves from the storms of life. Our survival is found in this space. The mask of weakness allows us to exist, unscathed from the world's perception of who we truly are. Our scars live dormant here. The risk of exposure of the mask of weakness poses a threat to existence as we know it. Those who are unwilling or are unable to subject themselves to public scrutiny, only allow the mask of weakness to make appearances during quiet moments in order to relinquish pain. The mask of weakness hurts like hell and fuels our fears. It shows up unexpectedly in the presence of our greatest trials and tribulations. The mask of weakness can be described as a sweet dream or a beautiful nightmare.

Our ability to wear these masks is a resounding proclamation and testament to the alter ego that we each possess. We all have an alter ego that the world knows nothing about. It preserves the depths of our souls that sometimes even we would rather not see.

The mask of my alter ego has forced me to cast a part of myself into a sea of forgetfulness for many years and for so many reasons. The agony of doing so has at times brought me to my knees in humility. The journey, composed of steps into a land of untruth, is a dead end. Nothing lives or grows there. There can be no evolution in that space.

The pressure from the weight of the mask atop my face has made it difficult for me to breathe. The burden of the mask has compromised the quality in my ability to hope, dream, and pursue. The internal battle that has ensued over the years has, on occasion, crushed my spirit; but still, like a Phoenix, I rise. The torment I have lived through, in the presence of my alter ego, could be a book in and of itself.

For me, that acceptance that I so greatly desired from the world, has come at the expense of the fullness of my truth. Like so many, I've lived my life in secrecy. I was unwilling to walk in truth for many reasons; the most prevalent among them was the prospect of being denied acceptance. Today, I ponder what acceptance it is that we truly seek. Is there an imaginary line that we are granted permission to cross amidst being approved? Is there a secret elite society that we receive more abundance from if we are acceptable in the eyes of others? The need to be accepted has held me captive in ways unimaginable.

I was threatened by the fear of my truth and what it would allow the world to make of me. I inherited the notion of going to the grave with my deepest secrets and the perseverance of the ideology that my parents often referred to as "Letting sleeping dogs lie." Albeit, I have determined that the weight of untruth is unequivocal bondage. The weight of my truth was like a noose around my neck and heavy laden on my heart. In full transparency, a defining moment in my life forced me to recognize that not walking in the fullness of my truth had the power to suffocate me until I took my last breath.

And as the cycle of life unfolds, we will all be faced with moments that take our breath away and those that change the trajectory of the choices we make when we arrive at the forks in the road of our journeys. The passing of my father was mine. When he gained his wings into heaven, I recognized that the wisdom he imparted within me would now allow me to discover a pair of my own. The single act of telling my story is equivalent to taking flight in so many ways.

I had been unwilling to come forward with the truest sentiments of my heart prior to my father's passing because I didn't want to hurt him. I longed for his acceptance. I longed to make him proud and for him to see that I was a reflection of all that he was. He lived his life according to the scriptures of the Bible, and for so long, I questioned if I had been the total opposite. His passing broke the weakest link of my chains and confirmed that the wings that he had given me were given unto me that I might soar. Soaring for me also means giving all of who I am to the world. My commitment forced me to do so, with vigor and the fullness of my whole heart.

And even though I have relinquished the need for acceptance, I must admit that in my quiet moments, the act of peeling back the layers to tell my story has caused me to consider what the world will make of me. The act of telling my story represents an act of great sacrifice. The quest to walk in and discover the truth has forced me to dig into some of the deepest pockets of my heart, to restore memories of hurt and pain that I had buried. It has allowed me to see the stars amidst the darkest nights of my life. The trials and tribulations are often too traumatic to allow them to take up space in the cache of our memories, but my greatest discovery was the poetic justice of it all. For every pain, joy prevails. The silver lining is ever present if we choose to wear the rose-colored glasses that reveal the rainbows, which appear after the rain. My greatest joy is knowing that life is worth living for so many reasons. I've learned that God will dip his brush into our deep wounds and ugliest scars and paint a masterpiece. It is with admiration and appreciation of His holy work in me that I walk boldly into the sunset of my story. In these moments of truth, I have decided to blaze the trails of righteousness that you might discover the embers in the fire to blaze your own. I am no longer bound, broken, and wrapped in chains. I am free.

—Elgin Charles

ACKNOWLEDGEMENTS

TREMENDOUS THANKS to all of my family for your unwavering love and support. There are far too many of you for me to name individually, but, to my son, Frank, my precious grandson, Kydyn, my aunts, Uncle Albert, my nieces & nephews, and all of my wonderful cousins, I love you more than you could ever fully process.

Thank you to my very best friend, LeVester Cornelius aka my 'brother from another mother,' your loyalty and friendship has held me through the decades.

To Christopher Wesson, your benevolence and ardent support of all things *Elgin Charles* is greatly appreciated.

To every client and staffer who has ever crossed my threshold, my success is directly tied to all of you. Thank you so very much.

To my *industry mother,* Diahann Carroll, your love, guidance, and sage advice has helped me navigate the crazy world of Hollywood and life in general. You are a priceless jewel. I love you endlessly.

To Vidal Sassoon, Michael Jackson, Prince, Magic Johnson, Oprah Winfrey, Michael Jordan, Barack Obama, and The Avant Family, you have served as beacons of light to millions of people around the globe, including yours truly. I have been gifted with the distinct honor of not only being able to consider you sources of inspiration, but to also consider you my friends.

To ABC, BET, Bravo, CBS, E!, FOX, HBO, Oxygen, Style Network, VH1, Chris Rock, and Wendy Williams, you provided platforms for me to be seen by global audiences, and for that, I am eternally grateful.

To 13th & Joan Publishing, and CEO, Ardre Orie, your commitment to excellence in service, seamless attention to detail, professionalism, and your loyalty to the art of storytelling far surpassed my expectation. I would not have wanted to entrust the production of my literary efforts in the hands of any other team of professionals. Simply stated, I thank you with my heart.

To my creative team, Dwight Jenkins, Bobby Quillard, Sebastian, DaRico Jackson, Marc Littlejohn, Lacresia Marcus, Curtis Sabir, and the uber fabulous Philip Brown, Jr., your masterful work provided an aesthetic backdrop that beautifully compliments my words. You are truly the best in the biz!

To Carol Gillie, Lori Myers, Gianna Drake, Kim Gregory, Faye McClure, Bettye Dixon, Spruce Storgaard, Anita Hansen, Barbara Rudd, Val Carnes, Barbara Kohler, Dee Horne, Winona Parks, Brenda Andrews, Felicia Wesley, Christie Maddox, Kevin Spicer, Pat Miller, Joyce Corrigan, Ro Rochester, Cookie Johnson, Star Jones, Holly Robinson-Peete, Jackée Harry, Gayle King, Anita Baker, Debra Lee, Yvette Nicole Brown, Regina King, Marla Gibbs, Tifphanie Griffith, Sean Cameron, Lolita Goods, Katrina Atkinson, Chaz Ebert, Lela Rochon-Fuqua, Gelila Assefa Puck, Dr. Gail E. Wyatt, Verdine White, LaTanya Richardson Jackson, Angela Bassett, Natalie Cole, Roxie Roker, Jenifer Lewis, Sheryl Lee Ralph, Joy Behar, Meredith Viera, Clifton Davis, Elgin Baylor, Bobby Womack, Billy Dee Williams, Beverly Todd, Hattie Winston, Anna Maria Horsford, Rolonda Watts, Serena Williams, Keri Hilson, Teena Marie, Mo'Nique, Samuel L. Jackson, Denzel Washington, Pauletta Washington, Vivica A. Fox, Tatyana Ali, Tanika Ray, Megan Good, Adrienne-Joi Johnson, Maynard Matthews, Maisha Oliver, Tara Love, Joan Collins, Vanessa Williams, Tonya Hart, Janet Zeitoun, Nicki Minaj, RuPaul, Donna Taylor, Shirlina Allen, Debbie Pierce, Stella Davis, Paris Vaughn, Nene Leakes, Tami Roman, Shaunie O'Neal, Doris Mosby, Lafaye Davenport, Karen Faye, Dawn Joi, Oscar James, Damone Roberts, Sam Fine, Ken Barboza, Alakazia, Brenda Richie, Denise Nicolas, Denise Williams, Elaine Boozler, Luenell Campbell, Tisha Campbell, Tichina Arnold, Martin Lawrence, Emmitt & Pat Smith, Regina Torres, Darnell Threets, Robin Givens, Chaka Khan, Ken Reynolds, Whitney Houston, Diana Ross, and Nancy Wilson you will always hold a special place in my heart.

INTRODUCTION

POWER, PASSION, PURPOSE

"We have been formed with God's hands and are, therefore, called to walk in the power and fullness of purpose."
—Elgin Charles

GOD OPENED UP the doors for me to come forth. He
put me in front of people for a reason.

Today, more than ever, we all need something to believe. We
need messages that encourage us to be who we are without apology.
We need to be reminded that freedom is ours for the taking. So
many of us, suffer in isolation, believing that we are the only ones
experiencing a given trial or tribulation. We often feel as though
we are alone. I've often wondered why God has always seemed to
isolate me in so many instances of my life. Was I meant to discover life alone?

When you've been called to do a thing, God will place you
amidst quiet moments, simply so that you can hear. Writing this
book is the greatest acknowledgment of the fact that I have heard
the calling of my life, loud and clear.

Today, I recognize now more than ever that there are elements
in my story that prove that you are not alone. There are truths that

had been kept secret that are healing for your soul. At times, I wished that someone had done the same for me. My life, and this book are a living testament to the fact that none of us are meant to live life alone and that each of us is purposed to tell our stories that they might empower the next person.

If we all took the time to imagine how many people are hurting for so many reasons, we would be flabbergasted. I've long pondered the tremendous hurt that floods the beautiful souls of the world rooted in people feeling like they cannot be themselves. It pains me to no end. I know this feeling all too well. We deserve better. We deserved to know that we must first accept ourselves before placing such high demands on others to do so. We must feel comfortable in our own skin before succumbing to the, sometimes harsh, notions of others.

I've appeared on TV, was married to a Hollywood starlet, and I've been at the pinnacle of the hair and beauty industry for well over three decades. My face is recognizable, and I've commanded the attention of many on some of the largest stages in the world. With all of that, I've often wondered if there was ever any one person in the world who has actually known me, Elgin Charles. I wonder if there has ever been anyone who has known the true motives of my heart? The most abundant revelation among these truths is that up until this point, I had never felt free. And although I've searched within myself for answers, there was one solution, looming in the distance. I will always hear my mother's voice, with a resounding conviction, imploring "the truth shall set you free." Today, I desire to walk in unprecedented freedom and peace, I see no other way to live my life. My normal is for me to decide and I proudly proclaim that yours is too. End of story.

TABLE OF CONTENTS

PROLOGUE

MASK ON

AS I STOOD PEERING out of the window of my Beverly Hills Salon, I could not help but reminisce over the memories of the years of hearty laughter. I could see every face that had ever sat in my chair. I could see the face of every stylist that I had ever given an opportunity to chase their dreams. I could see all of the faces that had come through the door, in search of knowledge and a chance to create a better life for themselves. Among the things that I am most proud of, the fact that I never turned anyone away in business or in life ranks near the top. Throughout my life, the presence of the sentiment of abandonment had rung so loudly in my ears that I never wanted to be responsible for producing that sound in another soul. I can now rest in the fullness of the fact that I have held true that.

I knew from a very young age that I would build a place great enough to be filled by many, and that I would stand at the entrance with my arms outstretched, welcoming those in need. This image became the backdrop for my life. And no matter how much freedom I created for others, I had never quite seemed to crack the code on how to create it for myself. The bustling salon, overlooking Rodeo

Drive was a constant reminder. The name Elgin Charles on the front reminded me of self-imposed bondage in many ways. It was my most astounding gift and curse.

In the story of my life, freedom is a peculiar phenom. I've often wondered if I was ever really free. Are any of us? For so long, I was trapped in a series of closets with doors that seemingly led to other doors, but never an exit. I've been aimlessly in search of freedom for so long that my definition of it is far too skewed for reality. Today, I question what freedom is, and how our access to it defines who we are or what we become. And maybe that's just it. Maybe, life maintains an invisible barbed wire fence around us, to help us turn to God, when we approach lines that should not be crossed. Maybe we aren't supposed to roam the Earth without feeling the consequences of our actions. Maybe we aren't supposed to be so wild and free that we believe that we are actually in control.

The freedom came with the discovery of the fact that for too many years, I had worn a veil of happiness that never really belonged to me. It was a borrowed remnant of the life I thought I wanted, until recently. The freedom that we never knew existed, rests on the discovery of the fact that you survived. The freedom rests in the fact that what was meant to break you, only made you stronger. The fact that I've lived to tell the story deserves a mutherfuckin round of applause. I mean it. Stand to your feet ladies and gentleman and clap for these series of events that I romanticize as my life, I now share unto you.

CHAPTER 1

Young, Dumb, and Well, You Know the Rest

"There are times that we discover who we think the world wants us to be, and there are times that we discover who we truly are."

—Elgin Charles

I ARRIVED IN THE City of Angels at the age of twenty-one, driving a two door, powder blue Mercury, with rectangular lights on the front. My father had purchased the car, brand new off the lot for me and told me that the upkeep, maintenance, and payments, all belonged to me. Prior to my leaving my hometown of San Antonio, Texas, he had made it crystal clear that I was now responsible for myself and that was exactly what I intended to be.

Nestled in the car with me were my Aunt Nilene and three of my cousins. I had agreed to drive them back to Los Angeles from San Antonio, as I knew that it was a justified way for me to get out of that town. I wanted nothing more than to leave San Antonio, it had been suffocating the life out of me. We had been driving a straight stretch for hours on end, but even if the signs hadn't said so, I knew that we had reached Los Angeles because the traffic was just as I had imagined it to be. Cars were stacked like dominoes, one in front of the other and the mix of haze and residue from car exhaust made the visions of the palm trees blurry. I had never seen traffic like that back in San Antonio. I remember sitting in grid-lock and thinking to myself, "Where are all of these people going?"

We had taken the I-10 West for the entire trip and I was in search of the Arlington exit. Arlington was right before Crenshaw, which many who lived there had affectionately named "The Shaw." If you made a left, you would venture further south into South Central. If you went north, you would venture towards Baldwin Hills, where more of the well to do blacks resided. I didn't care who lived where, the city was just so beautiful to me. The palm trees and looming sun represented the freedom that I so desper-ately needed to become acquainted with.

I was more than ready for a change of scenery from the rural opulence of San Antonio, Texas. If I hadn't left when I did, I believe San Antonio would have eventually swallowed me whole. In full transparency, I was just like any other twenty-one-year-old who was ready for the adventures of an adult life, with a little more fire beneath my wings. To say that I was young, dumb, and fearless would have been a grave understatement. I was in search of con-quests both personally and professionally. Lust was all over me.

Back in San Antonio, on many occasions, my appetite was fed with small bites from girls that I had dated, but nothing had ever come from any of the encounters; at least nothing promis-ing enough for me to consider the continuation of a relationship amidst the pursuit of my dreams. The truth is that even after eating a hearty plate, you can still find yourself hungry a short time later. My wonder years had left me unsatisfied. And let me tell you, I was still hungry.

Even though, my appetite for pleasure was ferocious, it would eventually pale in comparison to the dreams that I would relentlessly chase towards my destiny. All I knew was that I wanted to see my name in the Los Angeles lights! I could feel a calling on my life to be and do more, but I knew that if I didn't venture out, I would never get to the promised land, wherever that might be. I was determined to do everything possible for it to manifest. Los Angeles had my name written all over it. I figured that there was enough food there to satisfy any craving or appetite that I desired.

Albeit, I would not have cared if I had to sit on that highway for another hour, with no motion. What I knew in my heart was that Los Angeles was a far cry from all that I had known, and I was hell bent on coming for everything that I believed that life owed me. I was there to chase my dreams, let my hair down, and most importantly, discover myself.

Growing up, I always felt like I was on an island by myself. I was different in so many ways. I felt that my morals didn't always align with those around me. I had a need and a desire to help others, much to a fault. I was a deeply caring and feeling creature, and many times, I wore my emotions on my sleeve, but I was okay with that. I just never wanted to see anyone hurt.

I enjoyed the same past times as all of the other kids my age. I was athletic and wildly popular in school. I had the kind of personality that allowed me to get along with everyone. All of my teachers in school thought highly of me and showed me favor, and I was my mother's prized possession. The irony of it all, is that even with all of the winning attributes that guided my life, I somehow always felt a little lost. I always felt like I didn't belong or that I was in search of something within myself that the world knew nothing about. Now, much older and much wiser, I understand that we are all in search of something from the world that can only come from within but life must be experienced to attain the fullness of that notion.

For many years, I couldn't understand what led me to feel so different, but as I grew older and adolescence presented itself, I realized that my feelings were the direct result of my search for purpose and a sense of self. I felt like my desires and intrinsic motivations were even different. Eventually, this led to the discovery that perhaps even my sexual preferences were different. The more different I felt, the more effort I put into feeling normal. My father was such a straight-laced man that my desiring anything other than a woman was not up for discussion. I remained silent to that end. My silence led me into a lifetime of hiding the fullness of who I was. Even though it was hidden, there was still something inside of me that needed to connect with something, anything familiar. I would read books, peruse magazines, and watch movies in search of a glimmer of anything that resembled what I felt. I always came up empty. And while I was attempting to turn a blind eye to my overworked emotions, the world around me was doing the same thing. I am certain that even my family would say that there was always something that was peculiar about me. That same difference that I speak of was the elephant in the room. Although curious, I never acted on anything physically so as not to appear abnormal. I vowed to outwardly walk a line that was straight and narrow. What I knew for sure was that anything that resembled different was unacceptable in my hometown. Like every other guy my age, I had been with women. I had maintained relationships and friendships with the opposite sex and I was the better for it. I had always been intrigued by the softness and the scent of a woman. There was nothing quite like being loved by a woman. Their strength is uncanny. Even so, there was much left to be desired. That desire would not be something that I could remotely engage in satisfying in San Antonio, but LA offered the perfect backdrop to appease my search for more.

——PERMISSION——

IT DIDN'T TAKE me long to find work. After a brief placement with a temp agency, I was ready to sharpen my skills in the corporate sector. I had no idea that my new job at Crocker Bank would lead me to the well that I had been in search of. One day at work, out of the corner of my eye, I noticed a young professional man who was delivering mail to my office. He was tall, dark, slender, and attractive. He wore a pair of round frames, and was dressed in neutrals, which gave him a sleek corporate look. He was a little geeky, but nevertheless cute. There was something about him that intrigued me. Maybe it was that I wanted to explore with him. I know it's not quite politically correct to say that he looked gay— but he looked gay. His movements were graceful and dainty, but it was obvious that he was no damn ballerina. There was still an heir of masculinity about him that couldn't be denied. I'd say, that if there were a spectrum of masculine gayness based on appearances, ranging from hard to soft, he was at the far end of the softer side. Nevertheless, I liked what I saw. That day, he eventually noticed me too. When our eyes met, I didn't look away. I didn't want to. I wasn't shy or afraid in my conquest. I wanted him to notice that I was drawn to him. In the moment, he smiled a little. It was then that I felt a little rush. I had never felt that before, at least not with any of the girls that I had encountered back in San Antonio. I watched him as he turned and walked back through the door that he had entered through and I continued working.

The next day, like clockwork, he came in to make his deliveries. After about a week of noticing each other from afar, fate would have it that I had mail that needed to be delivered to my desk. This was the closest we had been to each other. As he set down the mail on my desk, he reached over my shoulder to do so. For some reason, I noticed his hands and the crease in the arm of his shirt. I could see how well he took care of himself. There was no dirt under his well-kept fingernails. I could tell he was meticulous. I turned around before he could walk away, and our eyes locked. The fact that he had just flirted with me was second to the energy that I felt when I looked at him. By nature, men are hunters, and I was in search of prey.

The chain of command is a funny thing when it comes to human interaction. There are times when I believe that the prey desires to be hunted. All I knew, was that if he kept prancing his ass around like a damn deer, he was in danger of getting caught. Our eye contact from that day, led to empty conversations and more mail being delivered to my desk, some of which was not even addressed to me. I would find parcels stuck inside of the stack given to me, that were for an office adjacent to mine. I didn't give a damn if he felt the need to make up an excuse to get to me. Hell, I welcomed it. Through our repeated exchanges, I learned that his name was Keith and that he was from Buffalo, New York. That alone was interesting to me because I had never met anyone from there. Over the course of the next several weeks, our daily contact morphed into a series of vague exchanges as friends. Over time, that vague friendship transformed into an open invitation for flirting. We were now amidst a courtship. Nothing about my intentions had changed, and it was clear that we were operating on the same wavelength. It was only a matter of time before we would find ourselves entangled.

On a Friday, after a long workweek, he invited me to hang out with him near his apartment and I accepted. I arrived in the Santa Monica area where he lived, ready for more than the conversation that had been the cornerstone of our exchanges. That night, both my mind and my body yearned for something that I hadn't yet experienced. I had waited my entire life to experience what I knew he would eventually give me permission to do.

That night, we walked on the beach and talked about life. I did enjoy his exchanges and the companionship was meaningful, considering that I was technically in LA on my own. After our walk, and based on his actions towards me, I knew that I had his permission. It was what I had been waiting for. I mean, I didn't know what I was waiting for exactly because I had absolutely no experience with men, but if you are a hunter by nature, inevitably, your prey at some point will be captured. That's what he was in for.

We returned to his apartment and even in the heat of the moment, I couldn't help but notice that it was disheveled. The dilapidated building reeked of cheap sex and late-night encounters, such as the one that we would soon have. I didn't care. By the time we got to his door, the anticipation was amplified. He hesitated as he placed the key into the lock. It was as if he knew what would happen next. As the door opened, the hinges whined in desperation. We fell through the threshold and against the wall as he began to kiss me and place his hands down my pants. I'm not quite sure what he was looking for, but whatever it was, he got it. Our eyes connected as we stood there kissing. I could tell from his behavior that this was not his first time. He knew what he was doing, but I didn't—at least not with a man. Those moments would prove to be the only time that he was the aggressor. He began to unbuckle my belt and we undressed in haste. In that moment, it wasn't completely about romance. I would imagine that in those moments, our movements mirrored a quarrelsome exchange, which was a far cry from my engagement with women. Those experiences had been far gentler in nature.

Holding my hand, he led me into his bedroom, and there, he gave me permission to explore his body. He was submissive and although I didn't know what I was doing, he was patient with me. He motioned for me to sit back against the headboard and then he proceeded to pleasure me. It didn't last long. I didn't last long. He was noticeably pleasured from seeing that my thirst had been quenched. My body had craved satisfaction such as this.

Afterwards, we lay there, just below the cloud of smoke from our cigarettes that had now formed a haze above our heads. When I got up to leave, I was certain that I wanted more. I knew that what I had just experienced was an appetizer, but I also knew I was not ready for a four-course meal.

The following week, we continued with the usual song and dance at work. I always had mail delivered to my desk because he would find a way to get his ass over there. He was cute in that he continued to flirt as if he hadn't given me permission to have my way with him. It was not just a matter of time. The intensity of my lust was mounting. It was obvious that Keith wanted to find more ways for us to be together. He invited me over again midweek to hang out, but we both knew that hanging out would be an afterthought.

When I arrived, he playfully opened the door. I don't think that we engaged in conversation for more than five minutes before we were entangled in passion. I caressed him and turned him around.

I remember pushing his face into the pillow. He was humbly requesting more. This time, I was much more comfortable and felt completely in control. All I could think about was that I had discovered new territory, and I enjoyed it even more than I had imagined. I had discovered a truth that I had denied my entire life. I was enthralled in a level of freedom that I had no plans of letting go of.

All that I ever needed was permission to be myself.

After I got up the next morning to leave his apartment, I was overtaken with guilt. I couldn't control it. I imagine that my walk of shame was no different from anyone else who had engaged in such acts the night before. Then again, maybe it was. My guilt carried the weight of all the things that my mother had taught me about sin. I can recall her telling me the story of Sodom and Gomorrah and how God was so displeased with the immorality of the people. The stories of morally compromised conduct, with emphasis on the gay conquests, stayed with me and made my spirit heavy, but not enough to stop.

What Keith and I had was a good friendship and even better physical exchange. In spite of the moral guilt that I carried, I continued my escapades with him. As our encounters grew in frequency, it was hard for me to ignore the fact that he was developing feelings in the absence of mine. I enjoyed his company, but I had no interest in anything other than what we had been doing. I can't say that I was shocked to discover that he was in search of the fairytale; I just knew that I was in no position to help him carry it out. I began to dodge the conversations that lead towards considerations of deepening our relationship.

On many evenings after work, he would invite me over and I always obliged. One evening, he asked me to move in with him. I didn't agree to do so, but I did agree to stay over more often. It was the best of both worlds to have a friend that you could laugh with and also make love to. I learned more about him as a person and shared even more of who I was with him. Everything that we had was based on friendship.

After roughly six months of our whirlwind, I knew for certain that I wanted to explore beyond Keith. In my heart, I had come to LA to fulfill my fantasies, not to settle down. And even though I have always been the type to seek a committed relationship over one rooted in physical exchanges, I was at the peak of adolescence, and pleasure was my priority. In the end, Keith would realize that he had introduced me to an indulgence that would prove difficult to no longer desire.

CHAPTER 2

FROM THE BOTTOM UP

"There is not always a fork in the road. Sometimes, there is only one direction from which to travel."
—Elgin Charles

HAVE YOU EVER HEARD the saying, "Hurt people, hurt people"? I would eventually become the epitome of that phrase. I hurt Keith in ways that I never even fathomed because we wanted different things from life and from each other. For me, he was a way to scratch an itch and as ugly as it may sound, once that itch was scratched, I no longer needed him. He had introduced me to a world that I knew existed and for that I was thankful, but he no longer held my attention, sexually or mentally. He was just a good friend to me. I needed to move on but found it increasingly difficult to do so because of the true friendship that we had developed. By this time, I was practically living in his apartment. I was there that often. Even so, the fact that I was in search of more excitement, sex in a different way, and being stimulated by something more than what Keith had to offer was something that even I could not avoid. Like K. Michelle said, "Oh, I broke another heart today. I didn't care, just walked away." Story of my life.

I had become such a regular at Keith's apartment complex that even his neighbors became familiar with me. When you see people in passing on a regular basis, you begin to smile and engage in small talk that can eventually lead to a genuine exchange, or at least that is what always seems to happen to me. One day as I was visiting Keith, a lady whom I had seen regularly happened to pull up at the same time as I did. As she got out of her car, I noticed that she had a ton of groceries. Because she lived on the second floor of the apartment building, it became obvious that she had no intention of coming back down to get all of her bags. She was dead set of carrying all of that shit at one time.

I walked over to her. "Hello ma'am. How are you today?" I asked.

"I'd be better if I had another set of arms to get all of this shit upstairs," she replied.

Immediately, I felt a connection with her and we shared a hearty dose of laughter. "Please, let me help you. It's the least that I can do." I guess I hadn't really taken the time to notice, but she was striking. She had an exotic look to her. Her skin was a dewy caramel and her hair was a fierce auburn. The contrast was interesting. She had these long eyelashes that almost looked like she was wearing false ones, but she had been born with fans for her eyes. Her nose was long and somewhat pointed and it hovered just above her thin pink lips. Even with the backdrop of beauty, it was her eyes that stole the show. They were two huge hard-boiled eggs that could read a soul. Her irises were the darkest hue of brown possible, making them appear black. Her hair was long and straight, with the exception of the curls that framed her face. I could tell that she tried to keep those pieces straight, but to no avail. Here natural hair pattern was curly, but she, like many women, wore the opposite of what God gave her. Either way, she was beautiful and

I felt like a giant in her presence because I was so much taller than her. She was a petite, yet statuesque woman. I had always been a sucker for a beautiful woman. And even a woman who might not be considered beautiful, I knew that I had the skills to transform her into a work of art. I had done it on countless occasions in San Antonio. I never saw a woman when she was standing in front of me. To me, women always appeared as works of art that could be molded, sculpted, and reconstructed into something worthy of staring. My mind was just wired that way.

I realized that my mind had been wandering when I turned towards her. She had been staring at me, and I smiled and dropped my head a little. I wasn't embarrassed, just caught a little off guard. She smiled and began to pass me a few paper bags filled with groceries from the trunk of her car. I laughed to myself because she was not shy about accepting my help. She began handing me all of the heavy shit. A milk jug, two gallons of water, and a bag filled with canned goods. Later, I would be asking myself what the hell I was thinking by offering to help. Shit, I said I wanted to help, not break a sweat. But it was ok. After all, she was cute and there was something about her that I liked.

As I carried the bags up the stairs, I gazed over at her and caught her looking at me. A little wisp of her hair fell into her eyes and I found it sexy when she gently whipped her head to move the hair out of the way. We smiled again, but it was that fake, nervous kind of energy that only strangers exchange. There was something there; some energy was present between us. I'm all about energy. I am a firm believer in the exchange of energy, and I've learned over the years that I am pretty good at reading people's vibes. I guess you could call it intuition. Although I don't always listen to it, it is a silent, yet highly recognizable voice in my ear.

Before I knew it, I had walked past Keith's apartment building, which was the neighboring building and we arrived at her door. She set the groceries down and reached for the keys from her purse. After unlocking the door, she invited me in to bring the groceries into her kitchen. The setup of her apartment was much different from Keith's. It was obvious that she had cared for her living quarters. I know meticulous when I see it. I'd spent too many days back in San Antonio arranging and rearranging our house to not recognize someone who was meticulous in decor. You couldn't tell me I was not the king of Feng Shui. I used to be so bored that I would change the decorations in that house on a weekly basis. Rearranging furniture, pulling weeds from outside and making them into floral arrangements. Boredom will drive you crazy if you let it. I was a far cry from the backwoods, but I knew what a well-kept home looked like. And although it was modest, I could tell that she had taken care to decorate her apartment. I was, however, perplexed. How could Keith's building look like a shithole, but her apartment showed no signs of it? It was in the same complex. As I stood there, my mind must have begun to wander again, and I heard a voice say, "Can I get you something to drink?"

"No, I'm fine. Thank you so much."

"You can set all that shit over here. I will unpack in when I get to it." She sat down and let out a relieved sigh. "Whew. I'm tired as hell. It's been a long day."

I stood there peering out the front window of her apartment. It overlooked the complex's pool. For some strange reason, the way that her apartment was positioned, you couldn't see any of the other apartment buildings. From her place, there was no view of the damn near dilapidated building in the complex. Her view was actually really nice. I stood there thinking what a difference a change of scenery can make. It was almost like a confirmation that being with Keith was a distorted view. The upkeep of Keith's apartment was different from where I stood. It was almost as if he was ok living there. I thought that building was going to cave in, but he never even discussed moving.

"Hey. You must have a lot on your mind" she said.

"Oh. No, I was just thinking of where I was heading to next."

"Well, if you're ever interested, a couple of neighbors around here get together to play bid whist almost every night. You are more than welcomed to join us," she offered.

"Yeah, that sounds like fun. Maybe one day, I will. I'm going to head out now. Have a good one."

As I prepared to leave, she walked over toward the door, "Damn, we've been talking all this time and I never even told you my name. I'm Diane. What was your name?"

"Charles. I'm Charles."

She extended her hand and we shook in agreement that it would not be the last time that we would meet. As I walked away, I heard the door to Diane's apartment close, but for me it signified the door that I needed to close on my dwindling relationship.

That night, as I walked back to Keith's apartment, I noticed things that I had never noticed before. There was a clear divide of resources, amongst tenants. It was almost as if they had purposely placed tenants with lower income levels in Keith's building and those with more substantial resources in other buildings. I was a dreamer and I realized in that moment that I had been so caught up that I hadn't been dreaming. My attention shifted back towards what my next move would be. Life for me had always been about forward progression. Although I was new to LA, I wasn't new to the concept of working to build a future for myself. When I arrived at Keith's apartment, he was ready to do what we always did. I wasn't the least bit interested. I simply wanted to lay in bed and take time to visualize what my next move would be.

The next morning, as I was leaving the complex, I drove past the building that Diane lived in and noticed that there was a small sign staked into the ground that read, "Apartment for Rent." At work, the vision of that sign stayed with me, and I tossed around the idea of moving from my apartment to Diane's apartment building. Where I was living wasn't as unkempt as Keith's apartment building, but there was no question that Diane's building was a step up. I was ready to make a move. I couldn't wait any longer.

After work, I went to the leasing office that was housed in a well-appointed apartment that appeared to have the same floor plan as Diane's place. As I walked in, I was greeted by the property manager. She explained to me that each of the buildings was owned by different real estate investors. This explained the startling contrast between Keith's building and Diane's. I must have appeared eager to learn because she went on to explain the concept of staging, which gave me insight into the immaculate decor of the unit that we were standing in. It was my first time being in a "model home" and all I knew was that I wanted my apartment to look just like the model unit. I was taking notes on decor just as much as I was taking notes on the prices for the various floor plans. "I'll take it," I said, and before I knew it, I had jumped head first into my first major financial commitment since arriving in LA. I was nervous and excited at the same time, but if there was anyone that I could count on, I knew that it was me.

Even though I was amidst transition, it was happening. I was in pursuit of a dream that was larger than my circumstance and one that would prove to be larger than life. Although, at the time, I had no idea how it would all unfold. After signing the lease on the new place, I immediately rushed back to my apartment and spent the night packing my belongings. The next morning, I remember Keith being upset because I hadn't called or even stopped by the night before. It seemed like we were transitioning into an arranged act of ships in passing. Even our run ins at work were diminishing. I had been so caught up in packing and the exciting new goal that I had set for myself that Keith was an afterthought. Eventually, things between he and I would fizzle completely and he would accept the fact that what we had shared was a thing of the past.

By the time I moved into my new place, I was becoming a regular at the bid whist parties that Diane had invited me to. And believe me when I say, I was exposed to a whole new world of possibilities. Some were good and others... well, let's just say, all we thought about at the time was having fun.

It was the 80s and man, the world was just coming down from the decade of free love. Sentiments like freedom and liberty were the guiding principles of life, love, and the pursuit of happiness. In LA, happiness meant sex, drugs, and rock and roll. Well, for me that would have been sex, drugs, and R&B. But the exception to all rules was gay love. Let's just say that everybody, whether they were in or out of the closet, was tasting the rainbow. Gay men and women were coming out of the woodworks, BABY! Now I can't speak for gay women as a whole, but what I know for sure is that gay men were discovering love in every nook and cranny of the city. A new era was upon us and I ushered it in.

The same pool that I saw for the first time when I stood in Diane's apartment, evolved as one of the major hangouts for the socialites of the apartment building. On any given night you could find Diane, Fred, and Tracy, all of which Diane had introduced me to, hanging out there. They were the regulars. There were also a ton of riff raffs who would just stop by for fun. By which I mean coke, weed, and liquor. Now, if you mix any of those elements together, free love also becomes a part of the equation. When we weren't at the pool, we were at Diane's apartment.

One night, after I returned from a long day at work, I decided to just stop by Diane's apartment. I could tell that the gang was all there. I knocked on the door and Diane answered. "Hey boy, get yourself in here. We ain't doing nothing but what we always do: having a good time." She gave that same old snicker that I had become accustomed to and wrapped her arms around my neck and kissed me on the cheek. She and I had become great friends, but there was room for more. "You should get in on a game, Charles."

I laughed. "I just might." As I walked toward the table, it was obvious that people were partying. By which I mean snorting coke, smoking weed, and drinking liquor. There were lines on the table ready to be snorted. It was crazy to think that someone could just walk over and snort a line of cocaine, right next to where a game of cards was being played. Everyone was just living for the moment. There were a few people smoking cigarettes and vibing to the music on the record player, and those not playing cards were on the couch just enjoying the cocktail of drugs that they had indulged in. A few of the people present I didn't recognize, but that was always the case. For one reason or another, my eyes connected with a gentleman who was seated at the table. He was focused on the game, but not enough to not have noticed me. Our eyes locked and he wasn't backing away from staring. Me on the other hand, I dropped my head first. I was admittedly a little coy. When I looked up again, everything inside of me wanted to not look at him, but I couldn't help it. I was curious as to what he saw. He was still staring. I had never been in the presence of someone so forward.

"CHARLIEEEEE!" Diane was dangling over my shoulder, holding a glass of wine. She dangled the glass in such a way that it appeared some would spill out onto her tan carpet, but she clearly had it under control. That shows how regular our extracurricular activities of alcohol, drugs, and whatever else you could imagine had become. "Charlie, that's Joe. Joe, meet Charlie." She nodded her head as if she knew that there would be more to the story of Joe and I upon her introduction. I guess she sensed the chemistry. If there was one person who knew what was going on in the room, it was Diane. She was so intuitive and never missed anything.

Joe stood up and walked right over to me. He was short and even from the small distance that he had to walk from the table to where I was standing, I observed that he was bow legged. He had a little pot belly and wore black, round, metal glasses. There was nothing spectacular about his looks. In my mind, he looked like an insurance salesman. He had a regular haircut, but I noticed that he was thinning ever so slightly on the top and he was clean shaven. Though he appeared to be very unassuming, he was forward and direct, and I could tell that he was much older than I was. When he reached me, he stood there, admiring me. I wasn't quite sure how to handle his approach, so I just stood there, dumbfounded. The normalcy of gay men had not quite set in for me. In San Antonio, there was just no place for it outwardly. But there I stood, being lusted after by another man, and not one person in the room even paid us any attention. It was the new normal.

Eventually, he stepped into the realm of my personal space and although he didn't say anything, he made it quite clear that he was interested in me. I'd be lying if I said that I wasn't curious.

"You should come with me," he said.

"Come with you?" I didn't know what to say or do. I was caught off guard.

"Yeah, my apartment is just upstairs, let's get out of here." I was too afraid to not go and I was too intrigued to not be excited about his invitation. "We'll be right back. Y'all keep playing without me," he yelled to the rest of the people playing at the table.

We engaged in a bit of meaningless small talk as we made our way to his apartment. He was just trying to get to know more about me, I guess. When we got to his apartment, he invited me inside and I played coy. I really did feel shy, and I didn't quite know what to do. There was a profound moment of silence as we stood face to face. Before I knew it, he had me pinned against the wall and we were kissing. It was passionate, and I felt him get excited. I was so turned on, but my nerves got the best of me. In a panic, I muttered, "I think I should get back." He stepped back a little and let me rush out. When I looked back before closing his door, he had a smirk on his face. It was almost as if he knew that this wouldn't be the last time. Knowing him as I know now, he had every intent to pin more than just my hands to the wall.

That moment alone was a fresh perspective. There were more layers that I had yet to uncover with men and I wanted in. If it wasn't clear before, it was apparent now that my conquest of Keith had been just that: a conquest. I'm a Pisces and we are sensual creatures. Even though my mind directed me towards focusing on creating a new life for myself in LA, my body directed me towards exploration and now with Joe's aggression, it was staring me in the face. We wanted the same thing.

I will say that life is a fruitful teacher if you stick around long enough to learn. Whatever you desire, all you have to do is ask.

And then there are times that you get exactly what you ask for, not knowing that you might need to one day, mark that shit, "Return to Sender."

—=Keeping House=—

HAVE YOU EVER WANTED something so badly that you were willing to risk yourself for it? Of course, you have, and if you say that you haven't, you wouldn't be being honest with yourself. We've all been there. I was now twenty-two and willing to risk it all in order to satisfy myself and live freely. We've all tested murky waters to appease our curiosity, even if for only a moment. A man by the name of Joe Taylor would prove to be murky water that I would eventually wade in.

From continued observation, I would discover that Joe knew everyone and was the social butterfly of the apartment building. I'd also learn that not only did he know everybody, he was also engaged in extracurricular activities with everyone. That man had very loose limits. Boys, girls, young, old, you name it. And of course, I didn't know all of that when I decided to dive head first into a pool of love, emotion, and well... physical consummation with Joe. Like anyone who is in search of something, you notice the red flags along the way, but you ignore them. I know I did. I've always believed the best in people and felt like I had the power to love people past their circumstance.

Without cause or reason, I had fallen in love with Joe. That's a powerful statement. Life and love began moving so fast that my head was spinning. Let's be clear—I was in search of what I had never experienced. All things considered, I had waited my entire life for such a time as this, or so I thought. I had always wondered if the sexually driven motives that I had towards men were real.

Joe put every curiosity to bed, literally and figuratively. He was so experienced that he had me doing things that I never even imagined that I would do. The first time with him… well, it took my breath away. He taught me about "tops" and "bottoms" and so many concepts that I had never heard before. I had no point of reference and the time I'd spent with Keith was one big science experiment. He just let me do whatever I wanted with him. Joe on the other hand was always teaching me. He was a Leo, which meant that we could make love, multiple times a day, until our bodies gave out. It was a match made in heaven if you ask me. I did realize that I was a top. Life on the bottom was not for me.

Things were going so well between Joe and I that I started playing house with him. I mean, I let him drive my car and come and go as he pleased. Who does that? I guess it's true that love is blind. It would have appeared that I had turned a blind eye to Joe's indiscretions. I had not. He was still just as social when we were together as he was before I met him and I believed him to be who he said he was. He and a group of his friends would always attend these parties, but they wouldn't invite me. I would be sitting in my apartment, waiting for him to come back home to me. I didn't need the party scene in that way. And when I would ask about the parties, he would just shrug me off. "You don't need to be coming to stuff like that, it's not for you," he would say. Even though I didn't want to admit it, he was right. Such engagements were not in alignment with who I was. Even though I was at a point in my life where my sexual exploits guided many of my actions, I had found someone whom I thought I could create a lasting relationship with. I was no longer in search of a piece. I considered creating a long-term life with Joe. I've always been that way to tell the truth. I don't believe in sleeping with everyone.

My prude disposition landed me a seat alone on the couch on many nights when Joe didn't come home. Now, Joe still maintained his apartment, which was not far from mine. I would find myself doing the things that you do when you are jealous and scared of what could be. I can recall one evening popping up at Joe's apartment and discovering a letter on the mat just in front of the door. I picked it up and attempted to read through the envelope, but to no avail. My curiosity couldn't be curtailed, so I opened it in haste. I was so embarrassed to discover that he had been planning a surprise birthday party for me with some of our mutual friends. "You should be ashamed of yourself for not allowing me to surprise you. I don't know what's wrong with you, Charlie," he said.

Little did he know, I didn't feel bad one bit. It's hard dating a hoe. You never know what you could run up on. I always knew something was up but could never quite put my finger on it. And those little parties that he would go to without me, those were orgies. Of course, I wasn't invited. I guess I also felt like there was only so much I could say. It was the 80s after all, but I was no doormat. On the one hand, I questioned my motives because I realized that this era was for all of the men who'd lived under a shell, in fear of what the rest of the world would think of them. On the other hand, I felt completely justified in holding the person that I was in a relationship with accountable for their actions and loyalty to me. We were ushering in a new era. And when I wasn't worrying about Joe's cheating, I was enjoying the way that he loved me. We were opposites. I was more reserved, while he was wild and crazy. His spontaneity was attractive and I liked that he brought me out of my comfort zone in so many ways.

I was never one to go out or be adventurous by myself, I was too scared, but not Joe. That's what I admired most about him. I would even go so far as to say that I looked up to him. He would take me all over the city. He loved downtown LA on Main Street. One night, he took me to this small, low down, country ass place. The little building resembled an old warehouse. As we walked up, I could see people stumbling out drunk and some had no teeth. They looked like they had been to hell and back. Even the women reminded me of little demons. "What kind of shit is this?" I asked myself. I couldn't figure out who the hell these people were. They had the music bumping, and they were in there partying like they were in a mansion. The environment was too run down for me. I remember looking down and realizing that the warehouse didn't even have floors. I was literally standing on the ground. You could see patches of grass that had been trampled so badly that nothing could revive them. I was mortified just being there. Joe on the other hand resembled a regular. He was as comfortable as a frog on a lily pad. He left me standing there as he went to get some drinks for us, and all I could think about was whether or not I would risk drinking from a cup that came from that nasty ass place. As I stood there a man came towards me and I could tell he was smitten. He walked up to me almost the same way that Joe had when he first approached me. He put his hand up over my head and leaned in close to me. He looked like something from the Twilight Zone. I honestly wondered if this nigga had ever taken a bath. I didn't come to LA for this. This was not my scene. The dirty man kept flirting with me, and truthfully, he scared the shit out of me. Eventually, Joe returned and said a few words to let the intruder know that I was taken.

"Don't worry. He ain't going to mess with you. I will protect you."

That was some skid row kind of shit. I couldn't believe that Joe liked that type of crap and felt comfortable there. The more I got to know him, the more I realized how low rent he was. Despite the fact that Joe was highly educated, he seemed to favor engaging in the bottom. I think after that night, my eyes were opened in a way that they had not been before. I was smitten with my heart, but my mind began to wonder about Joe. I began to realize quickly that there were some significant differences in our moral fibers, but I was now two years deep into the relationship and letting go was not really an option for me at the time. The one thing that we could agree on was the bid whist parties at Diane's. They became our pastime together, and even though we were all doing drugs, and smoking way too much weed, it was a level I was comfortable with

In that safe space, we could show our love without fear of what those around us would think, even so, we still operated with caution. We both maintained lady friends for appearances sake. Around that time, I also started to recognize that my recreational use of drugs was a drop in the bucket compared to Joe's use. He was using cocaine heavily and it affected his judgement and his temperament. Truth be told, he had a drug problem.

Snooping was just as normal for me as snorting was normal for Joe. One evening, he left me at his apartment as he attended another one of those "parties" which I wasn't invited to. I capitalized on the opportunity to see whatever the hell I could see. He always kept tons of pictures. I found a few that appeared to be meaningless amongst a huge stack. There must have been at least a hundred photos. I didn't see shit worth looking at and prepared to return them to the shoe box that he had placed them in. As I was opening the box with one hand, the stack of pictures that I was holding in the other hand fell. "Shit." I was trying to move as fast as I could because I didn't know what time he would be back. As I was cleaning up the photos, I noticed one that was a little strange. Joe was sitting on the sofa and a young boy was beside him with his head in Joe's lap. At first glance, the picture could have appeared to be innocent but I knew Joe's ass. After a closer look, I realized that it was one of the kids that Joe had introduced to me from his volunteering with Big Brothers, Big Sisters. To this day, I'm unsure of the story behind that photo, but I sure as hell have my suspicions. Without question it was wrong, and I have my doubts about whether he was truly mentoring those young boys. What I knew of Joe was that he could read people like nobody's business. He could recognize if you had a little sugar in your tank in the blink of an eye.

I was disgusted. I now questioned the levels that he would go to, when attempting to satisfy his flesh. That night, I felt sick to my stomach. The orgy parties, the cocaine, the lack of respect for me and my well-being was getting to be a little too much for me. I was now underwhelmed by whom he had shown himself to be. In retrospect, I think that Joe's moral lines were blurred. That was never a problem that I had. My father had taught me to be a man of my word and to respect people as much as humanly possible. If you are going to mentor someone, it should be exclusively mentorship. I don't care if there are two adults, business should remain business. It's never right to put people in compromising situations. In my heart, I might not have admitted it immediately, but eventually I would come to my senses and acknowledge that I believed that Joe's desires superseded our relationship, and that he could not be trusted, not even with young boys.

Just as Joe's eyes and attention began to wander, so did mine. I didn't feel the same about him after all that I believed to be unraveling. I began to consider other options, and Jeff would prove to be one of them.

CHAPTER 3

A Part Down the Middle

"If the theory of evolution ceased to exist, what might the alternative be?"

—Elgin Charles

AS MY PERCEPTION of Joe began to change, I took time to reflect over my past relationships with both men and women. Anyone who is truly honest with themselves, knows that we all have moments where we want to explore without limits and, in those moments, the shackles must be loosened at all costs. And no matter who you decide to explore with, you're not a bad person for doing so. There are times amidst these phases that people do get hurt. I found a similarity between Keith and myself: I was now in love with someone who was not capable of returning love in the same way.

Unfortunately, this cycle of our lives is often at the expense of someone else's heart. I would never intentionally set out to hurt anyone, but that's the way love goes, sometimes. I knew that Keith and I had ended things on good terms, but if I were honest with myself, I also knew he had hoped for more, just as I had hoped for more with Joe. Hope was a dangerous drug. It could lead you down a winding road to nowhere. Keith wasn't what I wanted in the long run, and I recognized that I could not change Joe's internal wiring to have him miraculously become faithful.

I must not have been paying attention because I had fallen for Joe at the expense of my common sense. There are times when your heart and your mind don't speak the same language. It happens to the best of us. What had drawn me to Joe so unequivocally? I guess when you are introduced to new things, you become intrigued by them. If those new exploits feel good, you want more. I was captivated by sex with Joe. What he lacked in emotional value, he overcompensated for in other ways. I had been deprived and frustratingly curious for so many years. I had suppressed anything that I remotely felt, for fear of what others might say or how they might react towards me. With him, I never had to even concern myself with it. Joe further legitimized that what I had felt in secret while growing up was real and it validated me in many ways. Even though being with Joe cost me, it also gave me permission and resources to afford the price of opening Pandora's Box. It was almost as if the stench of intimacy was something that he could not wash off; it turned me on. I knew that at any given moment, we could quench the thirst of our testosterone. I can't lie, it had a hold on me.

I was willing to learn and most importantly, I was willing to love. I came into the relationship in search of a physical connection, but I ended up finding a friend and a partner as well. Joe just knew what he was doing. He embodied a dominance that made me surrender. Love will make you do some crazy shit and for me, this was one of them. I wanted with Joe what Keith desired with me, I always had. When you meet someone who is sexually skillful, you have to know that they've learned through experience. And while experience is an amazing teacher, those who are experienced might find it hard to curtail their curiosity while in a relationship. Joe didn't always want to be just my teacher; he was a hunter by nature and always in search of his latest conquest.

The discovery of the photos was the straw that broke the camel's back. My feelings for him began to change and I began to slip back into consciousness. The light was becoming more obvious and I began to consider what would be best for me. It is often stated that if you stand atop a mountain, the air is fresher and the views are better.

——THE MOUNTAIN TOP——

AFTER BEING STUCK in the muck with Joe, I was left to search for a fresh new perspective. A mutual friend that we shared by the name of Jeff evolved into a confidant. He was newly divorced and had three daughters. It was my assumption that around the time his marriage got rocky, he began attending the bid whist parties as a way to unwind from the perils of his personal life. Both Joe and I would sit in conversation with Jeff for hours on end and we would encourage him in any way that we could.

He was a classy man, who was well groomed, with manicured nails. I couldn't tell if he had a light coat of clear polish on them or not, but it didn't look strange because he was very masculine in so many other ways. The first time we met him, I was sitting on the couch and Joe was at the table playing bid whist and being boisterous as usual. From where I sat, you could see anyone who came through the door. When he entered the room, I immediately noticed his yellow linen pants suit. The yellow was a pale hue and he paired the pants with a tan belt and tan shoes. I remember thinking to myself that he was debonair. He had very little facial hair and a thick mustache atop his lip that was trimmed to a t.

This was a man who took care of himself. He was without question a metrosexual.

Out of nowhere, Diane, holding her usual glass of endangered wine, swooned over. "This is Jeff, everybody. Make him feel welcome. This is his first time with the crew." She pulled him farther into the room. "Come on in, love. You know we've got it all. Whatever your pain is, we've got something for your pleasure. Indulge. You only live once. Ain't that right, Charlie?"

I told you Diane didn't miss a damn thing. Now, I can't say that she saw the way that I was looking at Jeff, but I had to check myself in the moment. Although disengaged, I was still there with Joe and I knew that I had to find my way out of the relationship with him because my attention span was getting shorter and shorter for his antics. My intuition became much sharper as my head was no longer clouded by the physical attraction Joe and I shared. I could now tell when he was checking out other guys in my presence and even when he intended to engage with someone else. That night as Jeff stood in the threshold of the door, I don't know who was staring harder, me or Joe with his lurking antics. Like I said, I needed to check myself until further notice.

Diane escorted Jeff over to the couch where I was. What did she want me to do? In a normal situation, where there was not an attraction, I would have been the perfect person to help someone new feel comfortable in a room of strangers. It would have been in a civilized fashion, but by the time she walked him over to me, I had already undressed him with my eyes.

"Jeff, this is Charlie. Charlie, Jeff. Help him get acquainted, Charlie. Make him feel at home. You know how we do," said Diane. She had that sneaky look again on her face. She was so high that the glass of wine and the cigarette was all that her tiny hands could hold. She knew what was going on though, I have to give her that.

"What's up, man? Nice to meet you," Jeff said. He extended his hand to shake mine and I returned my hand in kind. He had a very strong grip and just as I pulled my hand back in, I saw another hand extending from my peripheral. I knew it to be all too familiar.

"Hey, Jeff, welcome to the crew. I'm Joe and everybody calls me Joe." He laughed harder than anyone else with that dry ass joke. He now disgusted me. He hadn't even allowed me to speak two words to Jeff. I wished he had stayed at the card table.

Joe's continued presence felt like an act of intrusion to me. I leaned back on the couch and Jeff sat down in the high winged chair adjacent to me. Joe propped himself up on the arm of the couch and rested his elbow atop of my shoulder. He was like a dog peeing on a hydrant in a desperate attempt to mark his territory. We continued to sit, talk, and laugh. We even snorted a few lines of cocaine. I knew immediately that it was not for me. Joe's ass snorted enough for everyone at the whole party. Classless. Jeff, on the other hand, came from a different place and I liked his style. He shared with us that he was in the process of divorcing his wife of nineteen years. He even showed us pictures of their three beautiful daughters.

That night, in the short time that we talked, I could tell that there was more to Jeff's story. He was hiding something. I saw a part of myself in him. I'm sure Joe could sniff the aura of his orientation. We must have sat there talking for at least two hours. Now, I'll admit Joe had some bomb ass conversation. He could speak on any subject and although ignorant as hell, he was also educated and gave great insight on many things. Most of all, he was wise from all of his years of living, and he had a great deal of experience from which to share from.

We were all still getting acquainted with one another when Jeff looked down at his watch and realized that it was already two o'clock in the morning. "Aw, damn, I have to get out of here. Man, I have truly enjoyed myself. This was just what I needed. I'm definitely coming back. I've got to go though. I'm still technically married and I need as much peace in my life as possible," he said with a laugh of sarcasm. He reached out to shake Joe's hand and then mine. When he grabbed my hand, he said "I will for sure make my way back over here. I think I've found the outlet that I've been looking for." He was definitely making a pass at me, but it was so obvious that it wasn't obvious. Even Joe and his territorial antics didn't catch that one, but I sure as hell did. And right there, at that minute, thoughts of much more than a handshake crossed my mind.

As the weeks passed, Jeff became a regular at the parties, anytime he could steal away from his wife and kids. We all started to get close and he knew that I was with Joe, so we maintained limits that would not emphasize the attraction that we shared. I'm just not morally wired that way. I truly would have wanted to get out of the relationship with Joe before developing any bonds with anyone else. I will admit, however, Jeff was tempting. The more time we spent together, the more I learned. At the parties, Joe didn't seem so hard up to stake claim to his territory because he saw our interactions as innocent. It almost seemed as if Joe was glad that there was someone to entertain me in a space that would allow him to keep an eye on me, but still be social and entertain every new potential lover that came to the party. While he was busy, I learned that Jeff knew exactly what he wanted and that he was hoping to discover it in the arms of another man. I was blown out of the water to discover that he desired to be a bottom. I almost couldn't believe it. This man had been married to a woman for nineteen years, but he desired to be manhandled. I had to admit that learning about that side of him made me even more curious and turned me on, on another level. The whole "top" vs "bottom" discussion is still one that the world can't seem to get just right. Jeff's desires were baffling to me. It was during that time that I realized that I wasn't weird for being attracted to both men and women and all of the nuances that the world imposed upon such feelings were just that: nuances. I realized that whatever satisfies us during intimacy is what we have to come to terms with. Why should we allow society to place us in a box? How was it that I was just as turned on by Diane as I was by Jeff? How could it be possible for me to share time, space and energy with them both? This was my truth. It was possible that I could be attracted to a man and a woman. It was possible that I could climax from engagement with either one. Although I had not been intimate with Diane, I had always thought about it and I know that she too thought about me. We had just never crossed the line. She had been there through my whole relationship with Joe, but the chemistry and the attraction had always remained present. For so long, I questioned this notion. But in those moments, it was so and I now understood why.

For me, it was a climactic moment. I was amidst an era of personal self-actualization. I wasn't gay. I was bisexual. What a revelation.

──✦An Open Invitation✦──

I HAVE ALWAYS HAD women, and I've never had to work hard to get them. They have always flocked to me. Even the guys in school, back in San Antonio, including my brother, would get jealous because the girls paid more attention to me than many of them. I can't really say what it was. I was handsome, I guess! Even so, I gave San Antonio nothing as it pertained to my being a bisexual. Public displays of bisexuality simply didn't exist there. I had suffocated that notion, without ceasing. Moving to LA had given me the time, space, and opportunity to research and make decisions as to what my preferences would be. Furthermore, no matter who I had been in a relationship with, I had never ended anything on bad terms with anyone. It was just who I was, to always keep people's dignity intact and to never burn bridges. You never know who you might need to call upon.

On occasions, my former life would make its presence known. One Friday afternoon, I was sitting on the couch in my living room when the phone rang. Joe was asleep in the bedroom, so I closed the door so that the sound wouldn't wake him.

"Hello," I answered.

"CHARLIIIIIIIIIIEEEEEEE! Hi, baby. Oh my God, I've missed hearing your voice. Have you missed me?"

"Well, hi." I immediately recognized the voice. "Hi. Hi. Henrietta. How's everything going with you?"

"Oh, no complaints here. Just ready to see my Charlie. I can't go much longer without seeing you, baby."

Now, Henrietta was a big burly ass girl, whom I had dated in high school. She was a hue of cocoa and had these cornbread fed, thighs. In the heat of passion, she used to squeeze me half to death with them. She was even pretty solid up top, almost like a linebacker. She had a lovely face and very defined features, but it was her beautiful, long locks of hair that were her best asset in my opinion. Henrietta was as sweet as pie and we had immediately hit it off back in San Antonio. She was madly in love with me, but I hadn't received the same memo. She used to take the lead during intimate moments and she was, dare I say, rough. I mean, she never ever gave me a chance to show my aggressive side because she had enough for the both of us. When we would hang out at her house after school, she would tear my clothes off. On many occasions, I didn't feel like there was much that I could do but just sit there. I don't even know how or why she was so strong, but I knew if I ever had to fight her, I wouldn't be able to take her, so shit, I let her have her way with me. Before I left San Antonio to move to LA, she proclaimed that she would one day move there as well so that we could be together. Chile, I guess. Either way, on this day, a call and a visit from Henrietta was a reality that was staring me in the face.

"Charlie, I know you miss me too. You've always been so shy. I know you want to tell me all of your feelings. It's ok. You know I'm bold enough for both of us.

"Awe. Ok," I muttered.

"I'm working on getting myself there, baby. I just miss you like crazy. You know we need to get back together and do some of those things that we used to do. You remember how I used to…

I interrupted. "Hey. Hey. Hey, now, Henrietta."

"Oh Charlie, you don't have to be shy with me. We've done some nasty, freaky shit. You just wait until I get myself there. OOOO, baby." She might not have recognized it, but I was really just trying to get her ass to move on to something else in the conversation. "You're so crazy Charlie. So, like I said, baby, I'm coming to LA to see you."

"Awe, man. Ok. So, when are you thinking about coming?" To be completely honest, I had very little interest in Henrietta's visit. She had always been a good friend to me and I valued her in that way, but I wasn't buying what she was selling, especially when I was getting far more than I could stand in other places.

Even though Joe and I were on the rocks, I was living my best life amidst the revolutionary expedition that I had embarked upon after arriving in LA. Bringing San Antonio here was like bringing sand to the beach: there was no need, but I digress.

The call with Henrietta left off with her single handedly settling on a weekend to visit and a detailed explanation of what she was planning to do with me when she arrived. I wasn't moved. I was probably more scared of how she was planning to snatch me up more than anything. Woo, Jesus.

The next morning, Joe left early with no word as to his whereabouts or plans. I didn't care. I called Jeff and asked if he wanted to meet for lunch. We were becoming quite connected. He proved to be a good outlet and confidant while Joe did whatever he wanted to do. After lunch, I invited him back to my apartment for a few drinks, which proved to be desert. By this time, Jeff's wife and kids had moved out of their home, so he was ready to dip his toe into the murky waters.

While at the apartment, we got a little closer. It was the first time that we crossed the line of friendship that we had garnered. In minute acts of flirtation, he had been talking so much about the length of his assets. I had to see to believe. Men and their egos can be something else. That day as we sat nestled on the couch, where Joe and I had once enjoyed sitting together, Jeff encouraged me to take a closer look. My eyes would soon be led to discover that he wasn't lying. This was not a case of exaggeration. He possessed an exception to the rule. Even so, there was a tenderness in the moment. He needed for me to comfort him and to acknowledge that what he had been feeling was normal. I could relate in so many ways and I could see the hurt in his eyes from having to be who the world thought he should be. In that moment, he yearned to just be what he felt like being. I can't speak for him, but it is possible that his desire for being a "bottom" came from the pressure of always having to be in control of life for his wife and children and being in control led him to fantasize about someone controlling him. Maybe it was that he just wanted to let go and unwind, and this was his way of doing so. Who was I to judge? In that moment, I just knew that it might be our only chance to be together.

Right then, I had no consideration for Joe because he had been so inconsiderate of me and my feelings. I was desiring and I acted accordingly. I could tell that he was nervous, so I took my time with him. I wanted to protect Jeff, but I also wanted to experience the fullness of the passion in the heat of the moment.

There we were, suspended in time, together. A single stream of sweat dripped down his back and engrained the moment in my memory forever. It was just as important to me to be the source of his pleasure as it was to the recipient.

After removing myself from the entanglement with him, we both immediately began to redress. We knew that we were in danger of Joe arriving at any moment. The threat of his presence wasn't enough for us to not engage, but it was enough for us to cover up what had now been a significant source of relief for each of us. There was no holding hands or plans for future moments together. We were both deserving and we both indulged in gratification from the time that we shared. After about five minutes, Jeff mentioned that he had to leave to pick up his daughters from their ballet class. "Let me walk you to your car," I said. I wanted to see if anyone was hanging out by the pool anyway.

As Jeff and I were walking towards the parking lot, we rounded the corner and almost walked directly into Joe. He jumped back with exaggeration and let on that he was startled. We all stood there, staring in silence for what seemed like elapsed time. Jeff and I were facing Joe and Joe was facing us. It seemed like it was us against him, and I know he felt a way about it. The look on his face evolved from surprise to suspicion. Neither Jeff nor I confirmed or denied our prior terms of engagement. It wasn't Joe's damn business. And since he put his fingers on anything and everything, all he could do was speak in uncertain terms. "Where are you two going?" he asked.

"Oh, what's up man? I'm headed to pick up the girls from ballet," Jeff replied. Say, what are you guys getting into tonight? Are y'all going to Diane's? If so, I'll probably come back through a little later."

"Yeah, you do that," Joe said with a snarl. He was sniffing around like the hound he was, but trust and believe that he was not getting one clue from us on that day.

As Jeff walked off, he said "See you guys later," and he gave us both high fives. Joe's back was turned to Jeff as he and I stood face to face. I could see Jeff out of the corner of my eye. He threw up his hand to say goodbye again, but I could also tell that he was confirming that what had happened between us would be our little secret. My exploit with Jeff that day, proved that I too had the capabilities to share time and space with someone besides Joe. It was all the ammunition that I needed in order to take another step towards walking away from him altogether.

As my conversations with Jeff transitioned into daily interactions, Joe's conjecture transitioned into daily inquiries. He would say things like, "You want to screw him, don't you?" I denied everything. I guess it was a half-truth. It wasn't that I wanted to, I already had. My bitterness towards Joe was mounting by the day. Not only did I feel that I owed him no explanation, but I was also wise enough to know that nothing had changed about his actions. He did nothing to show me that he was remotely concerned about any of the extracurricular activities I might have been participating in. Well, at least not enough to forgo his. You would think that amidst suspicion, he would have been moved enough to be around more, to love me harder, to make sure that I knew without question that his heart resided with me. But to no avail.

Jeff and I had been in talks about taking a road trip, just to get away. Through our exchanges, I also learned that he had taken company with a new girlfriend. I knew that it was a front, but it didn't bother me because I recognized just how necessary it was. With Jeff being a newly divorced man, there was no way in hell that he could go parading around and screaming from the rooftops that he liked to be manhandled. That wouldn't have been decent. I knew that he needed a girl to sleep with occasionally, to at least cover up what the rest of the world did not have privy to. Essentially, he had enlisted the assistance of a beard.

That conversation also triggered me telling him about Henrietta and her upcoming visit to Los Angeles. We began to discuss the prospect of taking the ladies, both his girlfriend and Henrietta on the road trip in hopes that we could all be one big ass distraction from one another. We had to keep up appearances that way. And since Joe really had no proof that Jeff and I were anything other than friends, there was really not much that he could say. It was settled. We were hitting the open road. I was actually looking forward to doing something different. It would be a welcomed change from sitting in the house and waiting for Joe to come back to me. Those days were over.

When the weekend for the trip arrived, I woke up to find that like clockwork, Joe had left before the sun had come out. I didn't care. I got up, showered, and placed the last of my things into a black leather duffle bag. My bag was packed with care and every item was folded like so. It made me feel better to have my things in order. After sitting down and enjoying a cup of coffee, I took a moment to bask in the rays of the California sun that always made their presence known in the morning. I had been in such a rush to get here, make friends, and start a life that was different from San Antonio, that I wasn't even sure if I had ever taken the time to just admire the beauty of the land. California was a beautiful place. It made me even more excited about the road trip because I would now get to see more of it, as we were headed to the mountains.

As I stood, staring out of the window, I heard a knock and some unexpected noise at the door. I went over to answer, but I opened it instead of looking out of the peephole of the apartment door. There stood three of the biggest smiles that I had ever seen. It was Henrietta, Jeff, and his girlfriend Rachel. Henrietta barreled through both Jeff and his girlfriend with her arms extended to the heavens. "CHHHHHHHAAAARLIE!!! Look at my baby, y'all. Oh my God!" She kissed me on the lips with her mouth closed for what felt like a whole fifteen minutes.

"Well, hello, Henrietta. It's really good to see you. Really good," I said.

"Charlie, you have no idea how much I've missed you. Lord Jesus," she screeched with a throaty voice.

"Come on everyone. Come on inside. I just need to get the rest of my things." When we were all inside, Jeff introduced me to his girlfriend.

"Charlie, this is Rachel. She's the one who I have been telling you about." Jeff looked me square in the eyes as if to say, "If you say or do anything that is suspicious, I will kill you." I had no intention of doing so. We were both in the same boat. The women served as distractions from the fact that we would have much rather been taking this trip alone.

"I have heard so much about you, darling. It is so nice to meet you," I said, as I kissed her hand.

Rachel was lovely and very statuesque. She had a massive head of curly, naturally textured hair. She looked to be a mix of black and Hispanic. She wore very little makeup, but her beauty shined through.

"Rachel, what do you do here in LA?" I inquired.

"Oh, I'm an actress," she replied with confidence. I imagined that she was like most of the young women in LA: waitressing tables and going from audition to audition in the hopes of landing a breakout role to become a star.

"Enough of the small talk, Charlie, get your ass over here to me. Boy, I have been waiting to put my eyes on you. Stand there, let me see how you lookin. WOWOWEE! Boy, look at that ass. I tell you, Charlie, we need some time together. Alone," she hissed.

Henrietta was a ball of laughter just waiting to be rolled around. Both Jeff and Rachel broke out into laughter at her antics. It was an indicator that we could make it through the weekend together. I was thankful that Henrietta's backwoods ass would not be a deal breaker. She was actually a great deal of fun, which was why she and I had spent so much time together in the past. I was now really excited about our getaway.

"Ok, everybody. Are we ready? Let's get this show on the road," I proclaimed.

While on the road, Jeff and I exchanged more than a few lusting looks and stares. Unbeknownst to the women, he and I had more of an attraction to each other than either of us had to them, even though they were there to accompany us. The drive there was filled with beautiful scenery and the sun that you just couldn't escape, nor would you have wanted to. We belted out hearty laughs for days. There wasn't one person in the car whose personality didn't become a magnet for the comical mood of the day. Any bystander would have assumed that we had all known each other for years. With the miles behind us, I recognized that it was good to have taken a breather from my convoluted thoughts about Joe.

When we arrived, we planned for a relaxing night in. The views from the condo that we rented were breathtaking. I knew that no matter how much I attempted to avoid Henrietta, I would have to sleep with her that night. I was really unsure if I would even be able to muster up the strength to do so. In many ways, I felt that I was doing her a disservice because she didn't know about the men in my life. I had to be cognizant of karma. It is usually the most innocent and pure person who gets mixed up in things they don't deserve. Moreover, I was far more interested in another round with Jeff. From the looks that we exchanged throughout the weekend, I knew with certainty that he shared the same thoughts and desires that I had.

I'd have to say that the trip was uneventful because it was just a series of moments in which I desired to be doing something other than what I was doing. At one point, we were all sitting at the dinner table and Jeff and I had gotten so lost in each other's eyes, I thought for sure that Henrietta suspected something. "Boy, if you don't focus right here on all of this. I already told you what I was going to do to you, Daddy. Tonight, is the night." I let out a big sigh of relief behind a forced smile. I wasn't ready.

It simply would not have been possible for me to sleep with Jeff, knowing that the ladies were present in our environment. I have an unprecedented amount of respect for women. I couldn't be disrespectful in that way. Women are a trigger to my moral compass every time. I'm not sure if it is the voice of my grandmother that I can still hear, softly whispering in my ear, or the piercing words of my mother that stuck with me so deeply. I just valued women and knew that it was my responsibility to keep them safe at all costs.

Men, on the other hand, have a different level of strength and conviction as it pertains to relationships. Men are sexual creatures by nature, and I knew that it was more about me being straightforward with my intentions and what I desired from the relationship. End of story.

There were so many moving parts within my heart and my mind. I was facing my own personal journey. When we returned, we all said our goodbyes. Jeff and his guest got back into his car and went about their business. There was very little time for Henrietta to do anything other than kiss me goodbye and prepare for her drive back to San Antonio, as she had work the following day. I bid her adieu and genuinely wished her well. I cared about her well-being. I kissed her on the forehead as I watched her drive away. I motioned to let her know that I would call her to ensure that she had endured the long drive. She was in need of a clear direction for the simplest drive home and I was in need of a compass to navigate the winding road of the never-ending maze of my faltering relationship with Joe. Quite frankly, now that I had really seen Joe for who he was, everything had taken a turn towards a fork in the road. I knew that continuing to date him, wouldn't end well for me.

And if you sit in shit, eventually you too will begin to smell. I was at the point where I was just sick and tired of being sick and tired. Joe's lying and cheating ways began to push me to the point of no return. Eventually, it would all hit the fan, and no longer be about love, the pursuit of happiness, or the celebration of the freedom to love as we saw fit. Not only did Joe's swindling ways have me feeling used, but his excessive use of cocaine began to take center stage amidst our relationship. He no longer even pretended to put me first. I knew that I was worthy of far more, especially when I was making sacrifices to be a loving partner.

If I'd been honest with myself and allowed the light of the truth to shine through, I would have acknowledged Joe's absence long before I actually did. Even when he was there, Joe was not really with me. He was a hoe. He belonged to everybody. When he was with me, he was always plotting and figuring out ways to get out of the house. I had given so much of myself to him, and I couldn't really explain what I had to show for it in return. Love can disorient you in many ways. On the one hand, a part of me wanted to leave, but the other part of me was strung out on the hope that he would be, or could be, who I had wished for.

It wasn't until I caught Joe in the act of cheating that I accepted the truth that I had been unwilling to see. The reality was that there was no grand story. I simply walked in on Joe, in the act with another man. It forced me to admit to myself what I had already known, but sometimes turned a blind eye to. I was both hurt and relieved in the spirit of confirmation.

I wanted Joe to pay me in tears. He had hurt parts of me that I never even knew felt pain. My heart wanted to hate him, but my mind had to take responsibility for what I had allowed. I knew that Joe had shut me out of so much of his life because he didn't want me to be a part of it. He thought that I was much too good for some of the activities that had become second nature to him—and I was. On the one hand, he valued me, but on the other hand, I saw how much more he treasured his own needs, wants, and desires. I hadn't accepted the times when he disrespected me without a fight or the exercise of fury. In hindsight, I think that my desire to love was so great that I rejected the notions of his transgressions with other men because of what we shared. When Joe and I were together, I believed we shared the love that my heart had so desperately been in search of. But your heart has the ability to trick you into believing something is there when it isn't and that it wants something that can actually destroy you. I had chosen carnage, even if only for a moment in time, and now, I had to find a solution befitting of my worth and my value.

The trouble with heartbreak is that the agony is steady. It's enough to kill your soul, if you let it. The difference between me and many people, is that my somewhat passive aggressive nature allowed me to sit still as I watched things play out, before showing any signs of a reaction. Even today, I possess an ability to remain silent, but I am never misinformed. Ever.

After that night, I drew a mental line in the sand and decided that I would open myself up for other options. With Joe's antics at the forefront of our relationship, I felt like I deserved better. Hell, I knew that I deserved better. And since I hadn't found anyone better, I granted myself permission to explore, free from the guilt that might have otherwise taunted my conscience. Joe had taken me for granted for far too long, but everything would soon change. My new mindset and disposition would now be equivalent to pouring water on a parched desert.

Contrary to the way that things looked to those around us, I was really the one with the power. I always had my own money, my own apartment, my own car, and my own financial stability. Even though it seemed that he was the dominant one in our relationship, Joe had been benefiting from my toil, driving my car, and frequenting my apartment. Joe needed me more financially than I needed him. On the flip side of the coin, I thought I needed him more emotionally, but I was wrong.

As my eyes began to open, my view would eventually shift from Joe's wayward antics to my own greener pastures. By this point, I had every intention of moving forward with my life, without Joe, but I was just not sure when it would happen or who it would happen with. I'm not sure why I didn't just break if off with him immediately, but I was numb to his antics and in those moments, it was about what I wanted, he became an afterthought. I was looking for trouble and another chance to get my feet wet. It turns out that when you go in search of trouble, you are sure to find it. Eventually, I would get more than my feet wet after a night of hanging out at Catch One, which was a hot spot, frequented by gay men, during that era in LA. All of the who's who could be found there. Fancy cars and flashy clothes were all the rage. People weren't afraid to showcase their lavish lifestyles in LA, and I was becoming more accustomed to seeing it. From Cartier watches to David Yurman jewelry. You name it and, honey, the people were wearing it. I was here for it in every way. I had come from such humble beginnings, but the sights and sounds of Los Angeles gave me something to aspire to.

While Joe and his friends continued their orgy parties, which I wasn't invited to, it became a pastime of mine to go out on my own and just take in the Los Angeles breeze, vibes, and people. On many nights, I left the club empty handed and that was okay with me. Very few, be it man or woman, had the ability to spark my interest, but when I saw something that I liked, I immediately knew it. One night in particular stands out from the rest because

I stumbled upon a man that would go on to become the love of my life. That night, I had decided to leave the club early. I had an extremely busy week coming up and I wanted to be ready. As I was awaiting valet to bring my car around, I heard a raspy, baritone voice coming from behind me.

"Excuse me. Hey, stop. Hey. What's your name? My God, where did you come from?" I turned around out of sheer curiosity.

The voice that had stopped me dead in my tracks belonged to a charismatic spirit named Cory. When my eyes gained full focus on his face, I exhaled. Oh my GOD! I had never seen anyone that looked quite like Cory before. Los Angeles is filled with beautiful people and models, but Cory set the bar higher. I was in absolute awe. His skin revealed an unforgiving, dark hue of melanin that was so deep, it appeared to be illuminated by the moonlight. His smile offered the presence of a warm personality, and his lips resembled a pale pink rose. They were almost too light for his face but the sharpness of his jawline and the precision of his goatee made it all come together nicely. I noticed everything. He was speaking but I couldn't focus on what the hell he was saying. Cory was a sight for sore eyes in more ways than one. He was the embodiment of the tall, dark, and handsome phrase. It was like he emerged from the night and the closer he came to me the more I realized that he towered over me, such that the waves in his hair appeared to graze the sky. He must have been standing on stilts. He had legs for days. I allowed my eyes to move up his thighs, and I couldn't help but notice that his hands were large. WOOO! He had my attention, that's for damn sure. And even though his exterior was to die for, it was the appearance of his soul that seemed to steal the show. He was a gentle giant.

"What could you possibly be doing here all alone? I mean, how is that even possible? Look at you." He was sizing me up and I liked it. I tried to play coy, but my mind was racing with at least a thousand other things that I could do with him besides the conversation that we were both engaged in.

"I come here pretty regularly alone. I just haven't found the right person as of yet," I muttered.

"I would say that you have," he replied. I snickered like a little schoolboy and instantly knew that I wanted to know more about him. "So, tell me your name. Who are you? I mean, where did you come from? I've never seen anyone as fine as you," he proclaimed.

"My name is Charles, but some of my friends call me Charlie." From out of nowhere, I heard a man yell, "Cory" and he immediately turned around. I thought to myself that it was probably his boyfriend, summoning him to leave. I didn't have much faith in men after dealing with Joe's. I kinda felt like all men were whores and dogs.

As I was processing my thoughts, he grabbed me by the waist and said, "Wait. Stay right here. I will be right back. Promise me you won't leave." I shook my head and before I knew it, he leaned in to kiss me quickly on my lips. Although I was shocked, I didn't stop him. Our eyes connected and I smiled. He touched my hand. "Stay right here. Just give me one second." I kind of rolled my eyes, but he was too gorgeous for me to not at least see what was up. Wouldn't you know it, the guy calling him was the valet who had just pulled his car around. One look at the car and my breath caught... OH MY GOD! Cory had a hunter green big bodied BMW. I could tell that the car was custom just by looking at the rims. I tried to keep my calm, but in my mind, I was excited as hell. A car like that made me think that Cory had some money.

As far as I was concerned, you didn't drive a BMW, unless you had the coins to afford it. I was stricken and I stood my ass right there to wait for him as he requested that they pull the car to the side in the parking lot. I could hear him explaining to the valet that he wasn't exactly leaving and I watched him give the man a tip. Having squared that away, he jogged back over to me. Can you imagine what I saw when he was running? He was a damn goddess. I could have stood there watching him all day. "So, where were we?" he flirted. He leaned in to kiss me again and this time we remained in the moment. I could have stood there kissing him for hours. It amazed me that he showed no shame. He was not concerned with anyone or anything around us.

Finally, we both knew that we had to call it a night. Before we left, Cory asked for my number, and of course, I gave it to him. I didn't hide the fact that I was in a relationship with Joe. I did, however, let Cory know that I had every intention of bringing that shit to an abrupt end. Cory didn't seem to mind.

We kissed goodnight and vowed to keep in touch. "I'll give you a call sometime, ok, baby?" We hugged and bid each other adieu. That night, standing there talking to Cory, I had forgotten all about Joe's regular shmegular ass—that was until it was time for me to open the door to my apartment.

━━◆Hot Tea◆━━

AFTER ARRIVING BACK from the club, I opened the door to see Joe sitting on my couch in my dimly lit living room. He appeared to be bothered: his arms were folded and he wasn't smiling. He immediately jumped up and charged towards me. "Where have you been?" he screeched.

"I just went to hang out. What is wrong with you?"

He must have gotten wind that I was outside of the club talking with someone. I mean, hell, the circles that we ran in were big, but small at the same time, and everyone knew everyone.

"I'm going to bed. I'm not dealing with this shit tonight." Just as I attempted to push past him, he reached back and hit me, slapping me right in my face. It shocked the shit out of me. We had argued before and things had gotten heated, but he had never put his hands on me in that way. Tears began to stream down my face and I started crying profusely. My tears became a river, wet with all of the pain that he had caused me. All the pain that I spoke and that in which I remained silent about. The taste of the tears was salty and added insult to the wounds of what he had put me through. He had taken advantage of me in so many ways. From driving my car, to impeding upon my finances and all of the lies and cheating that I had ignored. He preyed upon me because I was young and he tried to break me more than help me to flourish. I became enraged as all of his past transgressions spun like a carousel in my mind. The tears became flames of rage. We stood there and it was as if time stood still. The sound of my heartbeat was deafening as the anger filled my mind, body and soul. I could now see the concern in his eyes because he had never seen this side of me. If only, I would have been granted another minute of elapsed time, I can't say how the story would have ended, but I do know that it would not have been good. In haste, he grabbed me and hugged me, binding my arms. I couldn't move and I felt too weak physically and emotionally to do anything. So, I sat there and cried in his arms. He allowed me what felt like hours to do so. And in those tension filled moments, I let go. I let go of all of my pain. I allowed it to escape my body like smoke under a doorway. What Joe didn't know was that in those moments, I also gave myself permission to let go of him. I let go of the hold that he had on me. Being close to him while doing so was cathartic. I was in the midst of a purge, and the weight of needing to be loved by Joe miraculously slipped away from my body. My soul was now free to soar.

Far too often, we allow ourselves to be underestimated. That had always been the case for me. Joe was no different, but his time was up. The next morning when I awoke, I realized that we had somehow made it to the bed. We had made love and I couldn't even remember it. I was so jaded from the series of events that had taken place. Joe had his arm around me as he always did, trapping me next to him. I lifted his arm and pushed away from him. When I rose from the bed, I realized that nothing had changed in my heart of hearts; we had come to the end of the road. I stood up and felt as light as a feather. I couldn't remember the last time I had felt so clear about anything. I went to the bathroom to get my robe and then walked to the kitchen to make myself a cup of tea. The honey that I used to sweeten the tea tasted surprisingly sweet that morning. I could see the sun peeking into the living room that had been so dim the night before. The light became another confirmation of my freedom.

Without hesitation, I headed back into the bedroom. With my tea on my hand and my robe tied in a perfect knot, I began to tap Joe on his shoulder. He was snoring like normal, but I wanted him awake and out of my home. "Joe, get up. You've got to go."

"Huh? What? What do you mean?" He sat up in the bed, confused and lethargic. "Why are you waking me up? It's seven o'clock on a Sunday morning."

"I don't give a damn what day it is. You've got to go. I want you to grab your things, right now—this moment—and get the hell out."

"Oh, so you're just gonna put me out? You're just mad. Calm down."

"As you can see, I am calm, but I'm also serious. Get your shit and get out!"

He began to mumble under his breath as he rolled out of my bed. He paced around the room, aimlessly looking for the small remains that he had there. He had never left his apartment and moved in with me, so there really wasn't much. As I stood there, I thought to myself that how little he had at my place was also a reflection of how much he had truly committed to our relationship. I was even more convinced to put his ass out.

He attempted to put his arm through his shirt and struggled a bit. I noticed his fat stomach and it disgusted me. How could I have even allowed myself to let someone like him overtake me? His time was up in my head and in my heart. I can honestly say that I didn't feel anything while I was watching him go. He couldn't fight it either because he knew that I deserve so much better than what he was giving.

When Joe walked towards the door, he stopped in his tracks and faced me. "If you do this, this is it for us. I'm not coming back," he said.

Before I knew it, I blurted out, "Nor would I want you to." I couldn't believe that I said it, but it was exactly how I felt. I was done protecting his feelings and putting him first. From this point forward, it was about me. Joe walked across the threshold of my apartment and out of my heart. Just like that, it was the end of a chapter and I was more than happy to turn the page. As Joe made his exit, Diane made her entrance for what proved to be a one time exchange of love and lust. That's another story for another time!

CHAPTER 4

INSIDE OUT

"Proof of love is when we give pieces of ourselves to someone, knowing that we shall never get them back."

—Elgin Charles

I HAD LOVED AND I HAD LOST. As piercing as those words are, they were the good kind of pain. I had been in search of a love that I had only imagined. The depth of my soul had sent me on a search to discover it and to fill my cup with it and even if for only a season, it had runneth over. As I closed the chapter that included my relationship with Joe, I did so with empty hands. I had nothing tangible to show for the time, energy, and space that I had given to him and to us. Nonetheless, I had touched love in a way that proved that it was real. And although I had chosen to walk away, I had gained perspective.

Today, I recognize that perspective is often one of the most powerful tools that we can use to move ourselves forward. When we are stretched, we are granted access to the possibilities of what could be. This pattern of thought has proven to be powerful in both my personal and professional life. And while at that time, my personal life was on a brief hold, the pendulum of my professional life was in full swing. The way my ambition was setup, I was in search of forward progression and a path that led to professional wins that would allow me to grow and climb the corporate ladder. But even the best laid plans don't materialize according to our plans.

The more I worked to prove myself at Smith Barney, the more I found myself attempting to scale a slippery slope. My father had managed to break through many racial barriers due to his ability to remain almost racially neutral. More importantly, he was smart and the companies he worked for needed him and his thinking power in every equation professionally. My level of respect ascended for him during this point in my life; particularly because I now recognized that what he had made look effortless was almost impossible for many. Being a black man in corporate America was no crystal staircase.

I had conquered so many tasks at my job. I oversaw the accounts that the traders acquired and made sure that the necessary documents were filed and I had mastered it. What I knew, was that I was capable of so much more. The trading desk was where the real action happened. Men would stand there and aggressively acquire municipal bonds for their clients. Not everyone was granted access to work there, but admittedly, I had my sights set on the trading desk as my next move. Complacency was not a part of my DNA.

Up until that point, I had not come face to face with the good ol' boy system, but it was now more apparent than ever. Even after excelling in my role and being requested to train others to excel, I was denied access to the trading desk. My work's track record and its associated numbers spoke for itself. My attention to detail wouldn't allow me to be anything but thorough. For the life of me, I couldn't understand why everyone apart from me had been promoted to work and thrive at the trading desk. Then, one day it hit me: I was the only black male.

If I decided to stay, I would be the only one not promoted. It wasn't a risk that I was willing to take. Being isolated and being placed in shackles once again was not my idea of progression. I became easily angered at the thought of not being given a fair shot, simply because I was black. It took a toll on my overall being. I had played the game, dressed the part, shook hands with enemies, smiled in the face of adversity, paid my dues, overcome obstacles that had been thrown my way, and even transferred the knowledge that I had acquired to ensure that the company had professionals who could do the job, yet boundaries were still set on how far I would be permitted to run, and it hurt like hell. For every black man, it hurts like hell.

We hike through life, carrying an invisible cross uphill, only to realize that the peak of the mountain, leads to another uphill climb. This cycle is endless in America and we often recognize the American dream as an American nightmare. This silent epidemic leads to depression, exhaustion, and emotional anguish. No one talks about it. No one. And black men suffer in silence for fear of not appearing strong or being accused of laziness, and I most certainly was neither. I'd venture to say that many of us are not what society has deemed us to be. It simply boils down to a lack of access to equal opportunities.

I knew in my heart that if I continued at that pace, under those constraints, I would have nothing left to give myself or anyone else for that matter. During our toughest times, God always sends a glimmer of hope. This time, for me, it was in the form of new love.

—◆A Cup of Joe◆—

IT WAS MONDAY morning and I was preparing for work as usual. My routine was very meticulous and the fact that I was no longer in love with my job had no bearing on my outward appearance. The corporate environment allowed me to get suited and booted daily and I loved it. I had no need to do so back in San Antonio, but in LA it was free reign. From my tie, to the crispness of my white collared shirt, and gray slacks with the cuff, I left no detail unnoticed.

As I stood in the mirror, tying my tie, I looked at myself. For the first time, I noticed myself in a way that I hadn't before. I saw myself... like really saw myself. I saw a man who was smart and capable and filled with fight. I recognized in that very moment that I had to devise an exit plan that would allow me to chart a new course for myself. I was not going to allow that job to strangle the life out of me and leave me desolate when I had so much to offer. But where would I go next? What would I do? What was I good at? How else could I make a living? These were all real questions that deserved real answers. And even though I didn't have the answers, I did know that I wanted something in my life to change and that I would be responsible for changing it.

I nodded back at myself with certainty and headed towards the kitchen for my morning cup of coffee. I never missed it. I turned on the coffee pot just before getting in the shower so that everything was timed perfectly. It would be ready as soon as I was finished getting dressed. Timing was everything. Just as I went to the fridge to grab the milk, the phone rang. I was rather shocked as my phone never rang at that time. I figured that it must have been something important.

As I walked over to the phone, thoughts of my mother raced through my mind. Usually, if someone from the family was contacting me, it meant that my mother had fallen into one of her depressions and refused to get out of bed. I hoped that this wasn't the case. "Hello, this is Charles," I spoke slowly.

"Aw, man. I can't believe you picked up the phone. I'm sorry if this isn't a good time. I just... I just have not been able to get you off my mind. I mean... I have not been able to stop thinking about you."

I stood there in shock. The silence was awkward.

"Are you there?"

"I'm here. Wow! I didn't expect you to call. It's really good to hear from you. I've actually been thinking about you too." The voice on the other end was Cory. Our chance meeting at the club, ended with fireworks and I was quite intrigued by him. I don't believe that I really ever thought that anything would come from it because I had told him that I was in a deteriorating relationship with Joe. His call gave me butterflies.

I sat on my couch, talking to Cory about absolutely nothing until I was forced to end the call, so as not to be late for work. The call was just what I needed. His voice and his timing could not have been more perfect. I don't think I had ever smiled so wide. I mean, my cheeks were hurting after our call ended. Just before saying our goodbyes, he invited me to dinner the following week and I accepted. Just like that, I was ready to open my heart to the prospect of love once again.

As foolish as it may sound, there are some people who exist to love. I am one of them. This want, need, desire, and quest for love is embedded so deeply within me that I've never stopped believing in its power. I don't fault myself for being this way, yet I embrace the beauty of being a hopeless romantic. It is poetic justice of sorts.

By the time I had arrived at work, I realized that I had forgotten to drink my coffee. I needed that coffee to get through the morning with the corporate thugs that I worked with. I dropped my head before walking in the door and heading towards my office. When I opened the door, I took a huge sigh of relief to encourage myself that I could make it through until my lunch break. As I got closer to my desk, I noticed that there was a large Styrofoam cup with a note that read, "Drink Me." I removed the plastic lid and discovered that the cup was filled with coffee. On the other side of the note, it read, "Can't wait to see you. Cory."

I dropped my briefcase strap from my shoulder and plopped down in my chair in disbelief. Was this really happening? Was I really exchanging with someone who would cater to me? Was this even real? It all felt like a dream. It had to be too good to be true, but I was willing to take the chance to find out.

That day, I didn't give a damn what they did at the trading desk. All I could think about was dinner with Cory. My time at that job was on a downward spiral, but I had a feeling that whatever developed between Cory and I would withstand the test of time!

——NATIVE TONGUES——

THE PACE OF MY LIFE began to pick up as I continued planning my exodus from corporate America. I learned that it was possible to take a mental health sabbatical that would provide you with a sustained income if the you were under tremendous stress or anxiety. I knew that I had to chart new territory, but I was still very unsure of what that looked like and I knew I had to conduct more research before I could leave a well paying position. Around this same time, I made a decision to become room-mates with Diane. I knew that it would be a phenomenal way to save money. Our friendship had far surpassed everything that hap-pened between Joe and me. Although Diane had introduced us, we shared an unspoken love that trumped all. The same week that we began to move our belongings was also the same week that I was to meet Cory for dinner. Each evening, I would drop items off at our shared condo and Diane would do the same. The night of the date, I followed the same schedule. When I opened the door, I yelled "Honey, I'm home."

I heard a voice from the back of the apartment yell out, "Boy, be quiet." Diane came sliding towards me in her flip flops and gave me a big hug. That was my girl.

"I'm going on a date. Can you believe it?"

She stood back and gave me a once over and rolled her eyes. "With whom?" she asked sarcastically.

"Cory. Cory. Cory," I said.

"Is that the same one that stuck his tongue down your throat in front of the club? Chile!"

"Well… ok, if you put it that way. I mean, it was a little more romantic than that to me, but clearly that's all you got from the story, then, huh?" I paused for a moment and she looked at me, square in the eyes and we immediately both burst into uncontrol-lable laughter. That was our relationship in a nutshell. She meant the world to me.

If I could have allowed Diane to be a fly on the wall during the date, I would have. She was such a good reader of character and people's spirits. She would have been able to tell me who she thought Cory was and if he would be good for me, just by shaking his hand. But I had to go this one alone; at least for this date. If he and I could survive the night, it would only be a matter of time before they would meet and I knew she would give me her entire opinion, even if it was not requested.

Diane adjusted my collar and I left to see what Cory was all about. I'd be lying if I said I wasn't excited. He was chasing me and I loved being pursued.

Everything that happened that night was honestly a blur. I just knew that he was smitten with me. It was so refreshing to have someone who was into me. He was very nurturing and attentive. Unlike so many men, Cory was not in the closet. He didn't care that people knew that we were there that night together. We sat at the table and talked for hours about nothing and everything. I learned that he had also taken a shot at leading a heterosexual life, in a monogamous relationship, and it hadn't worked out. He had also been previously married and together with his ex-wife, they had brought life into the world in the form of a baby girl.

Cory was born and raised in LA. He was a native and that was different for me. All of my assumptions about the people who were from Los Angeles were silenced. I had really only seen the affluence of LA in terms of the people who lived there. With the exception of my ex-boyfriend Keith, I had no idea that Los Angeles had a great history of disparity and poverty for people of color. I had seen the bottom life that Joe enjoyed being around, but that had all been by choice.

Cory told me about his experiences as a student at Crenshaw High. From the drugs to the violence to the police brutality, he had seen a great deal. And the hopelessness of a people can only be intensified when the hills of Hollywood are just within reach, but out of touch due to societal imposed poverty. The truth is, Cory was raised around Hollywood, but couldn't get there because he was in the hood and so was his family. Even so, he possessed an unspeakable joy. It was the same joy that I had known. When you come from humble beginnings and you get a taste of anything sweeter than what you had, you delight in it.

As we sat at the table, I could not take my eyes off of him. He was drop dead gorgeous. His dark skin always appeared to have a golden undertone that glowed. Maybe it was his light, I don't know, but whatever it was, he was simply beautiful. I don't even remember if we actually ate our dinner, I don't remember what the waiter or waitress was like. I don't even remember what I ordered. What I do remember is how we sat and looked into each other's eyes in silence. I remember how he held my hand under the table. I remember how he kissed me, right there in the restaurant, with no regard for who was watching. I remember thinking that this could be more than what I had expected. That night in the restaurant, seated at a dinner table, with plates left unattended, I had discovered love.

—◆From 0 to 100◆—

FALLING IN LOVE WITH CORY was blissful. I know that it is not healthy to compare relationships, but I can honestly say that with Cory I found a protector of my heart. That was what I had been in search of with Joe, but he had come up short.

Cory was a very emotional creature. At times, the contrast of his masculinity and the proverbial capacity to feel, baffled me. Even so, our relationship was built upon a mutual courtship and the bond of friendship that rapidly grew. No matter how perfect a relationship may seem, the flaws are what determines its ability to withstand the test of time. I can say that the levels of intensity that we shared for each other were not equally matched. I had been branded by the hurt of love and the smoke of the scorching of my heart was still prevalent in more ways than I let on. I was all in, but cautiously so. Cory was at the complete other end of the spectrum. There were times that I felt he allowed his emotions to overtake the need for rational trains of thought.

During the first two years of our relationship, I kept quiet in those moments, so as not to rock the boat. I had finally found who and what I was looking for, and we were doing life together. Why would I begin to pick away at the fibers of our relationship because he loved too hard? It almost didn't make sense, but there were so many underlying themes that I hadn't quite grasped. Furthermore, I didn't want to hurt Cory's feelings in any way when all he aspired to do was to love me. There were times that he would burst into fits of uncontrollable crying and I could never understand why. I also knew that I had cried so many tears in the absence of Momma that I had very few left to give. I was aware that my levels of sensitivity had been muted through my experiences and it would have been unfair to impose them upon him or anyone for that matter. To see a giant like Cory be so emotional was at times unnerving. He would call the radio station and dedicate songs to me and I would hear them playing on the way to work. He always added the element of surprise and spontaneity to our relationship by leaving surprises on my desk at work, in my car, and in the bedroom.

I knew without question, that he was willing to do anything to make me happy, even if it meant that it had to be done at his own expense. After my relationship with Cory was considered to be longstanding, we made the decision for him to move in with Diane and me because he was there all the time anyway. An extra roommate also meant a decrease in the bills and neither of us was opposed to that.

I began to learn that Cory's financial disposition was not what I had once assumed when I saw that green BMW he was driving the first night that I met him. His money was not long, in fact, it was short and he was working to get by. Even though I was making ends meet with my corporate job, I had no intentions of allowing that to be the case for any long period of time. I was saving money where I could and I had always kept my eyes and ears open to the prospect of new opportunities to increase my income. Somehow, someway, Cory would come up with his portion of money for the bills and to be honest, I didn't really ask a whole lot of questions. I knew that he had a steady job working for Lorimar Television Productions. What I did not know was that Cory was secretly writing checks from the company to himself. This embezzlement of the company's money, eventually led to a warrant for his arrest and a stint in jail.

Cory's departure resurrected so many of the feelings from my past that I had worked in desperation to shut out. I was left alone, again. And while I knew that Cory wanted to do what he could to begin creating a life with me, I had never requested that he do so through illegal means. It was not something that I believed in. I am not in the business of judging anyone because I am not perfect, but there are certain lines that my moral compass will not allow me to cross.

All things considered, I was angry with Cory and the respect that I once had for him began to diminish. Visiting him in jail was not something that I wanted to do. Quite honestly, I wanted no part of that shit. I felt like he had gotten himself into that mess and it was up to him to get himself out. He had taken me to meet his family on several occasions and each time I had felt uncomfortable. There was an undertone to the conversations—almost like subliminal messages—where on the one hand, they were pushing for me to support Cory financially and help his current legal position, but on the other hand, they wanted me to maintain a distance, so as not to confirm his gayness as it could pose a threat to his safety in jail. This was the type of shit that angered me to no end. Now, I was supposed to financially support him with some bitch-ass hope that he would return to me upon his release. Honestly, I felt like they all had me way too fucked up for words.

I gracefully allowed my calls, visits, and interaction with him to diminish until one day, I stopped. I began redirecting all of my time and attention towards a new career venture that would change the trajectory of who and what I would become. I was prepared to cleanse myself of anything and everybody that did not align with my future goals, even if that sabotaged my search for love.

——BABYLON——

WHEN CORY RETURNED home after his release, he assumed that everything would be just as it had been, but my feelings had shifted. I had hidden my head in the sand once again and I was not sure that I trusted him any longer. He was not who I had fallen in love with. Moreover, he had realized changes while being in jail. I did not know what pain or torment he had endured while there, but I knew that he was different as a result.

As the days passed, I knew with certainty that I wanted to break all ties with Cory. I called him and requested that we meet when he returned to the apartment that evening, so we could talk. It hurt my heart deeply because I knew what I was planning to tell him. Making the decision to part ways is never an easy one.

When he arrived, we hugged tightly. He patted me on the back as if someone had died. The look on his face spoke to the fact that he knew that our relationship was taking its last breaths.

"I just think that we have grown apart and gone in two different directions. I mean… I'm just not sure that we share the same values."

"Listen, Charlie. I know that things between us haven't been perfect, but all I've ever wanted to give you was the world. Haven't I shown you that?"

"I mean, you have. I… I… I just don't love you the same. It was hard for me to stomach the thought of you doing something illegal. I trusted you and you put both of us in danger."

"I know that I might have broken your trust and for that, I'm sorry. I just think that maybe if I give you some time, we can work through things. Would you at least be willing to take a break before making this decision so final?"

"I think that's fair. I just can't make any promises," I said intently.

As he stood up, I noticed the tears streaming down his face and it killed me. Against the will of my heart, I stood up and walked toward the door. I stood holding it open and my eyes were a dead giveaway that the levels of compassion that I had once owned for him had diminished.

Cory eventually got a place of his own and after a brief visit to collect the few belongings that he had at my place, he left the condo and our relationship behind. Just as Cory pulled out of the parking lot, I heard a loud voice yelling, "I love you!" I thought that maybe Cory had circled back around the parking lot, but as the voice drew closer, I realized that the voice belonged to the face of someone who had once been an intricate and intimate part of my life. It was Joe.

He yelled again as he got close enough to make eye contact from the driver's seat. "I love you, Charlie. I will always love you!" As fate would have it, on the same day that Cory and I placed a time-out on our relationship, I was standing there watching Joe profess his love for me.

Truthfully, I wanted nothing to do with either of them. I had finally realized that I was too good for Joe's antics and that I had no interest in Cory's lies and self-inflicted run ins with the law. I smiled vaguely at Joe but gave him nothing worthy of stopping and so he didn't. I watched his car exit the parking lot and my life forever.

What I didn't know was that that would be the last time I saw Joe alive. As I walked slowly back to my place, I began to exhale. I knew that no matter how badly I was in search of love, I now needed to take time to determine where I had gone wrong. I knew that I had to own my part in what was not right in my relationships. It was going to take some significant time and some significant thinking to arrive at any conclusions, and I had every intent to allow myself that time.

The number seven represents completion. For me, it represented the time spent with Cory. Although my heart did not agree, my mind recognized that our time together had expired.

The gut punching truth was that he hadn't been honest enough with me, and we didn't match in ambition. Over time, those simple truths became deal breakers. The saddest part of it all was that he wanted to be a provider and he wanted to take care of me, but he was also willing to cross immoral lines to do so, and I was never ok with that.

What I will not do is ignore or discount my part in the pain that led to the demise of my relationship with Cory. I had to recognize that I was the epitome of passive aggressive. And as ironic as that may sound, there were times that I desired to be treated like a little princess only to turn around and become the sexual aggressor, like a man. Of all the men that I have ever dated, Cory was able to balance my inconsistencies the best. In complete transparency, I lost interest in us when he went to jail. I no longer held him in the esteem that I once had.

When I got back to the apartment, the door was opening for me. Behind it stood a smile that I could never resist. It was Diane. She was standing there, holding a drink that she had made for me, and a cigarette. She passed the drink over to me and closed the door. She looked me square in my eyes as she always had, to read my soul.

"So, how are you, honey? You've had a rough few years," she said with concern.

I let out a deep breath and said, "I'd be lying if I said that this love thing has been all roses for me, but I know one thing... I will survive."

"Hell yeah. Of course, you will, and I will be right here for you, honey."

"I know. You are my world. Love ya." I reached in to kiss her on the forehead.

"Love ya back," she said, and then pranced back to her room.

I smiled to myself. She would always hold a special place in my heart. I had never really opened that compartment because I wasn't quite sure what to do with it, but I knew her friendship was unlike the rest and I wanted to hold onto it for dear life.

I made up my mind that I was going to harness all of my energy towards solidifying a financial future for myself and discovering success, whatever that meant for me. The following Tuesday, after returning home from work, I plopped down on the couch to watch TV. I needed to decompress from the mounting stress at work. The first station that came on was a local news station and it was buzzing with breaking news alerts.

It was on that day that I, along with the rest of the world, learned of the retirement of Earvin Magic Johnson. The news that one of the most prevalent and untouchable men in Los Angeles—and possibly the world—had contracted a disease from a sexual encounter was shocking. Magic Johnson was HIV positive and I was shaken to my core.

Prior to his announcement, the disease had been reserved for gay men. And all anyone knew or acknowledged about it was that it was a death sentence. That night, I could hardly sleep. If Magic could contract HIV, then none of us were as invincible as we pretended to be.

In retrospect, after Magic went public with his announcement, shit all around me began to hit the fan. Eventually, I would go from hearing Magic Johnson's story, to learning of the passing of my friends and people who I had known or worked with. Gay men were dropping like flies. The world began to establish a negative stigma surrounding the disease. Magic Johnson was the scary exception. HIV was now known as a gay man's disease.

During this same era, I received word that Joe had moved back to Dallas to pursue a second career. He called on rare occasions just to check on me and I was thankful for that. To my surprise, one of his calls was out of concern after having watched the local news in Texas. It broke as a story of a woman who had been murdered in San Antonio. The woman was identified as Hispanic, but he wanted to be certain that I had not had any connection to the lady. I was thankful that he had cared enough to check on me in this way. During that call he never mentioned being unwell, and because I no longer saw him on a daily basis, I was unaware of his dire physical state. Eventually, I received a call that he too had passed away from HIV.

My heart had taken another blow. Not only was I sad to hear about Joe, but I now feared for my own life. My mind reminisced over all of the orgies that Joe had engaged in, only to come back home to lie with me. I couldn't quit the replay of the sexual freedom that we had all once indulged in. We had all been in search of a love that the world was so adamant in denying us. And now, it was as though the world was frowning upon those with the disease, almost as if it was the perfect punishment for not living according to God's will. The walls felt like they were closing in on me. I would wake up in the middle of the night in cold sweats from nightmares of what could be. I was frightened and for good reason.

My fear became a reality in many ways when I went to Cory's apartment to visit. We were still very much in love and I was so attracted to him that it wasn't possible to keep my hands off of him. He looked different, but I initially thought that he had just done something different with his hair. I couldn't quite put my finger on what else had changed; I just knew that I still loved him. Although not in love with him, I never stopped loving him. We started kissing and eventually, ended up in his bedroom. I began to undress him and as he stood up to take off his pants, my nightmare was before me. He was a vision of skin and bones. He had lost so much weight that he appeared to be rawboned. Seeing his body and his face, took my breath away. I felt like I was in the twilight zone. Not Cory too, I thought to myself.

"I can't do this. I'm so sorry Cory. I… I just can't do this."

"Baby, what's wrong. I know I'm not the same, but it's still me. It's still me, Charlie," he pleaded.

I grabbed my things and rushed out of his apartment, full of tears. I was enraged. I felt like there was an entire bed of lies that he had withheld from me and that they transcended his illegal activity.

When I got back to my apartment, I plowed through the door in a rage. Diane was on the couch, watching TV, but she knew me too well to not notice that I was upset. If there was one person that I wouldn't be able to hide from, it was Diane.

"What's gotten into you Charlie? What's wrong my love?"

"Nothing, Diane. I'm just fine, ok?"

"Ok, Charlie, honey. I'm here if you need me, love."

"Thanks," I said, sarcastically. I knew that she didn't deserve that, but I was beside myself. I was losing my shit. I laid on my bed and wept. I must have cried for over an hour and after that time, I knew that I had to make a decision about my future. That night, with bloodshot red eyes, I stood in the bathroom in my apartment, staring in the mirror, making a decision to choose me. I had put the need to love before my safety. I had put the need to love before my salvation. On that night, I resolved that I would put the need to preserve self before everything else. Like an ostrich, I buried my head in the ground and washed my hands of Joe and of Cory, and any existing notion of what we had shared. It was all dead to me.

I was now in my twenties and I recognized that the era of sexual freedom that we had all indulged in had come to a screeching halt. When death knocks at your door, you leave that muthafucker closed.

BY THE WAY

MOTHER EARTH AND FATHER TIME

IT IS IMPOSSIBLE TO understand where you are going if you haven't taken the time to feel the fullness of the conviction from which you came. Everything that has happened to me has been a part of my story. Whether through laughter and happiness or sorrow and pain, it has been my destiny to unfold. I have walked this journey with the intentions of living every moment to the fullest. It has never, under any circumstances, been my wish to look back over my life, after all has been said and done, and see it as mundane. It would be dismissive to whom I've been called to be. All that any of us will have at the end are precious memories. I desire memories that are the most vivid colors and those that reflect a soul who lived and longed for the passion of feeling alive. I want my breath that so many have taken for granted, to actually mean something.

I was born to a woman whose personality was colorful and to a father whose muted hues brought about a subtle balance. I am the intersection of their rainbow. Careful dissection of all that they were, gleans tremendous insight as to who I became. Taking the time to ponder the significance of it all, has required me to dig deep into my cache of memories to recall my formative stages.

Whether we choose to acknowledge it or not, every decision that we make, stems from who we are preconditioned to be and who we believe we are. And as simple as that may sound, it is mystic truth.

CHAPTER 5

FORMATION

"Coming together is the alpha; keeping together is the omega."

—Elgin Charles

"YOU'RE THE UGLIEST one in the bunch." Who wouldn't long to hear words such as this? They were spoken by the matriarch of the family, Honey. Honey was my mother's aunt, but more like a grandmother to all of us. And by all of us, I mean all of the first cousins, who shared a bond like siblings due to the closeness in our ages. There were eight children, including me. One of my mother's first cousins, Gene Marie, had five children and my mother, Charles Etta, had three. My mother had a total of four siblings, three sisters, Joyce, Nilene and Elaine and one brother, Albert.

Honey made sure that the bills were paid, and the kids were fed. She took care of her own daughter as well as all of us. Honey was old school and placed value on people based upon their skin tone. She was color struck. That pattern of thought was so ingrained in her psyche that she would treat people according to such standards. Even as kids, she called us in to eat by order of skin tone. Those who were of lighter hues were called long before those of darker hues. Honey and my brother didn't get along for this very reason. He sensed the injustice in her actions and he always felt slighted because of the richness of the melanin in his skin.

Even so, we all felt the brunt of the societal imposed hatred that had plagued people of color for generations. Within our family, the presence of traditional put downs were alive and well.

I was young, but I always felt like I was tough. I felt like I had to be. "I know I ain't ugly. Don't get me talking about your ugly black ass." This would be a typical response and although I didn't really mean it, it was a response worthy of clapping back. We were the true embodiment of the notion that we could bother each other, but anyone outside of the family would not be granted permission to do so. We had each other's backs.

Honey was one of many strong female examples that I had seen growing up, and I recognized that the strength that we all possessed was a direct correlation to what we had witnessed of her. She would even fight off the boyfriends, who made attempts to come around with empty promises of courtship.

When Stephanie's first child was born, she came out looking like a white girl with blue eyes and since she was born in the same month that Honey was, she loved Karisha. Sadly, Honey up and died out of nowhere. It was devastating to the fiber of our family structure. The dynamics and the way in which we interacted changed when we lost our matriarch. Unfortunately, there was no one willing to step up and fulfill that role.

Honey's house had been the backdrop for much of our lives and was considered our retreat from the world. That refuge was left wide opened and somewhat unattended. There was no one around to sustain it and even when my cousin Marsha was there, she felt too alone and afraid to stay long. Because the home was situated in the projects and so many had frequented its walls, no one was even certain who had the keys.

My mother was fortunate to have her blood relatives on one side, and the home that my father had used his resources to create for us, on the other side. In my father, she had assurances that her sister did not. My mother was a keen woman who had wisdom beyond her years. And even though her actions might lead you to believe that she was unaware of many small details that dictate life, she was in full command of the elements around her.

Often called "Charlie," Momma was a feisty Scorpio who would sting at a moment's notice if she needed to. Her frame was thin and statuesque. Her dark, silky hair framed her fair hued face and illuminated the sparkle in her eyes. She was the most beautiful woman that I had ever seen. It was as if she glowed. As a child, I would look up to her as she peered down at me and the vision of her face blocked the sun from hurting my eyes. She was my protector from everything; my guardian angel in many ways. In her presence I felt safe and secure from dangers seen and unseen.

When she was a young girl, my mother weighed just under one hundred pounds. She was often teased for her white girl shape. The truth was that she had inherited her frame and her skin complexion from the white side of the family. I remember her retelling the stories of how she had been terrorized by her peers.

"These girls, they mess with me. They try to talk about me with their fat black asses. They just mad because they wish they looked like me."

Although she was tough and knew the streets, she was never promiscuous. Momma bore all of her children by one man. During the era of her upbringing, many men communicated their emotions with their fists. She was a far cry from subordinate under any circumstances. If the demands being imposed were not in alignment with her will, you were unlikely to get anywhere with her. Any attempt to physically force her under control, was a grave mistake. Momma could fight a man and be the victor. Throughout her life, she fought for the principles she believed in. Time and evolution would serve as proof that her most triumphant battles would be rooted in discovering herself.

——BABY HAIR——

MY MOTHER WAS SPECIAL to me because of the way that she loved me. I am well aware of the fact that most everyone can conceptualize the overwhelming sense of fulfillment that a mother's love provides. For me, the ability to define, commit to memory, and encapsulate the feelings evoked by her love would prove to be vital for my life as a whole and eventually my survival.

Growing up, I listened to all of the stories about my birth. According to my mother, even the way that I came into the world was different. I'm not sure how much of that was her and how much was me, but I do know that I have never met, nor will I ever meet anyone like Momma. I was born Charles Elgin Williams and I was told that from the moment I was conceived there was something special about me, or at least my mother believed this to be true.

"The world will open doors of opportunity for you. You are special and smart and handsome. What you have been given by God will set you apart from many. Never be afraid of your gifts. God has blessed you to be fruitful." The powerful offering of words such as these were etched into my psyche.

"You was breached when you were born. I screamed so loud during labor with you. After all of that you came out ass first. I knew right then, after all you put me through that you was something special. Giving birth to you even flipped my uterus. The doctor said I would never be able to have any more children after you."

She'd tell that story a million times and let out a hearty dose of laughter afterwards, gleaming at me with delight. I knew that I was her pride and joy, and I absorbed every ounce of the love that she gave me. I thrived on it. During the earliest years of my life, we were inseparable. She showered me with praise and special anointings, and her words gave me confidence, building me up and answering the deepest questions of my soul.

Those words that I clung so dearly to, were spoken by the lips that had given me life; the same lips that would eventually serve as a whisper in the distance, rather than a resounding proclamation up close. And even though Momma had the capacity to fill me up, she had witnessed a few things in her own childhood that tore her down. Many of her aunts were teachers and they would beat her and make her stand in the corner, holding books, when she didn't appear to grasp concepts at the same rate as her peers. As the offspring of educators, it was implied that she was supposed to be smart and she was, but not always to their standards. It was eventually discovered that she needed to see words backwards to comprehend what she was reading. Doing so opened new doors of possibilities for her ability to read and write.

She would write from right to left in order to read her letters, and later in life, when she would write to me, I would have to place her writings up to the mirror in the bathroom to read what she had written to me. Momma would also pick up a book and read it from the back to front.

In addition to hardships in school, Momma was all too familiar with hardships on the streets. There was something about the streets that called her name, and on many occasions, she answered. Later in life, it would prove to be at the expense of both her husband and children.

Momma was a blues singer among many things. She was raised during a time when women had raspy voices and the grit of the air could be heard in the music. The vibration of the blues was a color that stained her heart. And although Momma knew the ill of heartbreak from life in general, my Daddy wanted nothing more than to be the cure.

Daddy fell in love with Momma in a small town called Whyma, Texas, while at the NCO club. They were polar opposites from the very beginning, but Momma thought a man in the military was a good catch, and the older people in her family were eager to marry her off. As a young child, I wasn't aware of how their differences were affecting their relationship. As I grew, those distinctions became apparent, especially when it came to raising me and my siblings. When it came to rearing children, they each believed in different value systems and methodologies.

More often than not, when it came to the story of how they met, it was Momma's side that I heard. I'd sit at her feet as she spoke about the peculiar union that she shared with Daddy. She would start with, "I was just a country girl," and then say, "All he saw was a light skinned woman that he could have kids with. I think that is the only reason he married me. He wanted some light skinned kids and when he showed me to his momma, they decided that I fit the bill. I didn't even get to finish high school. Before you knew it, I was married, barefoot, and pregnant. But only one of you came out like me," she'd say while staring at me with a twinkle in her eye before finishing the story. "The other two look just like him."

And truthfully, that was the case. My brother, Edgar and sister, Holly looked more like my father, who was of a darker complexion. I, on the other hand, was the spitting image of Momma. The four of us lived together as a family for as long as Momma could stand it.

By the time I was six years of age or so, Daddy had built us a beautiful, four bedroom, brick home with central heating and air. He thought maybe Momma's desires to chase her singing career, and the desires of her heart that didn't align with raising kids and playing house, would quiet from a storm to a whisper. Daddy yearned for Momma to be happy as a housewife and recognize him as a sound provider. But Momma was just not wired that way. She felt like the world had something that she deserved and it pulled at her heartstrings so much that it caused her to abandon the very children that she had birthed. By the time I was in second grade, Momma no longer lived with us. With no other choice, Daddy had to assume full responsibility for rearing Holly, Edgar and me. Momma's departure changed my life so profoundly. I would not recognize all the ways that her actions created a sense of abandonment within me that served as a backdrop to much of my life.

Daddy worked tirelessly to fill in the gaps for us. His goal was to never miss a beat, but it was inevitable. He couldn't cover all the bases in the game of life when he was missing a major team member. Daddy prioritized education, honesty, stick-to-it-iveness, and most importantly being responsible. He wanted for us to never feel as though we were alone in the world and for us to recognize that we had the ability to achieve whatever we put our minds to.

Unknowingly, I found many ways to cope with Momma's departure. I used to scratch my skin profusely, sometimes so much so that I bled. To this day, I can remember saying to myself, "You need to stop." I was in search of comfort, and although Momma would remain in our lives, she never returned to live under the same roof. We were all left with no choice; we had to keep moving forward. School allowed me a proper escape to do so. I excelled mentally, even if I was suffering emotionally. My cousins and siblings would always speak on how much I cried. According to them, I cried all the time, but it was a reprieve. The tears represented the pain of missing my mother's tender touch upon my face and the showering of words that I had held so dear.

In second grade, I excelled and skipped to third. By the time I had reached fourth grade, I was put back in third because they believed me to be too young. I was more than capable of handling the work, but they were attentive to my socialization needs. The school system in San Antonio was a high performing district and I was making straight A's. It helped that the teachers were very loving and they made it a point to teach us anything that we desired to learn about. The school set a foundation for me to succeed in an environment that mirrored the love of a family. I always became the teacher's pet. They were the ones to first put me on stage for programs, plays, and dancing. Because of the teachers, I evolved into a great dancer and would even win contests.

Momma continued to live her life, according to her own rules. One day, out of the blue, she and her new boyfriend came and picked us up to take us all to the laundromat. She gathered all of our clothes and some of our belongings and settled us in the car. We drove for what seemed like an eternity, until we reached a town named Brackenridge. It was ironic that we were supposed to be going to the laundromat and Momma just kept driving, until we were in another city all together. When we arrived, we kept passing one home after another. The town was clearly a place where there were very few people that looked like us. Our stay was short lived, and eventually, Momma would tire of the full-time toil associated with raising children and return us to Daddy.

It was after that when Momma left and went to live in Arizona near her mother. My mother's mother was an Evangelist and a bible toting woman. She was always preaching the gospel and trying to rebuke the devil out of you. It was odd to me that Momma moved back with that type of structure in place when she sought freedom. There were so many things that I was too young to understand.

There was no presence of peace to help us understand Momma's revolving door antics. She and Daddy had a hard time getting along under the circumstances. I never saw anything specifically, but I heard the story of Momma having gotten a black eye. To this day, I can neither confirm nor deny if that happened. Upon the acceptance of the realization that Momma would not stop living for herself or attempting to carry out her dreams, Daddy was determined to invest in the assured stability of his children. He demonstrated in many ways that he would not allow us to fail in her absence. His commute into the city was one hour there and one hour back, but he did so every day without complaining because he wanted to be a reliable provider.

Recognizing that he could not control Momma and that focusing on her whereabouts was pointless, Daddy began construction on a home in the backwoods of Pleasant, Texas.

Momma attempted to remain in touch through phone calls. She would tell me how much she loved me and that the reason she left was so that I could get a better education. But, no phone call could hold a candle to the impact of having Momma in my presence. To make matters worse, there were times that Momma would return to San Antonio and not make it a point to see me. I'm not sure which was worse—to love someone that you can't have, or to have someone that you can't love. Either way, Momma was not there for me to love. Her absence caused me to cry so much that other children would stand in a circle around me and chant that I was a cry baby. Within my home, I was also teased that I was the milkman's baby. In my earliest stages, I had always been covered in the protection of Momma's loving arms, but that was no longer the case.

In middle school, I missed Momma but spent much of my time trying to navigate adolescence. School was a place of refuge and I learned to make friends while there. The skill of socialization proved to be beneficial in so many ways, including the success I've seen throughout my career. My optimism allowed me to always see a glimmer of hope. Finding creative ways to entertain myself and experiment with hair, kept me engaged and on my toes.

Hanging on to my mother's words and longing to be in her presence, if only for a moment, I caught a Greyhound Bus to visit her in Chandler, Arizona at the age of seventeen. Doing so, allowed me to see Momma in a different element. She was a far cry from the woman playing house with Daddy. In Chandler, she was encapsulated by the essence of the streets. When I arrived, she had this little bitty house where she had set up the garage like a living room. Flanked by a coffee table, television, a rug, and a wood burning stove, Momma had constructed a custom cave according to her desires. On any given day, Momma could be found sitting in her chair, watching TV, sipping a hot cup of tea with a hint of the moonshine that she had crafted. She'd be draped in a mink stole with a bevy of rings on her fingers—some real and some fake but shining nonetheless. Her adornments and mindset were the perfect mix of luxe and low tariff. I had never met anyone who was so unapologetic about living life according to their own terms. It was almost as if you could not fault her for doing so.

The city was heavily populated with Native American people and culture. The norm in business and pastime was the act of boot-legging alcohol. The city was home to a bar that Momma would frequent and play the guitar at. She was a hustler. When I could not find her, I learned to look to the streets. She could usually be found in an alleyway shooting craps with guys and drinking until her steps became stumbles. In those moments, she would exclaim "Steady Going, Moving Forward." My cousin Buggy and I were always motivated to find her when she was in that state because we knew that we would be met with little resistance in getting some money from her. She would hustle like a man, squatting down and tossing the dice with cockiness. She was a pro. She hit seven or eleven with ease. Many times, she would be so into what she was doing that she would forget that I was standing there or that I was her son. I will never forget the time that I stood just above her, naive of the unspoken codes of the street. I attempted to reach down to pick up the money that she had won, but she grabbed my hand ferociously. In an instant, she snapped back into reality and released my wrist. She handed me the money she intended and I left as quickly as I could. There were no limits to Momma's antics. On a different day, I approached her as she was enthralled in a huge argument with a man. I was so nervous for her as the fight turned physical. Before I knew it, the man began to back away and run with haste in the other direction. To my surprise, he was wailing. I never knew him or met him, but that day, I must admit that I had a scary feeling. Why was he crying? Maybe he was jealous of the fact that she had a son. I could never quite wrap my mind around what happened that day. All I knew was that Momma took shit from no one.

Momma just had this way of making people do what she wanted them to do. It was like the whole world was at her mercy. She was also pimping the hell out of me. On occasion, she would even ask me for money. She would wrap her arms around me and say things like, "You're my baby. You are the one. You're going to have the keys to it all."

She placed so much pressure on me to recognize myself as the one who would be financially stable. I always felt like she didn't apply such emphasis on Edgar and Holly. She truly believed that there was some sort of special calling on my life to take care of others. To this day, I have done so to a fault. I would venture to say that there was some part of me that wanted to live up to the words that Momma spoke over my life.

Momma taught me what she could about the streets. "You can't let the streets give you a bad rep. You have to be strong and hold your own." I knew how to fight. I had been forced to learn. People didn't expect it from me, but I was more than capable of kicking someone's ass if I needed to. I am not a fighter by nature. I believe myself to be a defender, who stands up for what they believe is right. This mentality seemed to earn everyone's respect.

After I became an adult, no matter what profession I was in, I always made sure to send money back to momma, wherever she had decided to live. After moving to Los Angeles, Mom came to stay with me. She stayed as long as she could. My life in Los Angeles was not even close to aligning with the streets that held her heart.

Momma relocated back to San Antonio to take up residence. A short time later, due to what I thought was depression, the doctor began giving her Valium. Despite the medication, her drinking continued and when she got her hands on alcohol, she often became another person. There were times when she would go on binges and drink all day. She wouldn't leave the house or even comb her hair. Eventually, I would get a call from a family member, informing me that she was in the middle of one of her "fits." I knew that when she reached that point she would only leave the bed to go to the bathroom. When she was like that, I would have to leave LA, to go and revive her. I was the only person who could. Once there, I would talk about faith, get her food, and do her hair. My goal was to always spark new life in her.

Our relationship continued to evolve, such that Momma let me into her world. I'll never forget the day she let me listen to her record. It was a forty-five and she was singing her heart out. My review was brutally honest. "Wow, Momma. Your voice is very heavy. It almost sounds like a man's."

"Yeah, Lito, I have a deep voice."

After hearing her music, I recognized that all those years, Momma had been singing the blues in her heart. She was the embodiment of the genre.

I have never, nor will I ever, meet anyone like my Momma. From both her presence and her absence, I learned so much. Eventually, Momma picked up the Bible and the word became her sword. I can hear her saying ever so softly, "If you live by the sword, you die by the sword." It would be a lesson that I would never, under any circumstances, forget.

BY THE WAY
I Forgive You

I T WOULD BE SIMPLY impossible for me to ever, under any circumstances, question your love for me. It was you who made me feel that I was the most important person in your life. More times that I can count, I felt the warmness of your heart. Your love felt like the fresh mist of morning dew. I thirsted for your presence and drank from the fountain of security that you bestowed upon me. I bowed in your presence, for your positioning in my life garnered an unprecedented hierarchy of respect.

When you left indefinitely, I was desolate, famished, and searching for answers that had been cast away into a sea of sorrow. Your absence became the source of the wounds that injured my ability to think, to thrive, to hope, to love, to wonder, and to heal from the vicious war that was waged on me by the world. Life as I knew it would never be quite the same. I was forced to fully encase myself in armor I knew nothing of. I was dropped amidst a battle that showed no signs of retreat and I was without the skills to earn a reprieve. I was alone, fending off evil spirits without the one warrior by my side whose artillery was heavy enough to silence it all.

You must know that your actions brought me to anger. You deserve to feel the weight of my hurt. But after the rain, the sun is sure to shine. Through my pain, I discovered a power that superseded all that I had been in search of. It caused me to hasten toward my power in Jesus. God's great love allowed me to see your pretty face in the distance and to smell the sweetness of your skin. His love gave me permission to free myself from the self-imposed interrogation of why you left me if you loved me. I discovered that I was most safe in the arms of the Lord.

Today, I live to play peek a boo with the moments of poetic justice in life. They never fail to prevail. And although you will never understand how much torture I endured due to your absence, I thank God for every moment that you gifted me with your presence. You saw a light in me, and through the love you gave unto me, it never dims.

You are the most regal being that I have ever had the honor of witnessing, and it has been my greatest honor to be a direct descendant of all that you are and all that you have been. I thank you. I forgive you. And most importantly, I forgive myself.

With Heartfelt Gratitude,

Lito xo

—Daddy's Eyes—

I DON'T BELIEVE THAT YOU can truly know a person unless you know who their heroes are. Daddy was without question the only man that I have ever hailed as my hero. He stood at about 5'6" and was the absolute smartest man that I ever met. A trained biochemist, he was appointed as the lead researcher at Brooks Air Force Base. In the later years of his career, he was chosen to be the Safety Administrator. He never ceased to amaze me with his wit. Like all of us, Daddy had many fascinating sides. The intellectual in him knew what seemed like everything there was to know about chemistry and formulas. If I ever had any homework to this end, there was nothing that I couldn't ask him. I would even attempt to ask him questions that I believed were more challenging than my homework, but he always somehow knew the answers.

I can recall times when he would bring my siblings and me to work with him. He mostly worked later shifts. I now recognize that he'd had no choice in bringing us because there was no one to watch us at home. Thankfully, he didn't mind us being there, learning and watching what he did. It definitely expanded the scope of our thinking. We tried to be quiet so as not to embarrass him. It was the same when Daddy made the decision to further his education by attending classes at Trinity University. There were times where he would have to take us there as well. Today, I still have a sensitive spot for people who are trying to work with their children in tow. I realize that sometimes that is the only option.

I remember that there was a monkey launched in a rocket, sent to the moon. Daddy wrote many of the official research documents needed for that to happen. A true milestone in his career was when he took us all to meet President John F. Kennedy in Dallas. Daddy's work broadened our horizons in many ways.

As a term of endearment, Dad nicknamed me Cha Cha—short of course for Charles. When he used that name it truly revealed his sweet side. And even though he was a tender-hearted man, he rarely showed it. He was a leader by nature and when it came to instilling values and a work ethic within us, he held nothing back. He had every intention of feeding our brains with life lessons, whether we wanted them or not.

He was adamant about us learning to speak well and think for ourselves. He would say thing like, "Don't be one of those black men, stuck in a rut, blaming everything on the white man. Get your ass up and work. If you have intelligence and you know how to talk, people will respect that and doors will open." Everyone admired him. Even in what we referred to as the hood. He was Mr. Williams, and his name was held in high regard.

He would also say things like, "Sit down, and read the instructions first, so that you can know what the hell you are doing." On occasions, Daddy would cook us a hearty breakfast. He would start at 9 a.m. and not be finished until 1 p.m. We would be hangry by the time the meal was ready, but as a chemist, he was used to taking his time and reading the directions carefully. Those meals may have been slow and methodical in the making, but they were special all the same.

There was a real no nonsense side to Daddy. I would come to recognize that at times he led with an iron fist. He wanted to ensure that we understood how to find our way towards success.

I'll never forget an incident that occurred before we moved to the country. My mother and father were still trying to make it work at the time. One particular day, Edgar and I were down the street playing with friends. We were swinging on the swings and we had a goal to see who could jump the farthest from the swing. First Edgar jumped and his friend was next. When my turn came, I jumped so high, that my left arm hit the side of the house. The pain shot through my bones like lightning. I ran home crying, overtaken by the agony.

When I arrived, Daddy said, "Let me see." But there was nothing to see; the injury was internal. All I knew was that I was hurt. After careful examination, he said "Boy, shut up all of that crying. We will take you to the hospital in the morning if we need to."

Needless to say, I wasn't able to shut up. I knew that something was gravely wrong. Eventually, they took me to the hospital and discovered that my arm had been dislocated and that I was justified in my acknowledgement of the pain. Even then, he had a textbook response, but there was no sign of emotion. I've always wondered why he had me in pain the whole night instead of taking me to the doctor immediately. Maybe it was because he had known pain of his own.

—JOY AND PAIN—

THE DEPARTURE OF MY MOTHER, on her own terms, was a loss to my father that compared in magnitude to that of a death. He was left feeling angry and resentful. And although introduced to heartache by Momma, my father managed to discover the blueprints that help one overcome unfair circumstances in life. Yet, he was not a stranger to pain.

I didn't see a reflection of myself in my father. My brother Edgar was a spitting image of him. He was a very handsome man. When we were out, people would ask, "That's your dad?" We didn't resemble one another, but I felt more like him in my heart than either of my siblings. The fact that I didn't look like him, made his approval all the more important and I was forever seeking it. A true Aquarius, he was not concerned with feelings. He would always say "I am responsible for training my knuckle headed sons to be successful and productive in the world."

Our home housed a great deal of subliminal tension in the absence of my mother. I can't imagine how frustrated my father must have been. Being left to raise three kids alone is something that I don't wish upon anyone. And although he handled it with dignity, grace, and class, I can recall some moments where it was just too much and the stress felt like raging winds. In those moments, there were always casualties of war. I can't even recall what I was doing or why it was displeasing to Daddy, but he beat me so profusely that the belt popped. I can still hear the snap that resembled electricity striking a tree. The belt's destruction was so loud that even Daddy stopped at the moment. It was almost as if he was unaware of what he'd done. I was overcome with anger, but mostly fear. There we stood, in shock, and it was as if time stood still. We were at a fork in the road of our relationship. He had beaten me for the pain that he felt from the broken heart that my mother had rendered him. He had beaten me because I was a way that he could remotely channel her. I was encased by my own hurt, now seemingly left responsible for carrying the weight of what should have been hers.

The look in my eyes spoke directly to his heart and he realized almost immediately that he had made me into a victim of the senseless turmoil that had waged between them. Even if he never apologized with words, his soul screamed it much louder. He hadn't meant to hurt me and I hadn't meant to be the vision of my mother. We had both been placed into situations that were inescapable. We were both out of control.

——ROOTS——

MY FATHER'S MOTHER BOOTSIE, lived in Madison, Illinois. Gang violence was the backdrop for the era. Everyone had guns, and talking trash was a way of life. We had to visit Grandma Bootsie during the summers, so that my father, who cared for us, could have a glimmer of a break. Grandma Bootsie had a friend, Charles that lived in the house with her. And although we knew that they were not married, we also knew that they were together. He was a big ass man, who loved to wake up in the middle of the night and eat ham sandwiches. His shadow appeared to skim the ceilings when he walked around the house in the late hours after the sun had gone down. You could hear the imprint of his feet, pounding into the hardwood floors. That was always how I knew where he was in the house.

My mind is drawn towards pain, when I recollect the moments that my brother Edgar would join forces with Charles to tease me. For some reason, they loved to fuck with me, while I was sleeping. I would wake abruptly, to Charles grabbing me by the head and putting me in a headlock, essentially choking me. Grandma Bootsie, worked the graveyard shift and wasn't there to run interference on my behalf. The torment didn't stop there. There were times when we would run minor errands in the car and while in the backseat, they found it humorous to put all of the windows down and freeze me half to death. I can recall on other occasions I would wake to find Charles and my brother tickling me and it would go on for hours. It was torment.

I attempted to explain to Grandma Bootsie what was occurring in her absence in hopes of attaining a reprieve, but to my dismay, she brushed it off, believing that they were just playing.

Finally, one night, Charles' behavior was so agonizing that Edgar, who had been an accomplice, became angered. The teasing and tickling had gone on for what felt like an hour; so long in fact that all three of us began to fight. I had never been the kind of child who upset people and as such, I couldn't understand why I was being victimized in that way. Edgar knew my personality and that evening, even he knew that Charles had gone too far.

All through the summer, I dreamed of better days and hoped that in some strange twist of fate, my mother would rescue me from it all. And while some kids dread summer's end, it was my greatest desire to see it come to a close because it signified the end of Charles' torment. For me, the prospect of peace outweighed everything else.

When we returned home, Daddy made sure that school was the priority. When I was in elementary school, he would wake us up every morning like clockwork. Since he worked late hours, Daddy would drive us to school in the morning and then have us catch the bus back home in the afternoon. During my elementary school years, it seemed as though Daddy was working, just to make it work. He encouraged us to take everything that we could in terms of extracurriculars because he wanted for us to have a bevy of exposure and experiences from which to pull from. He would try his best to pick me up from school after my activities were finished, but there were times that I would be out there hanging around until two or three in the morning. Unfortunately, I had no choice but to wait. We lived nine country miles from the school, which just wasn't walkable.

As we got a little older, Daddy found a few ways to take a load off. One of them was the Officer's Club. There, he shared a drink with his cohorts and discussed all things military. When he stayed a little too long, that meant that I'd be stranded at the school for hours. A will to survive, allowed me to notice a Texaco gas station nearby that had a little cafe house. Instead of remaining at the school, I began to go there to wait for Daddy. There were moments that I just broke out in tears. Sometimes it felt as if being left was an undercurrent in my life and it didn't feel good. Many times, I arrived at the cafe hungry, but without any money. One late afternoon, while at there, a waitress said, "Honey, are you ok?"

"Yes, I'm fine. I replied. I'm just waiting on my dad."

"Is there anything that I can do?"

"Can I order something to eat and have him pay when he gets here?"

"Of course, love. That would be just fine."

When my father arrived, I nervously told him that I had ordered some food. I was unsure of what his reaction would be. Thankfully, he took it well. "From now on, just get something to eat and I will pay for it when I get here."

He insisted on our being independent and to that end once we were old enough, he purchased cars for us to ensure that we were never stranded. We were undoubtedly spoiled in that regard. Daddy even went so far as to have a makeshift basketball court designed at our home in the country. He was determined to keep us happy by any means necessary.

By the age of seventeen, the free spirit within me was asking to come out and play. I had always been a free spirit, but I often felt as though my father tried to keep me in a box of tradition. This was especially true when it came to my affinity for hair. In his mind, there was nothing traditional about a man who enjoyed styling hair. I even experimented with my own hair during that era. I was trying out new techniques and products to satisfy my curiosity. If you ask me, I had the best afro in the city of San Antonio. Having an afro of that caliber, required work and consistent maintenance. I knew how my father felt, which forced me to wake up early in the morning so that he wouldn't see me amidst my styling sessions. My customary routine was to braid my afro at night and then pull it out, early in the morning. The fact that I knew how to braid hair alone would have been mind blowing to Daddy.

One fine morning, I was meticulously unbraiding my hair and the door opened unexpectedly. When I turned around, I was met with a face that revealed disbelief, disappointment, and alarm. Daddy stood there, just long enough to confirm with his mind what he was seeing with his eyes, and then, he dropped his head and closed the door. I was petrified, but I was also one step closer to being free.

—⟐Next of Kin⟐—

WHILE SOME PARENTS, who have loved and lost, resolve to chart new territory, others are determined to remain steadfast in rearing children and providing sustainability for their families. This was true of my father. Daddy didn't bring a lot of women around us. If he was dating, we saw no signs of it as children. As I approached adulthood, I noticed that Daddy began taking calls, and time would reveal that he had indeed decided to fill the empty space in his heart.

Blondie was a Lieutenant Colonel in the Air Force. She earned her Master's in Nursing Administration and served as a supervisor at a convalescent home. She and Daddy entered into a lengthy courtship and on a summer day in July, their union resulted in a ray of hope. Crystal, their beautiful baby girl, was born under the sign of Cancer and from the moment she entered the world, she was as sweet as pie.

I've always felt as though Crystal's birth filled the void that Daddy had felt when Holly left home to create her life with Donald Ray. He used to call Holly "Kitty Kat" and now Crystal would be called the same. That was the sweetness of the love that Daddy had for his girls. By the time Crystal was born, Daddy had retired, which opened the door for him to be a stay-at-home father and he loved every minute of it. He had a chance to really spoil Crystal the way we all wanted to. Holly, Edgar, and I were so many years older that we were more like an aunt and two uncles, but that never mattered to us. There were times that I was teased by family members that I was jealous when Crystal entered into the world, but nothing could have been farther from the truth. She was a blessed light. I was overjoyed to see the manifestation of new life. Most importantly, it was among my greatest joys to develop a lasting and loving relationship with Crystal. After all, we shared the same DNA.

Daddy and Blondie went to the Philippines for five years and Daddy spent his time there caring for Crystal. When they returned home to the US, I got to know my little sister even better. Daddy kept us connected and I was so proud of all that she was growing up to be.

Blondie saw to it that Crystal always got the best education possible. As a student at the University of Texas, Crystal won a ton of awards, became a campus queen, and was even featured in the parade. I'll be forever thankful that Daddy finally got the family that he had always wanted. In my heart, I have always felt that it was the family that he deserved. As the old saying goes, God may not come when you want him, but he's always right on time.

BY THE WAY

I Love You
A Dance With My Father

WHEN I REFLECT UPON who you were and what you meant to me, I am filled with a slice of heaven. You were the most straight up, straight forward, no nonsense, no bullshit, optimistic, well-mannered man that has walked the face of this Earth. Anyone that was in your space was cognizant of your hatred of poor manners and dreadful grammar.

As a father now myself, I understand you even more. You were such a little man, but your strong presence made you monumental. I appreciate how you raised us. I want to thank you for giving me all that you had. In retrospect, it was the absolute best. You should know that you didn't miss a beat. Not one. Your intelligence was unmatched. I loved how you could enter into any circle, regardless of the ethnic makeup and be respected as a black man. You set the example for what a man is and should be. You taught me that there was nothing I could not accomplish if I worked hard and put my mind to it.

Thank you for the sacrifices. Thank you for abstaining from your life to be there for us. Thank you for thinking ahead and moving us into the country. Thank you for showing me how to treat a lady.

I do remember some of the good times when Mom lived with us. I recall the fur coats and jewelry that you bought her. You wanted with your whole heart to make her happy. I also know that the more you tried to show her love, the less she cared. I watched as she hurt you and left you to raise three kids on your own. And through it all, you sustained and I thank you. I need you to know that you created something special in Holly, Edgar, Crystal, and me.

You were the most gentle, caring, loving, attentive Dad that anyone could have ever hoped for. I have always thanked God for you. I am glad He chose you to nurture me and to give me wisdom. When I was hurt, you were there to protect me. I thank you for your prayers which helped through the years. You were my confidant and my inspiration. You gave me hope. Because of you we made it through.

You were there for every Christmas, Thanksgiving, birthday, and graduation. You made sure that I had new shoes and clothes, a nice home, and money in my pocket. You are the man that I aspire to be. You are my idol. I put you up there with Martin Luther King, Jr., MALIK, and Muhammad Ali. You are my president, a class act. I admire you and I love you

I am so glad that you found love with Blondie. God blessed you because of what you gave up for us. You were so deserving and brave and He knew that a new family would be the perfect gift.

I want you to know that I am aware of and sorry for the worry that I put you through with my love for "girly things." I could see how you detested it. It hurt you badly and that was never my intention. The dolls and the hair, the secrets inside of me, were never meant to upset you. You saw these parts of me and you were so against them. I never had the courage to share the struggle I was having with my sexuality for fear that you would not accept me or that you would judge me. I have only ever wanted to please you, and I vowed to take my secret to my grave, so as to spare you from the grief.

There is a small part of me that recognizes that I hid behind the notion that you would not accept me. Now, I have to live with the fact that you will never truly know. Today, you are in heaven, and I know that you see it all. I can't help but wonder... would you accept me for who I am?

You were so happy when I was married. I'm glad I could give you that peace in knowing that I at least attempted to live my life in a way that was pleasing to you and society. I have no regrets, I'm glad I did.

Our inside joke was that you would live to see the tender age of eighty. Well, you did it. You made it to eighty-four. And just like every other part of your life, you beat the odds and exceeded the expectations. God will never make another you. It is my highest honor to have been your child. The very essence of all that I do is to honor you.

Humbly Signed,
Cha Cha

CHAPTER 6

An Ode to San Antonio

"It takes unyielding courage to grow up and become who you were meant to be."

—Elgin Charles

RURAL SAN ANTONIO was our stomping ground. Daddy resolved to keep us safe by moving us so far away from civilization that we were all in search of ways to make the quiet, country days go by faster. The weeds, armadillos, poison ivy, and sticker bushes made it hard to deny that we were anywhere other than the country. And while some might attest to the quiet, subdued environment and the fact that Daddy's theory was the best way to keep us out of trouble, I beg to differ in many ways. It's hard to live in the sticks. Aside from an ongoing desire to be in the presence of other people, inevitably, boredom is bound to strike. There were times that I would take my daddy's golf clubs and use them to cut the grass.

Simple things like keeping the sinks clean with only well water, was pure hell. There were times when the well water would clog the washing machines and I would be forced to wash my laundry in the sink and hang it up to dry. I would often find myself cleaning the house from top to bottom because I had nothing else to do. I learned that Daddy would give me extra money that way and that became motivation for me.

Cleaning the house was actually therapeutic and calming in many ways. The ability to maintain oversight of my own environment gave me back the power that I had lost in the absence of Momma. I've always liked for the things around me to be clean and beautiful. It is possible that I was subconsciously trying to create the home that I believe she would have made for us. My cleaning led me into a pseudo career as an interior decorator in the sticks. I would go outside and grab weeds and stems and make a bouquet. It was fabulous as hell. I would even take the time to look for various pieces of greenery that had hints of other hues to add pops of color to the arrangement. The more I decorated, the better I became at it. It just came natural to me. At the time, it was not about buying the most expensive crystal vase, it was about using whatever I could find to add elements of charm to our living quarters. Today, I know without question that I have the ability to take the simplest elements and make them look like a million dollars.

I also began to take pride in rearranging the furniture on a regular basis. If I walked into the room and the arrangement of the furniture was unbalanced, I felt a sense of urgency to do something about it. I would later learn that I had an affinity for Feng Shui, though I had no idea what that was at the time. It was my belief then, and it is still my belief today that we are all responsible for making the absolute best of what we have, while we have it.

There were four consistent bodies that inhabited our home in the sticks, including me. In the confines of our home, those bodies learned to work together, play together, learn together, and do life together. In the absence of my mother, we knew that we had to depend on those who were actually present. We recognized the need to bond, not because we were family, but because our survival depended on it. My father was the nucleus and the glue that held it all together, but my siblings were the extensions of me that shaped my perception of who I was and my role in the world. It was through their interests, love, and an undeniable attachment that was rooted in DNA, that I evolved. As I got older, I would better understand that they had their own crosses to bear. We all yearned for the love of our mother. We yearned for the kind of love that kisses you on your forehead and tucks you in at night. We longed for mornings waking up to the smell of hot food on the stove, the rattling of pots and pans, and the gentle yell of a woman whose voice was ever so familiar, requesting your presence at the table for breakfast. We all longed for Momma. We all knew without question that she loved us, but her absence left us all in search of the hug we so desperately needed. And while Daddy did everything that he could to create a good life for us, his time was consumed as the provider. Eventually, we would all embark upon our own individual searches for the one thing that every living heart desires: love.

——HOLLY——

HAVE YOU EVER TAKEN the time to notice how a loving father gazes into his daughter's eyes? I have found that the immense emotions that a man is overcome with when he becomes the father of a daughter to be quite profound. There is a gentleness that a father of a daughter embodies that is both unique and indescribable. Simply put, a daughter has the ability to make her father's heart melt. Holly was the oldest daughter of my mother and father. She was born on February 22nd and her gentle spirit preceded her. She was my father's pride and joy and the apple of his eye. It became apparent to me at a very young age that he had a vision for what her life would be.

In high school, Holly was a cheerleader and athletically inclined. Even though she was one of the few blacks on her squad, her beauty was profound. She was an obedient child and the bond that she and my father shared was unbreakable. In retrospect, I now know that Holly was the deciding factor when my father made the decision to move us into the rural confines of San Antonio. He wanted nothing more than to keep us away from the inner city. Like any father, he wanted to protect Holly at all costs. She was his princess. I often wonder if he felt the need to shelter her from many of the things that he believed my mother had experienced, to ensure that his daughter had a better life. My father was such a proper man and he had every intention of ensuring that Holly had the best of what he could give.

In many ways, Holly was a helpmate to him in the absence of my mom. She was a second mother to both my brother and me. I don't know how Dad would have done it without her. She was always so gentle and loving with us. On more occasions than I can remember, Holly extended the touch of a mother's hand that I so desperately yearned for. She was patient with me and unlike most older siblings, she never complained about having to take me everywhere with her. Holly cooked for me, cleaned for me. She taught me to be a cheerleader and to dance. Everything that she did, I did because I was always with her. She was my first example of many things.

In addition to being caring and responsible, Holly was smart. She excelled in school and truly had the potential to do anything that she set her mind to. With the rural, country roads of San

Antonio as her backdrop, Holly had an abundance of time to consider what she would want to have manifest in her life. And like most high school girls, the presence of adolescence had a way of creating a change of scenery.

I can recall one weekend in particular that Holly went to the movies at the local theatre with our cousin, Stephanie. That trip would change her life forever. The theatre was a local hangout for kids and provided a source of entertainment and a way for everyone to socialize outside of school. The teenage boys would line the corridor of the walkway that led to the doors of the theatre. They'd stand there and snicker, while looking at the girls and doing all that they could to get their attention. Some girls were curious enough to come closer when called by the horny boys. That day, Holly caught the attention of many of the boys, but her beauty was intimidating. Only one proved to be bold enough to approach Holly. As Holly and Stephanie neared the theatre doors, they heard a voice emerge from the noise.

"Hey, Miss Lady. Excuse me. Hi. Can I talk to you please?"

They kept walking towards the theatre, when they were stopped abruptly as a tall, brawny admirer appeared from the crowd. He towered over Holly and stood directly in her pathway.

"You are so beautiful. I just ain't never seen anybody as pretty as you," he said.

Holly dropped her head in modesty. He extended his hand to lift her face as she fought back her smirk. From that moment on, she felt flurries of butterflies in her stomach.

"I'm Donald Ray. What's your name, beautiful?"

She placed her hand towards her mouth and mumbled, "I'm Holly."

As Stephanie stood there in awe of everything that was happening. I would imagine it was a teenage girl's dream. I don't know if they watched the movie together or what happened from that moment on. All I know was that as the days passed, the whispers amongst the girls became louder that Holly now had a boyfriend. That day at the movies, Holly met the love of her life.

Donald muthafuckin Ray came into Holly's life like a storm in the night and he never left. The storm of life began to rage once my father found out because shit hit the fan. Do you hear me? Donald Ray was everything that my father had warned Holly against. Guys like Donald Ray were the reason my father had moved us out to the country to begin with. Donald Ray was the opposite of what my father had envisioned for Holly's life. He was not articulate. He was not well educated. He did not come from generational wealth. And the icing on the cake was that he was a ladies' man. Trust me, I watched my father warn Holly against Donald Ray on many occasions, but his words fell on deaf ears.

Donald Ray began coming to visit Holly at our house more and more often. He had to have fallen in love with her because our house was far as hell from everything else and he still managed to find a way there. I can recall one time, they were making out and I ran over to sucker punch him. I was so much smaller and younger than him that there was very little impact, but I sure did try. "Get off my sister," I yelled. I thought that he may have been trying to hurt her.

"Go and sit down Charlie, I'm fine," she warned.

From that moment on, I knew that she wanted him to be around just as much as he wanted to be around. That song by Marvin Gaye, "Let's Get It On" had been released around that same time. Everyone was sexually charged and I watched Holly fall madly, deeply in love, and in lust with Donald Ray. I can remember her friends laughing and giggling at the sight of him. They would say "What's that in Donald Ray's pocket?" or "Girl, how can you take all of that?" It wasn't a secret that Donald Ray was a lady's favorite, with a big Johnson to boot, and he drove the girls crazy. He was also a good dancer and did this James Brown imitation that drew attention. My father recognized that those were the only things he had going for him and he questioned how Donald Ray would be able to provide for Holly.

For these reasons, Daddy continued to voice his opinion, but it was to no avail. With no other options, he felt the need to draw a line in the sand. One evening, he and Holly got into an argument that was so heated it drove a wedge in their relationship. I could see that the way they looked at each other had changed. He had hurt her and she had hurt him and to witness it all made me sad. It almost felt like we were losing Holly and it reminded me of losing my mother. Holly may have been my sister, but in many ways, she had also been my surrogate mother.

Daddy had a clear vision for our lives, right down to how we would choose who we would fall in love with. But the real truth was that we were also our mother's children. We were wired such that we would fall in love with whoever we would fall in love with and figure the rest out later. Quietly, that is what daddy had done with momma. Maybe that is why he fought so hard against it. Even after that argument, Holly didn't stop seeing Donald Ray. In fact, it was almost as if she was drawn to him even more. Our father would soon learn that Holly's fate with Donald Ray would not only be solidified, but also irreversible when she revealed that she was carrying Donald Ray's baby. Holly got pregnant during her senior year of high school and it was very taboo during that time for a girl in school to be pregnant. The stares and the whispers in our little town were heavy. Holly, however, didn't retreat; she held her head high. With her growing stomach and new life inside of her womb, she was as beautiful as ever.

Momma was always in and out of our lives, but she was around for many of the crucial moments such as this. "You love him? You havin a baby by him? You need to go ahead and marry him. You'll work it out," Momma would tell her.

That's exactly what Holly intended to do. Shortly after graduating high school, Holly gave birth to a bouncing baby girl. Donna was named after her father, Donald Ray. With her baby in tow, Holly made up her mind to make a complete life with Donald Ray. She packed her things and moved into an apartment near his family. Now, Donald Ray's family lived in the hood. The irony that Holly had graduated and moved to the very place that my father was most determined to keep us away from, was overwhelming. Holly knew that no matter where he lived, Donald Ray had a good heart and she was determined to make it work.

Her determination would prove to be vital. Donald Ray's shortcomings couldn't provide a living for Holly and the baby. Eventually, Holly went to school to become a nursing assistant. It was almost as if she knew that she would need to be financially responsible for both of them and she accepted that role. She began working at the local hospital in San Antonio to provide for her family. When their funds got low, Donald Ray would go "catch a truck," which in San Antonio meant that he would pick up some day labor. When Donald Ray returned from his day labor, he would have earned about $30 on a good day. He would always stop by the liquor store on his way home to pick up a fifth of Seagram's gin and a pack of cigarettes.

Over time, Holly gained insight into all of the things that weren't revealed during their courting stage. Not only was Donald Ray a lover of Seagram's gin, but so was his father. I can recall going over to his father's home and seeing him sitting in a chair on the front porch in a stiff position with his eyes closed, mouth wide open, and head tilted back. Shit, I used to think his ass was sitting up, dead. I couldn't have been the only one because out of nowhere, someone would say, "Donald Ray, what's wrong with your daddy?"

"Aw, ain't nothin wrong with Pops. He's just passed out, that's all." This behavior was normal to Donald Ray, but not normal to us. We had never seen our father intoxicated at any point during our lives. If he drank, we never saw it.

Like father, like son. With his Seagram's gin in hand, Donald Ray would often pass out on the floor in the middle of the apartment. He would get so drunk that he would lay there for hours without moving. We all knew he was alive because he was breathing. You could see his back rising and falling as his body took gasps of air.

In addition to his love of gin and cigarettes, Donald Ray also had some strange eating habits. He loved to make chitterlings and hog maws. It all smelled disgusting to me. Daddy never fed that to us, so I wasn't that familiar with it. I called all that shit slave food, but Donald Ray loved it. I guess Holly learned to like it too.

So, regardless of his occasional day labor jobs, once Donald Ray had spent money on gin and cigarettes, he still brought nothing home. I can't imagine the strain that must have put on Holly. Having to provide for herself and her child and also Donald Ray's tired ass. I can't say why she stayed, other than the fact that she loved him. Well, maybe, that big body part of his played a part too, who knows. Together, their love would bring about the birth of their second and then third child, a son named Donald Jr. and a daughter named DaVonne. Despite their money troubles, their children brought them great joy.

Over the years, as with any marriage, they continued to learn about the person with whom they shared a bed. Like me, Holly was passive aggressive in many ways. She was witty and that couldn't be denied. Even so, she allowed Donald Ray to be the man of the relationship. Demands like, "Holly, get me some cigarettes," and "Holly, get me a drink, girl," were commonplace. Donald Ray would eventually discover that Holly was not as fragile as she appeared. I'm certain that with his drinking and antics, their arguments led to physical altercations.

Donald Ray was a trip. Shit. I knew he was crazy as hell when he invited me to go with him to pick up girls. Now, how in the hell does that make sense? I was Holly's little brother. Who the fuck asks the little brother of their wife to go search for girls? That was Donald Ray for you. One thing that was for certain was that our parents hadn't raised soft kids. We were built to last. Holly would have to be tough to endure Donald Ray and she was.

Her endurance of the marriage would not be without struggle, many of which I wished she had never had to endure. Year after year, Holly worked to make ends meet financially for her family and to keep her marriage to Donald Ray intact. It was never confirmed, but there were whispers amongst the family that Holly had to endure an attack at a local bus stop in San Antonio early one morning, as she was catching the bus to work. It broke my heart because I had always felt that if Donald Ray had worked harder to be any kind of provider for her, she wouldn't have had to go through things like that. She pushed through though, and never spoke of the attack. She wasn't one to ever play the victim even though she was in many ways.

And although Holly would always warn Donald Ray about his drinking, he never stopped. He was dead set on doing things the way that he wanted to. In my mind, I had nicknamed him, "Donald Duck, I Don't Give a Fuck," because that is just how he rolled. Unsurprisingly, Donald Ray eventually landed himself in jail and was forced to spend a year there after receiving a DUI. But we were raised to be loyal, and Holly was no different. She continued to hold down the home front and did a damn good job at doing so.

Donald Ray's woes continued after he was diagnosed with cancer. I'm not sure which of his vices caused the disease, but the combination of the gin and cigarettes proved to be detrimental to his health. Holly cared for Donald Ray after he entered the hospital to begin chemotherapy for his cancer. To everyone's surprise, he stopped smoking and drinking during his treatment and made an amazing turn for the best. Holly remained solid and her care helped him make it through. But ultimately, "Donald Duck, I Don't Give a Fuck" returned and the smoking and drinking resumed, until his death. Although painful for his family, it was predictable in many ways. His prized combination of cigarettes and alcohol poisoned his system.

After Donald Ray's death, Holly continued to do what she had always done: care for their children and now grandchildren. The love in her heart continued to multiply and serve as a source of comfort for her family. Her job at the hospital had spanned the course of over thirty years and because she was calculated and strategic, she had ensured herself a hefty retirement. After almost forty years, Holly would now be free to live her life according to her own wishes. She had served her sentence with Donald Ray. All the things that my daddy tried to instill in her had never departed. She had just lived her life according to the path that she chose for herself.

I've always been proud of Holly for making decisions and sticking to them. She is the embodiment of gumption. My sister will always be one of the most beautiful girls in the world to me, and it brings me great joy to see her live a life with no regrets. Today, she does not bear the burden of caring for Donald Ray, only her own hopes and dreams, just as daddy would have wished. In the end, she became all that he envisioned her to be.

——EDGAR——

THE YEAR WAS 1974 and I was an incoming freshman in high school. For many, this was an exhilarating time in their lives. There was so much to look forward to and the act of blossoming into a young adult was thrilling. In many ways, I was not so different from the other boys my age. I enjoyed sports and discovered was quite the athlete.

By this time, my sister Holly had moved out of the house to start her own family. Emotionally, I had always operated with a deficit, that was my life. I missed Holly like crazy, but I also knew that she deserved to pursue life the way that she saw fit. I longed for the affection that only a mother could give, but it never materialized. Mamma's presence was so inconsistent that I couldn't really count on her. I felt blessed when she did grace us with her presence and her love, but it wasn't something that I could even look forward to because of its scarcity. As always, Daddy remained vigilant in raising us. I can't remember a time when he wasn't there. He always overcompensated for what he knew we lacked in Momma's presence, and it was appreciated.

Edgar was now a junior and we spent a great deal of time together in the mornings before school. Our bond continued to grow and we established a ritual of stopping by what we called the Ice House, which was the local corner store. Each morning, en route to school, we purchased the junk food that we had come to adore. I don't think that we could have put into words the excitement that we experienced at the start of each day. We would each get a Big Red and a honey bun. Edgar would always get the grape flavor and I would always get the red one. When we'd get to the middle of it, we would switch, but not before carefully examining the tradeoff, to make sure that we were making an even exchange. If either one of us had eaten more than our fair share, all bets were off. I tell you, it's the little things that matter growing up in the country. Sometimes, the little things make the biggest differences in our lives.

After filling our bodies with junk food for breakfast, we would head directly to school. Edgar did all of the driving, and boy would he take his time. He enjoyed the art of being rebellious. The more I would encourage him to hurry up, the slower he would go. That year, Edgar and I had French class together the first period of the day. I did not want to be late for class, I detested it. Prior to that time, we had never had any classes together because of our age difference. This gave me an opportunity to see how he acted in class. Truth be told, Edgar acted a damn fool! I was a perfectionist and a teacher pleaser, so Edgar often embarrassed the shit out of me, but he was my brother and I could never have traded his ass in.

I had been playing in the middle school band but chose not to continue in high school as my athletic ability began to surface. Edgar was a jock in every way, so the notion of my athleticism was not far-fetched. His ability to control a ball was astonishing. He was hailed as one of the top athletes in San Antonio and it made me proud to be his brother. I too immersed myself in basketball and much like Edgar, I was a natural. I continued to grow and my height became a tremendous attribute on the court. I'd have to say that I was a force to be reckoned with. Hand, eye coordination felt like second nature. I guess that would also explain why learning to cut hair and precision was also quite simple for me to execute. On the court, I was an athlete in every way. Off the court, I was still mastering the art of hair; it was my first love.

At the basketball games, the crowd cheered for me relentlessly. I loved the attention I received on the court. I always felt like my purpose was to give the crowd a show. And, baby, I could do that. My skills on the court made me even more popular with the girls. I can honestly say that I wasn't pressed. After the games, most of the guys wanted to hang out and chase girls. I, however, wasn't obsessed with girls, I was obsessed with being the flyest. For some odd reason, this made girls even more intrigued by me. What did concern me was how big my afro was. During that time, the bigger the afro, the better and I had everyone beat. After the games, I couldn't wait to get home to texturize my hair. Since the days of playing with dolls, my curiosity for makeovers and making people feel beautiful was still present and my obsession was ever evolving.

Edgar and I were among the only black kids at the school. We got called all kinds of names, including nigger. My rebuttal would always be to call them wetbacks. For some reason, the word nigga never bothered me. I had more of a problem with them saying I had big lips because I knew I didn't. Overall, there were more Mexicans than whites in the school and I found myself being a liaison between the two groups on many occasions. My job as mediator allowed me to make friends and associated on all sides and I ended up one of the most popular kids in my class. My classmates were always voting for me to run things, which led to my becoming elected as the student council president. I had no idea what I was doing, but I somehow figured it out. To add to my popularity, my father had also purchased a car for me. That was an instant magnet for friends and girls. I would soon discover what adolescent boys did in their spare time, and believe me, we hit more than just the books.

—WATCH AND LEARN—

I AM AN AVID BELIEVEr in zodiac signs. After all the years that I spent managing people, I recognized the importance of understanding the heart of another person. Knowing how they are likely to respond to various scenarios, and react in different situations, places you at an advantage to develop a successful relationship with them. Even back then, I always took the time to learn when a person's birthday was and I paid close attention to their behaviors.

Joyce was a friend of my first cousin Marsha. She was an Aries and that could only explain her role towards me as the aggressor. I don't think that girl had a shy bone in her body. Aries represent fire and from the moment that we met, she had every intention of letting me feel the flames. I'll admit, she was cute and I took a liking to her.

My cousin Daryl, who was Marsha's brother, was dating a girl named Cynthia at the time. By association, he and I would spend time together. As his adolescence peaked, so did his relationship with Cynthia. The four of us, went from spending time at the house and doing innocent things like watching TV, to him inviting Joyce and me to come to the hotel with him and Cynthia.

The first time that I went, I was afraid. I had never done anything like what I knew they were about to do. This was no longer getting close with clothes on and kissing until your mouth was sore; they were preparing to take it all the way.

When he extended the invitation, I didn't quite know how to feel, but he was my big cousin, so I didn't say no. Joyce was ready, willing, and able to accept the invitation. When we arrived, Daryl got out of the car and told us all to wait there for him. He walked into the lobby, spoke with the person at the front desk, and received a set of room keys. The car was quiet and I was observant and yet inquisitive as I watched what happened through the motel's front window.

After receiving the keys, he walked back towards the car, with a smile on his face that let me know he was thrilled about what was about to go down. I was a little shocked that Cynthia returned the same smile. It was then that I realized that this was not their first time, it was mine. She extended her arm for the room key that was attached to a big plastic rectangle and Daryl hopped back into the car. He then proceeded to drive around to the back parking lot of the motel.

He and Cynthia acted like they had just won the lottery. They were both giddy as hell. Meanwhile, I was trying to figure out what I was supposed to be doing with Joyce. She was calm and seemed completely unbothered by it all.

As we approached the door, Cynthia held onto Daryl's shoulder as he wiggled the key in the raggedy ass door. When the door opened, they damn near jumped on top of each other. They were kissing and making out so profusely that neither one of them had even bothered to close the door. It was like Joyce and I were not even standing there. They were moaning and groaning and Daryl was lifting Cynthia's skirt. They were full throttle in preparation for sex.

Joyce didn't seem to mind and I had to wonder if I was the only person who was a little taken aback. Nevertheless, there was no way that I could keep myself from being aroused by the way that Daryl and Cynthia were carrying on. I tried to keep it cool and approached the bed adjacent to the one that Daryl and Cynthia were making a spectacle of. I extended my hand for Joyce to come and sit with me. Before I knew it, we were kissing and rubbing and touching too. We moved to the floor on the other side of the bed to give ourselves an inkling of privacy. It was there that we both undressed and in the blink of an eye, made the decision to have sex. It was my first time and the excitement of it all overtook me. I climaxed almost instantly. Joyce was understanding and continued to rub and caress me. I learned in that moment that she wasn't shy because it had not been her first time. Apparently, I was the only one in the room that night who had not yet experienced the act of having sex.

Once I had, it was a feeling that I craved. Joyce had opened Pandora's box and I wanted more. Not only did we begin having sex regularly, but we also developed an unbreakable bond through our friendship. When not in school or extracurricular activities, I was at her house. I would spend so much time there that her mother would often ask, "Boy, are you ever going to go home?" I had fallen for Joyce and that feeling was blissful.

In addition to her parents, Joyce had four siblings—two brothers and two sisters. I delighted in the fact that they all made me feel welcome and treated me like another member of the family. The more time that Joyce and I spent together, the closer we became. I had never really felt like that about anyone before. I couldn't see days without her in them. When no one was at home, we sat on the couch and did what adolescent kids did: make out. She let me experiment with her body and for everything that I didn't know, she was willing to let me discover it.

My having a car allowed us to go places and do things that many kids our age were only dreaming of. We would go to the movies and sometimes to the country to my house. After about a year and a half of being together, we began to take our partying to another level. We would sit in the car and smoke cigarettes while drink beer that we had sneaked from the local corner store. We were wild, crazy, and in love. Every night, we spoke on the phone until we fell asleep, only to wake up and spend as much time as possible together during the day.

I believe that time has a way of revealing details that you may have overlooked while your heart was occupied. I should have known that Joyce's friendship with my cousin Marsha was based on more than just the fact that they were two girls who went to the same high school. Marsha was and had always been hot in the ass. The commonality between Joyce and Marsha was that they were cut from the same cloth. They would go out together from time to time to see what attention they could get from other boys. Going out without Joyce was of no interest to me because if I had spare time, I only wanted to spend it with her. But I had seen how Momma enjoyed the freedom to come and go as she pleased, so I never really thought to speak on it with Joyce. I did, however, notice that she would do little things that were not consistent with someone who was in a committed relationship. Whether she flirted with a guy a little too much for comfort in front of me, or I found another guy's number on a piece of paper, I began to sense that Joyce was not always completely honest.

About two years into our relationship, there was a family reunion hosted in San Antonio. I got word that Joyce had kissed one of my cousins while there. When I confronted her about it, her reply floored me.

"Well, what are you going to do about it, Charlie? Aren't you going to hit me or hurt me? Go on, I'm waiting." She screamed at me in rage, almost begging me to cause her harm.

"No. I'm not going to do any of that. What would make you say something like that?" I asked in turmoil.

"I just figured that if you were a man, you would hit me and make me get in line."

It was in that moment that I realized that Joyce was not the girl that I had placed upon the pedestal. Joyce was like many other girls in the projects, broken.

In the projects of San Antonio, it was normal behavior for men to pimp the girls out and have them hoeing on Cherry Street. My reaction to Joyce was a reflection of who I was; and her reaction to me was a reflection of who she was. All of the time, energy, and love that I had poured into her had come up short in showing her that she had met someone who was nothing like any of the typical guys on the block. I was tormented by the fact that I had given so much of myself to her, only to be met with disgrace and disappointment. Why hadn't I seen this coming? Why hadn't I recognized that her not being afraid of sex, like I was, was a dead giveaway that she was able to pull from all of her experiences with other men? Why hadn't I accepted the fact that her friendship with my cousin could only have been defined by their goal to see boys as conquests? Had she not loved me the way that I loved her?

These thoughts angered me, but also took me back to the memories of Momma and how abandoned I felt. In transparency, I cried for days over Joyce. After I had cried myself a river, I said, "Fuck this shit." My goal became to indulge, but not to love; it was too great a pain to bear, and I was no longer willing to put my heart at risk.

After the harsh reality of the breakup, I found myself having random sex with random girls in the projects. I also found myself having to go to the doctor regularly in a desperate attempt to calm the burning sensation in my body. I kept contracting sexually transmitted diseases and every time I turned around, I had discharge coming out of my penis and it hurt to pee.

My father was instrumental in advising us to read about the things that we were curious about. As such, I found myself in search of any information that could help me better understand what kept happening to me when I slept with girls. Why did this seem to only be happening to me? I had never heard my brother or any other guys speak about this condition. Even though my hormones were raging, I was also in the midst of paranoia. I read about the urethra and buildup and a whole slew of allergic reactions that were possible during sex. I didn't understand what I was reading. And as crazy as it sounds, I began to believe that I was allergic to snatch. Even so, nothing could keep me away from it.

People sit around and talk about how dangerous a woman scorned can be, but I am proof that a man scorned is equally as dangerous. As I approached my high school graduation, I continued to excel in my academics and in the arena of athletics, but when it came to love I failed.

The girls were in rotation and my heart was no longer open to the kind of love that I had given to Joyce. I just couldn't muster up the strength to go through something like that again, and the exchange of infections had taught me that girls were not interested in loving as deeply as I had once imagined.

This was the era when the notion of notches on my belt became an understatement. There was Angie, who lived in an area that we called Lakeside. Angie was friends with Darleen, who also lived there. When my limited time with Angie didn't work out, I was on to Darlene. They knew each other and neither seemed to mind.

Darlene was a year younger than me. We would go to her house and sit on her couch. It was the thing to do when you were getting to know someone. Truth be told, sitting on a couch is still relevant today. I never saw Darlene's daddy, although I was told that he lived with her. And in true adolescent fashion, we had a lot of sessions that went all the way to fourth base. We spoke on the phone often, but nowhere near as much as I had allowed myself to talk with Joyce.

Darlene was fast as hell. One time during sex, she began to go to a place that I had never seen before. She was trembling and her eyes rolled to the back of her head as she squeezed me with a grip of death. I could barely move, but she motioned for me to continue. She looked like the girl from *The Exorcist*. I mean, she went ballistic and then out of nowhere she let out a deep sigh and collapsed onto the couch.

That was the first time that I had seen a woman climax. Witnessing her in the midst of what appeared to be an out of body experience, scared the living daylights out of me. Even so, that night I learned that I had the power to bring about unspeakable joy to a woman, even if for only a moment in time.

CHAPTER 7

THE PRAYER OF JABEZ

"Ask with your whole heart and believe with your whole soul."
—Elgin Charles

AT HOME, IT BECAME PAINFULLY apparent that Momma was not going to return. We would never resemble the typical family, living out the American dream. The faint wish that I had held in my heart for the day that my parents would reunite had diminished into an afterthought. The closure of that chapter occurred when Daddy informed us that he had found someone and she was to become his new bride.

So much had happened in such a short period of time that it was all a blur. On the heels of my high school graduation, my father had discovered love and I discovered a truth, which I had known since I was a little boy, transforming Barbie Dolls into goddesses: San Antonio was not for me. It's hard to put into words the feelings that you have when you discover that you've outgrown a place and you know that if you stay, the walls will eventually close in on you. I had known that San Antonio, and the mindset of foreverness that existed there, was not a concept that I could relate to. I was in search of a way out, sooner rather than later.

I am ever amazed at the comedic relief that the universe often presents. The whole "ask and you shall receive" sentiment is real. In a related series of events, my cousin Marsha had already left San Antonio and moved to Waco, Texas with my Uncle Winks and his wife, to begin working after graduating high school. Buggy was too scared to stay in the San Antonio house alone and so Uncle Winks' wife invited her to Waco as well, letting her know that she would have no trouble finding work.

Buggy kept saying, "Charlie, why don't you come on down here with me?"

Since I was itching to leave San Antonio anyway, I decided that her offer could not have come at a better time. It was official, I was leaving San Antonio to explore and chart new territory.

When I shared the news of my decision to move to Waco with my father's wife Blondie, she was in full support of my departure. I knew her eagerness for me to leave was due to her wanting a family of her own with my father. With both Holly and Edgar gone, I was the only one standing in the way of her American dream.

—◄As the World Turns►—

THERE WAS NOTHING memorable about my trek to Waco; I arrived safely and that was that. There were no emotional good-byes or moments of sadness between my father and me before I left, I was the last child to leave the house we had grown up in and so my father was more than ready for my departure. He demonstrated through his actions that he was confident in what he had instilled in me, and in his heart, he knew that I would find my way.

When I arrived in Waco, I came to the realization that much like San Antonio, I was surrounded by family. By the time I got there, Buggy had obtained a job at the local paper mill. Waco was not much better than San Antonio, in terms of room for growth and development in a career, but it was new, so it provided me the opportunity to meet new people. I was now at the onset of adulthood. More importantly, I was single and ready to mingle. The nightlife there proved to be a consistent pastime. One night, while at a local club, I noticed a beautiful dark-skinned girl from afar. She couldn't have been any taller than 5'4". She was as black as the night with unapologetic melanin. She was just standing there, observing everything that was going on in the club. I noticed that she was alone, and I mustered up the courage to approach her. As I got closer to her, I noticed that she had a head of long, beautiful, thick hair. She had it pulled back into a ponytail, with the end twisted. It was an instant turn on for me. As I entered her personal space, I extended my hand towards her and introduced myself.

"Hi. I'm Charlie."

She glanced up at me, as I was much taller than she was and she appeared to be instantly smitten. She smiled intently and lifted her hand to my lips. "I'm Shondra," she replied.

I asked her to dance and she obliged. If anyone allowed me to dance on their watch, mark my words the show would be instantly stopped. Dancing was something that I did better than anyone I had ever known. It was just a feeling that got into me when the music penetrated my soul. Shondra and I instantly connected and we shut the club down that night. We must have danced for at least five songs straight. The DJ earned every bit of his money. After I found myself breaking a sweat and I noticed that Shondra was also perspiring, I invited her to the bar for a drink.

Looking back on all of this, I must say, I was smooth as hell. I guess my father's finesse and my mother's comfort in her own skin had proved well for me when it came to socializing. We sat at the bar, drinking and laughing for at least thirty minutes. You couldn't tell by looking at her, but she was Stella trying to get her groove back. She was roughly twenty-six and I was only nineteen, but I didn't care and she didn't seem to mind. Our exchange turned into repeated bouts of laughter and before we knew it, the lights had come on and our night was about to come to an end.

"Well, Charlie, are you going to ask me for my number?"

"Of course. I would love to see you again."

She reached over the bar and grabbed a pen from the bartender's station. Taking my hand, she wrote her number on my palm and then placed the cap back on the pen. As she stood up to leave, she placed her hand on my leg and leaned towards my ear. "Call me now, Charlie. Ok?" She was sexy as hell and she knew it, and I couldn't wait to see more of her.

Consistent with all of my previous courtships, Shondra and I began talking on the phone regularly. I liked her because she was ambitious for her environment. She had her own car and her own apartment, but to my disappointment, she also had a son. I knew from the onset of our relationship that I had no intentions of becoming a father at that point in my life. I didn't want the weight of the responsibility. And even though both my heart and my mind were convinced that I did not want to be a young father, my loins spoke otherwise. Shondra and I had sex so regularly that it became a daily ritual.

I can remember the fullness of my sexuality even back then, although at that time, I had not explored it from every angle, like I would in the future. For instance, Buggy was dating a guy by the name of Big D, and I can recall flirting with him. I remember asking, "So, why do they call you Big D.?" Though nothing ever came from my innocent banter, there was something about him that made me feel as though he was interested in me. And despite the fact that neither of us had ever shown any attraction to anything other than the female sex, my curiosity was piqued. Regardless, I kept my focus on intimacy with Shondra.

If I dropped by during the evenings, Shondra's son was around. I never wanted anyone, especially a child, to feel uncomfortable in any way, so I tried to engage in father figure behavior, like throwing a ball with him outside in the yard, but in my heart, I was not ready to go any deeper. Though I began to like Shondra a great deal, I was still healing from the injury Joyce had caused my heart and thus unable to love fully.

I had obtained a job at a Marathon Battery Corporation factory in Waco, working as a Material Handler. The employees that I worked with made the decision one day to go on strike. So, aside from my diminishing job and thrill seeking with Shondra, my mind became attracted to other ventures in the area. Buggy and I began seeking out opportunities to participate in various modeling and casting calls throughout the city. This was the first taste of what I had seen in the magazines and on TV growing up. It was the closest that I had ever been to stardom. We also began entering dance competitions, which made our faces pretty well known through the city. We made a mark for ourselves in a short period of time. Even so, there was still something missing for me. We most certainly were not in the city limits of San Antonio but working in the factory made me realize that there was still an undercurrent of generations being born, reared, and employed in the same place. That notion of remaining in the city forever was not a pill that I could swallow.

Because of the strike at the factory, we were now being asked to work the picket line in protest. While doing so, I had an epiphany about who I was and who I was destined to be. I came to the realization, right then and there that Wako was not for me.

That night, I called Buggy to tell her that I was leaving Waco and going back to San Antonio to regroup. She was not happy with me, but she had known me all my life and she knew that something internally was calling me to a bigger stage. Shonda was also unhappy with my decision, as we were in the midst of something special. But for me it was a season that had ended, like all seasons do, and I was in preparation for the next chapter in my life.

When I moved back to San Antonio, the seasons came and went a little faster than normal. The women in my life appeared to be on a Ferris wheel. When one got off, another one got on. At the time, the recklessness of it all did not affect me in any way. I was just young and living my life the best way I knew how. We all were.

Although my personal life was in full swing, I would learn to master the art of keeping my professional life stable. In my mind, there was no other way. I immediately obtained a job at EG&G Automotive Research and began to work and save my money. Surprisingly, or maybe not so much, I found my way back to Darlene. We jumped right back into the physical relationship that we had indulged in before I left for Waco. Sex was a nightly endeavor and I was down for the cause. She was the aggressor, but I wanted it just as badly as she did. There was no method to the madness, just a case of young people, exploring sexuality.

As the universe would have it, no good deed goes unpunished. After finishing a long day at work, I decided to head home to my father's house because I had missed the opportunity to stop by Darlene's place. I unlocked the door to discover an empty home. Who knows where Daddy and his wife had gone, but I assumed that they would return shortly. As I settled on the couch the phone began to ring, but I was too tired to get back up and decided to let the answering machine catch the call. The voice I heard over the speaker was familiar.

"Charlie, it's Shonda. Please call me back. I have something that I need to tell you."

I was glad to hear her voice. It had been almost two weeks since we had last spoken. Forgetting my tiredness, I jumped up to grab the phone and began to dial her back. She picked up on the first ring.

"Hey, you! What's up? How have you been?" I said.

There was a brief pause. It was uncomfortable and I could tell in the silence that she hadn't called me for a good reason. She began to speak without answering any of my questions.

"Charlie, I have something that I need to tell you," she responded with a stern voice.

"Ok. What is it?" I would have given anything to get off the phone with her in that moment. I had never been the type to enjoy confrontation in any fashion. However, there was nowhere for me to go, so I had to sit in the moment.

"I'm six weeks pregnant," she revealed.

I was paralyzed. I had no words. I had known and demonstrated that I had no intentions of being responsible for anyone except myself. I wanted to be selfish in the fulfillment of my wants, needs, and desires. All my life, I felt like I'd had to yield to what others wanted. For the first time in my life, it was about me. That same train of thought afforded me some courage.

"I think we need to see about getting an abortion. I mean, how would you even know that you are already six weeks pregnant?"

It wasn't that I didn't care about Shonda or the possible life that we had created together, it was simply that I cared about my future and my hopes and dreams more. We hung up the phone, not in a good space. I'm certain that my response was not what she had hoped for, but I had given every ounce of what I had to give. I sat there, puzzled and working diligently to piece together a timeline for what had happened between us.

Truthfully, I never heard from Shonda again. Her time on the Ferris wheel was over and based on the fact that she never attempted to contact me again, I knew that she had gotten off by her own will.

—A LEOPARD PRINT THONG—

A VOLUPTUOUS BEAUTY BY the name of Angie stepped onto my Ferris wheel of love, just as I began to fully immerse myself back in San Antonio. Angie had curves for days and was rough to make you dizzy. She wore these long eyelashes and wigs and always had a full face of makeup. I'm not sure I ever saw her when she wasn't fully made up. I was so intrigued by her and all of her friends that would come around when I would frequent her apartment. She was, dare I say erotic. The things that she was into in the bedroom represented a different level of experience. She took me to school and I wanted nothing more than to become her best pupil. I knew that Angie worked at a club, but eventually I figured out that it was none other than Baby Dolls, a gentleman's club in San Antonio. There was no question on how she became so well versed in the bedroom.

Still in pursuit of upward mobility professionally, I took a job at EG&G, working in data entry. I also continued to update my headshots with a series of photo shoots in the hopes of advancing a modeling career. I wasn't sure which avenue would pan out, but I was in hot pursuit of success. The hustler in me would not lie dormant. I was always looking for new ways to make money.

Through Angie and her friends, I heard whispers of an up and coming club in the city, named LaBear. It was unlike the other strip clubs because all of the dancers were men. When I learned that all you had to do was dance in order to make tons of money, I thought to myself that I would be perfect for the job. I had seen the countless amount of money that Angie and her friends were bringing home and I wanted in. Since the dance floor was my second home, I figured that I had nothing to lose.

While at work one day, I decided to call the club on my lunch break. They asked me if I could come in for an audition, right then. I was nervous as hell, but I agreed. I told my boss that I would need to take a little longer lunch break so that I could run and pay some bills. Thankfully, he didn't question my request. By 11:30 a.m., I was standing in the middle of a stage with a spotlight on me, wearing only a G-string. The manager of the club cued the DJ to play the music and said, "Just dance when the music comes on, ok?" His voice and demeanor reflected the "I've seen it all" disposition, but he didn't know me. I was ready to set that stage on fire. I couldn't wait for him to turn the music on. I was prepared to give them a show like they had never seen before.

As soon as the beat dropped, I started shaking my ass like nobody's business. I did every trick I knew. I jumped up high in the air and came down on my chest. I thrust my body into a series of worm like motions. I gyrated and humped the air so much that I turned myself on. Shit, for a moment I forgot that I was auditioning because the music had gotten into my soul and I was free. It wasn't until I heard the sound of the manager's voice yelling out, "You've got the job," that I was brought back to reality. The DJ killed the music and the manager asked, "Can you work the 11:00 p.m. slot?"

I paused for a moment because my normal shift at work was until 11:00 p.m. at night. On the nights I didn't work late, I helped my cousin Pat with her kids and even stayed with her on occasion. In my head, I vowed to resolve these conflicts and responded to the manager. "Sure... I mean... Yes, thank you." I was still breathing hard from all of the ammunition I'd fired and the war that I had waged on the stage, but I knew I would return with a vengeance to work for my coins. I had the eye of the tiger when it came to making money.

In addition to my two jobs, I was also trying to sell weed. I would buy a $20 bag and create joints and sell them ready made. I saw it as a concierge service of sorts. I didn't deal with thugs though. I wasn't cut out to do so. I could still hear my mother's words, "You're fragile." My siblings and family members never allowed me to live those words down and the repetition of the phrase pissed me off. "I ain't fragile," I would respond, but I also knew that certain situations were not for me. I knew my lane and I drove in it.

My first night working at the strip club felt like a normal work day. I knew my reason for being there: I had a job to do. I wasn't well versed in the arena of stripping, but after watching a few acts before mine, I recognized a pattern and caught on quickly. From the onset of the song, I was to come out with my clothes on, then seductively take them off, layer by layer. After the second song came on, I would have on just my thong and I could move from one table to the next. If you wanted to make some real money, that was exactly what you did. You also had the option to do private dances and work the entire room.

One night at the club, I met Ramona. She was short and dark-skinned. She motioned for me to come and dance for her. She was such a good tipper that I stayed with her for almost the entire night. She sat back and watched me as if I was the fulfillment of her erotic fantasies. I was about my coins back then, so whatever she was seeking, I was willing to give.

As the night came to a close, she whispered in my ear, "Could I see you afterwards? I'll pay?"

That night in her hotel room, we had sex. Afterwards, she put $100 on the nightstand. This was during the era of pimps and hoes, and everyone was in some way exposed to the overarching themes of sex in exchange for money. This wasn't the case for Ramona and me because we began dating, which only went to prove that I was not cut out to be a pimp or a hoe. I wasn't as hard or as rough around the edges as I let on. Against my better judgement, my heart was still secretly in search of love.

I managed to balance both my daytime and nighttime careers by adjusting my hours and I began to save money to the best of my ability.

I didn't bother mentioning my night career to my father or my mother. Even though Momma was from the streets and I assumed that she would be more than understanding, I chose to keep her in the dark about my line of work.

Despite the fact that things were progressing towards the direction that I had placed my energy, I can honestly say that I wasn't happy. This lifestyle simply wasn't for me. I was a product of my environment and I was striving to make the best of what was before me. Momma may not have always been around, but her words of wisdom always rang loudly in my ears. She was well versed on the codes of the streets and often spoke about the differences between the laws created by man versus the unspoken law of the land. The law of the land was the street code that should never be violated. The bottom line was that I was not living the life that had envisioned for myself. Nothing that I was doing was what I had dreamt of and I knew that I was in need of a change of scenery.

Right around the time I turned twenty-one, I remember my Aunt Nilene, along with my cousins Jimmy, Bernard, and little bad ass Terrance, coming for a visit to San Antonio. They had moved to Los Angeles years ago and while sitting with my father, she planned her return trip back home to California. Everyone was in the living room, talking and catching up and I sat there in somewhat of a daze. I was exhausted from all of the hours that I had been working. Somewhere along the way, I heard her mention that she needed someone to help her drive back. I sat up and without hesitation, eagerly volunteered. It was the perfect opportunity to get the hell out of San Antonio, forever. Just like that, I had changed the trajectory of my life and my career. I had overstayed my welcome in San Antonio and the windows of heaven had opened up to pour me out the blessings of an unexpected exit.

——THE BOOK OF REVELATIONS AND—— INTRINSIC REALIZATIONS

WHAT I HAD GLEANED from my attempts at love with women was not promising. I had either been cheated on, been subjected to false allegations of fathering children, or had contracted sexually transmitted diseases that required medical attention. I was fed up with falling short with women and my urge to test the deeper waters of sexual exploits with men was on the horizon. I was and had always been in search of a relationship, built upon a foundation of love that would withstand the test of time. I now questioned if I was still interested in doing so with a woman.

The whirlwind of my rearing, my astute moral compass (instilled by my father), my affinity for hair, my internally aroused curiosity, and my intentions to discover the freedom to explore my sexuality were too powerful to contend with in San Antonio. My exit plan for the state of Texas became my priority.

BY THE WAY
WHEN THE BOUGH BREAKS

IT IS VIRTUALLY IMPOSSIBLE to chart new territory without careful examination of all that is around you. San Antonio represented my past and LA represented my future. I realized very quickly that I would need to fight tooth and nail to discover who I was destined to become, regardless of where I was physically planted. My father had always taught me about the power of visualization: how to will and work towards whatever we wanted to attain from life. I was curious to see just how the power of evolution would manifest for me. I had been through so much in such a short period of time and my journey was far from over; I was still trying to find my way.

The peak of my adolescence occurred during the heat of climax and curiosity. When it was all said and done, none of it had proven to be quite what I had bargained for. That era of my life had not served up the gratification that I believed myself to be in search of. I had been met with the perils that accompany the uncertainty of unsettled relationships and the pain that served as an accomplice. Pain has a way of influencing who we become, but the process hurts like hell. There is no around, there is only through. Everything that had happened to me, inclusive of my childhood, failed relationships with women, and failed relationships with men, had led me to this very moment. I was now at a crossroads and I needed someone or something to believe in. My soul yearned for the innocence of hope that had been slain from both my childhood and my sexual quests. I was in need of direction and a clearer vision for what my life could be. Even more, I was in need of a reprieve and clarity from the murky view that had now materialized in my presence. My moral compass had been compromised in many ways, and I wasn't quite sure that I alone had the tools to repair it. Sorrow had once again knocked at my door, but this time, I let that bitch in.

My mind was overworked and underprivileged. Even my work became too much mentally. I could no longer focus. Smith & Barney became a place that I dreaded going to because it meant more than seven hours of remaining idle. I couldn't remain steadfast on my tasks at hand, and it became noticeable to a supervisor. It was unlike me to ever let anything affect my work.

My father had always prided himself on being a stellar role model when it came to work ethics. In our home, it was unheard of to not perform well at your job, simply because you were experiencing emotional toil in another aspect of your life. That was not a luxury that we could afford nor was it honorable, but it was my truth. By the year of 1984, I had made the painful decision to take a sabbatical from Smith & Barney. I gave myself exactly one year off to order my steps. That meant that I had 365 days to determine what direction I would take, while standing at the fork in the road.

My mother's voice continued to resonate in such a powerful way. "Charlie, you need to stop all this and just go to beauty school. You are so good looking and you are so good at doing hair. Everything else is wasting your time," she would proclaim. Through it all, hair had been a constant theme in my heart. Although I wasn't doing anyone's hair when I moved to LA, my vivid imagination had not departed. I couldn't think of a single woman that I hadn't undressed and redressed with my eyes. And while most men are undressing women with lust filled eyes, mine were filled with ideas for makeovers and ways to enhance their appearance. I believed then and I still believe today that women are one of God's most beautiful creations. I love making people, places, and things around me beautiful.

In a desperate attempt to escape the reality unfolding before me, I made up my mind to conduct research on beauty school. Admittedly, I had looked down on hairdressers before addressing the ignorance that resonated within. I honestly thought that anyone could be a hairdresser. I also had no idea how much money they could make, which was concerning to me. My father had pushed the idea of my becoming a businessman. I was good with numbers, math, and chemistry. They were very practical skills, and I'd had every intention of putting them to use in order to become a mogul in corporate America. The real truth is that with my self-enforced sabbatical from Smith & Barney, I wasn't headed in that direction.

The notion of beauty school became a glimmer of hope that allowed me to transition my thoughts when I felt the despair that had overtaken me. I also knew that if I set out to do something, I would do it with my entire heart. During this era, I would venture to say that I needed hair more than it needed me. It was settled. I turned my mother's words into the fuel that I needed to ignite a fire that would become the epicenter of my existence. While standing at that fork in the road, I poured gasoline on the left, which represented the past. After I was done, I lit a match and set that bitch on fire. I was determined to let the past burn itself to death. The flames illuminated the right, which represented my future. With embers burning behind me, I walked with might, determination, and conviction into my future. God had a plan for my life and I now accepted the fact that I was worthy of fulfilling every ounce of purpose that God had spared me for.

With a new attitude and outlook on life, I fully immersed myself in the search for a beauty school that would accept me. I was so ardent about honing my craft that I wanted to live. And now, I had something to live for. A new beacon of hope was on the horizon.

CHAPTER 8

ALIAS

"When a blessing calls your name, answer."

—Elgin Charles

AFTER MAKING THE prolific decision to pursue a career in the hair industry, I knew that I wanted to be the best, whatever that meant. At no point in my life had I done anything with the intent to actualize a status of mediocrity. I was my father's son, made from grit. I knew that I wanted to take the industry by storm, but I hadn't the slightest idea of how that would manifest. How would I, Charlie from San Antonio, become a legend in an industry that did not even know my name? From the bottom up, that's how. I prepared to place my shovel in the sand and dig for dear life.

Prior to that time, I had a very limited scope of experiences from which to draw about the hair and beauty industry and the professionals in it. I can honestly say that I didn't have nearly as much respect for it as I should have. I had imagined that anyone was capable of becoming a hairdresser and that all that happened in the shops that I had seen during the days of old, when I visited the salon with my grandmother in St. Louis, was gossip. I thought that the salon was a gathering place for women to watch soap operas and talk about other people. I didn't have the slightest idea of the immense responsibility that comes with making people look and feel their best.

I began an evening ritual of riding up and down the streets of LA, looking at salons and dreaming with eyes wide opened. The prospects were becoming real to me and so was the notion of a renewal and healing of my soul. Eventually, my pseudo field trips would lead me to Hollywood. In what felt like the blink of an eye, everything changed. I stumbled upon and old magazine ad that triggered my recollection of Vidal Sassoon and it was game over. He was the embodiment of a trendsetter

Instantaneously, my territory was enlarged because my ability to conceive what could be had been stretched, allowing me to bear witness to new horizons. Vidal Sassoon was the epitome of the beauty industry. My eyes were now wide opened to the notion of becoming a mogul in the hair industry. We all need to be exposed to people, places, and things that teach us that dreams are real and that there is always something more that we can aspire to. Vidal Sassoon was not only revolutionizing the way in which hair stylists cut hair, with his infamous asymmetrical angles and exclusive lines of hair care products, but he had also managed to establish his brand as an entity. In the words of acclaimed actress Jenifer Lewis, "He was serving all." He was also the first stylists to be recognized as a celebrity. He was very famous. From beauty schools, overflowing with eager young hair stylists, to salons around the world; he was a household name. My continued intrigue and research led me to discover that he actually had an architectural background, which explained the cutting edge take he had on the haircuts he had introduced to the world. My cup runneth over with excitement when I learned that he had even managed to develop his own line of jeans. Jeans!

Vidal Sassoon single handedly shattered what I had once seen as a glass ceiling. I wanted to become my own version of him. I admired his business acumen and his ability to dream and work for the manifestation of those dreams. I knew with certainty that there was a place for me, my work ethic, and my larger than life aspirations in the hair industry. I didn't have all of the answers as to how I would achieve everything, but what I knew for sure was that I understood business and chemistry, and I most certainly knew how to transform a woman from drab to fab.

I can recall lying on my apartment floor, staring up at the ceiling with anticipation. This night was more noticeable than the rest because it was the first night that I had not cried. It was the first night of the rest of my life. I had discovered what my next move would be and I was beyond excited about what was in store for me.

The next morning, I woke up with the same sense of joy and excitement that I had gone to sleep with. With no formal job to report to, I set out to explore every opportunity to educate myself and blaze my own trail towards success. With my mind on my future, I thought back to a time when my coworker, Donna, made mention of a beauty school during one of our conversations. It was no secret that I had a gift for hair and beauty, but I was in corporate America, so at the time I swept the information under the rug. I decided to ask her to share that information with me again. If she could give me the name of a beauty school, perhaps I could stop by and explore possibilities. In haste, I decided to give her a call. As the phone rang, my nerves bounced with anticipation. What if she didn't answer the phone? Would that mean that it was a sign to leave it all alone? What if she thought I was crazy?

What if I appeared foolish for walking away from a good paying career with the potential for advancement? My mind raced as the phone rang, until finally I heard a voice say, "Hello?"

Hurriedly, I said, "Donna, it's me, Charlie. I know you remember me." I laughed under my breath.

"How could I forget? How are you, Charlie? How has everything been going for you?"

"Good. Good. I can't complain. I've just been thinking about trying something new."

"New?" she questioned.

"I don't know if you remember that day that we were talking about hair stylists in LA and you mentioned the name of a beauty school. For the life of me, I can't seem to recall it. Would you mind sharing the name of that school with me again?"

"Soooo, is this what you're planning next? Hair school? Ha!"

I played skittish. "It looks like it. I'm just letting God do his thing."

"I see. Well, the name of the school is Marinello. You should give them a call and see if you can schedule a tour or something."

"A tour? That's actually a great idea. It could be a way for me to really crack the ice. This is somewhat new territory for me."

"Well, Charlie, if I know you like I think I do, you will be as successful at this, as you've been with everything else. Let me know how it goes and you take care of yourself."

I thanked her for her time and her caring words and just like that, the ball was in my court and there was no turning back. I was on a quest to learn as much as I could about hair and the industry. My plan was to fully immerse myself into this new journey. I needed healing and retribution. Growing up, the act of creating and using my hands to make the things around me beautiful had served as my haven and shelter from the rain of my personal life. I needed to feel those drops on my life again.

Instead of waiting until Monday, I decided to search through the pages of the phone book for Marinello. If I found the number, I had already made up my mind that I would call right then. I traced down the pages with my finger extended. As I placed my face a little closer to the book, I discovered exactly what I was looking for. The words "Marinello Schools of Beauty" were in bold and they jumped off the page. I noticed that the school was located off of South La Cienega Boulevard. I couldn't seem to get to the phone fast enough. I took the heavy book with me; I needed to get the number correct the first time. As I dialed the numbers, I felt stronger than I ever had before. If I knew how to do one thing, it was stepping out on faith.

"Marinello Schools of Beauty. How may we help you?"

"Yes. My name is Charles Williams and I am interested in taking a tour of the school. Is that something that you do?"

"Thank you, Mr. Williams, we do offer tours of the school. If you would be willing to hold just for a moment, I can check the schedule of the director who handles all of our tours and new enrollments. Would it be ok if I placed you on a brief hold?"

"Yes. That would be just fine. Thank you."

"Thank you. Please hold."

I waited for her to return to the phone and I can promise you, I forgot to breathe.

"Mr. Williams, we actually have a cancellation on this coming Monday. Would you be interested in visiting on that day or is that too soon?"

"This Monday?" I said in shock.

"Yes, that is correct."

I could feel my heart pounding from excitement. "Yes… yes. I would be available this Monday. What time do you have an opening for?"

"Bright and early. Does 9:00 a.m. work for you?"

"Sure. Absolutely, I will be there at nine o'clock."

"We look forward to it."

"As do I."

When the conversation ended, I felt like a major weight had been lifted off of my shoulders. This was really happening. I mean… I was really doing this. After all of the years of doing hair for family members and friends back in San Antonio, I was now preparing to step into a new realm of possibilities. Little did I know at the time that I was on the heels of a career that would allow me to travel the world and break barriers that had never been broken. God's plans for our lives are always greater.

——What's in A Name?——

MONDAY MORNING ARRIVED and the California sun did exactly what it did best: illuminated the air with possibilities and what ifs. Los Angeles, California, the giver of HOLLY-WOOD, was filled with the essence of what dreams are made of. If you couldn't dream, or dared not to, the air alone would force it upon you. This wasn't a place that you could live, or even visit, and not be overtaken by thoughts of what could be. After rejecting the self-imposed bondage of my past and losing myself from the shackles, I set my sights on becoming the best. I recognized that anything worth having was worth working for, and I was no stranger to hard work. I was built to last and my time was now.

That morning, I found myself filled with a series of sentiments and emotions, but the most prevalent was of course anxiousness.

The time for me to tour Marinello Schools of Beauty and hope-fully enroll could not arrive fast enough. After laying in bed for what felt like an eternity, I got up, showered, and got dressed.

That day, I decided to wear all black, everything last stitch of clothing. I was no stranger to well-appointed dressing. My days in corporate America had taught me well. I also recognized that many hair stylists wore black and I had plenty of it. On this day, I decided upon a pair of black, silk blend slacks with a bottom cuff and a black button-down shirt that shared a similar texture to the pants. The details were what made everything come together. My black loafers had small silver buckles on the sides and were a mirror image of the buckle on my handmade, black leather crocodile belt. I even managed to find some black dress socks that appeared as regular dress socks, but they had silky tops, which felt like heaven on my feet. Of course, my hair was well trimmed and edged to perfection. I was sharp as hell and I knew it. Now, I just hoped that I would be well received when I arrived. I took one last look in the mirror before leaving and gave myself a nod of encourage-ment as I walked out the door.

When I arrived at the school, I turned the ignition off and just sat in the car. I needed a few moments of silence. So much had happened in my short, yet eventful life. I reflected over the many moments that had led me to be exactly where I was, and I real-ized I was once again at a fork in the road. If I made the decision to go inside, I could change the trajectory of the series of events unfolding for me in LA. If I allowed myself to be encapsulated by fear, I might never go in, and the career that I now longed for might not see the light of day.

"You're going to be something so special. God has something beautiful planned for your life. You're going to be exalted. I just know it. Look at you Charlie, you were made to do hair." Somehow, my mother's words played on repeat in my head and gave me the courage to move when I felt incapable of doing so. Her words carried me on many days, but on that day, they gave me the courage to simply move. In an instant, I took a deep, cleansing breath, grabbed my bag, and opened the door of my car. I placed one foot on the ground and the solid feeling of the pavement was the confirmation that I needed. It was a subtle reminder that I need only put one foot in front of the other to gain everything that was ordained for me. I didn't have vague plans about what I wanted for my career in the industry; I had very specific plans, and I was willing to do whatever it took to achieve that end.

There was a receptionist's desk on the left as I entered the building and I was immediately greeted by a young woman. She smiled. "Hello, welcome to Marinello. How can we help you today?"

"Hello, my name is Charles, and I'm here to meet with someone about your program for new stylists."

"Sure. Did you have a scheduled tour by chance?"

"Yes. I should be on the schedule." I was getting even more excited.

She looked up at me and said, "We have you confirmed for 9 a.m. Someone will be right with you. Feel free to wait in our lounge area. Can I get you any coffee or tea, while you wait?"

"Thank you, but no. I'm just fine. Thank you so much." I felt as if I was stuttering over my words. I was distracted by the sounds of the blow dryers and the snips of the scissors. It was really going down up in there. I mean, there were people of all races, immersed in hair, and it was a beautiful thing. I was captivated. This was for real. I had been doing hair all of my life and I while I was anxious, I also felt right at home. All I needed was to make this official and dive in.

As I began to settle onto the couch in the waiting area, I could hear the click of what sounded like heels walking towards me. I was both mesmerized and frightened by what I saw when I looked up. Boldly standing before me was a short, Caucasian man, wearing tight white bell bottom pants and a skin tight pink button up shirt, that was left unbuttoned from about the third button up. The area of the shirt left open, revealed the unruly hairs on his chest as well as a bevy of gold chains, some with medallions and others just dangling in excess. His skin was too tanned to be real and thus he glowed a pale hue of orange. As my eyes continued their assessment, I noticed his hands had a full set of long acrylic nails that were pink and rounded at the tips. The mix of the masculinity of his hands coupled with the feminine nails was unexplainable. His hair was bleached ash blonde, and the rays from the sun peeking in through the windows made it appear almost white. His attire alone caught my attention, but his full face of makeup sent my imagination into a convoluted tailspin. From the full lashes to the foundation, eyeshadow, eyeliner, blush, and a rose-pink lipstick, even Stevie Wonder would have been able to see that he was in full drag. He shook his head from side to side and used his long nails to gather and direct his long hair. I couldn't believe what I was seeing with my own eyes. Were they deceiving me? I had never seen anything or anyone like him; not even in my wildest imagination. Before I could actually process all that was standing there, he extended his hand and said, "Charles Williams?"

I was now forced to look him directly in his eyes and as I shook off the shock. I stood and replied, "Yes, good morning. I'm Charles Williams."

Although he was dressed in women's clothing and wearing a full face of makeup, he made it apparent in his mannerisms that he was a man. And although I had met and interacted with flamboyant men since my first days of being in LA, this was my first introduction to the notion of androgyny. I was taken aback, but there was no time for it at that moment. I was forced to disregard his bombshell appearance in order to allow my mind to focus on my purpose. I knew that this was my shot and I wasn't going to allow anything to disrupt it.

With a firm handshake he said, "Good Morning, Mr. Charles. I'm Shawn Michaels, the Director here at Marinello. It is my understanding that you are interested in enrolling in beauty school. Is this correct?"

I hung onto the words that he spoke; they were music to my ears. "Yes, I am interested," I replied.

"Great. I'd be happy to give you a tour of the school and afterwards, you can let us know if you'd still like to enroll."

I'm not sure why I felt so anxious about being accepted into the school. The truth is that they would enrolled almost anyone who wished to attend. I was just so determined that I never even thought about it in that way and truthfully, it wasn't important.

The school was exactly what I imagined. The tour revealed that the school had two distinct levels. The upstairs had more of a classroom atmosphere. As it was explained to me, this was where you acquired your textbook knowledge regarding the best practices and theory of cosmetology. The downstairs was designated to putting that knowledge and training to work. It was where all the action was taking place. As we walked around the bottom floor, I saw the students at work. They were cutting and blow drying; analyzing and coloring. It was a bustling circus, and I knew in my heart that I too had some tricks up my sleeve when it came to hair. I felt right at home. Mr. Michaels explained that the school accepted paying clients who were willing to have their hair or other professional beauty service done by someone trained from the school.

"This is also how you build your own clientele. If you can make someone beautiful, trust me honey, they will come back."

Even though Mr. Michaels had jolted me with his appearance, he was not to be mistaken for anything other than a guru in the industry. Years later, he would go on to become the Director of the Vidal Sassoon Academy. I didn't know it at the time, but we were all in good hands under his tutelage.

"Well, I have shown you Marinello. Now, it's time for you to make some decisions. Let's go to my office so we can review some information."

Before following him into his office, I turned around to take one final view of the school. As I stood there, I could see the range of the entire school. I closed my eyes for a moment and envisioned myself standing at my own booth, with clients coming in and out of Marinello like a revolving door. It was an out of body experience for me. I was standing there, cutting, blow drying, and laughing. I saw myself with joy inside my heart. This felt like home. I was in the midst of a peace that I wanted to surrender to. When I opened my eyes, that sense of peace remained embedded within my soul.

I was floating as I walked to Mr. Michael's office. As soon as I sat down in the seat closest to the door, he began speaking. "We can get you into a program that you can complete in ten months. You'd leave with your diploma and you would be fully accredited."

After recognizing that God had given me a clear vision of what I was capable of, I knew what I wanted out of my career as a hair stylist. I also knew that I had exactly one year to get this right. I would take those 365 days by the horns and work without ceasing until I reached my goal of not only becoming a stylist but working my way to becoming the most well-known stylist in Beverly Hills. Nothing else would suffice. My mission was clear and I knew exactly what I had to do.

I looked up at Mr. Michaels and he was sitting there, waiting for me to respond. "If I do decide to attend this school, I need to know something from you," I said resolutely. "I need for you to guarantee that if I do what I am supposed to do: follow the rules, work hard, maintain positive attendance, arrive on time, and whatever else you deem appropriate for my learning that you can assure me a position at a Beverly Hills Salon. I just need to know if this is possible?"

"Mr. Charles, if you become the stellar student that you speak of, I will personally see to it that you receive a placement in a Beverly Hills salon."

The sigh of relief that I exhaled, couldn't have contained the massive sense of purpose and direction that I had inhaled through my soul. This was it. The stars were aligned. "Well, then, I'm all in. All in!"

Mr. Michaels smiled assuredly and the corners of his mouth turned upwards. He looked proud and I hadn't even started. Maybe he saw something in me, or maybe he wanted to see if I would live up to what I had proposed. Either way, I was now officially chasing destiny and I was so glad about it.

That night, as I lay in my bed, I felt a sense of peace that had not been with me for as far back as I could remember. I had the consciousness to recognize it as more than just peace. I had discovered a path that would eventually lead me to the floor for my dance with purpose and destiny. Some search an entire lifetime to find such a thing and to call it by name, but there I was, preparing to par the course. God had shined His light on me and in due time, I would spread that same light to the rest of Los Angeles.

——DON'T SWEAT THE TECHNIQUE——

THE NEXT DAY, I spent time reviewing my finances and completing the application process. It was my intention to begin school the following Monday, which meant that I had less than one week to get my affairs in order. For me, ensuring that the business aspect of things was aligned was important. I had watched my father keep our affairs in order and I wanted to do the same. I recognized that nothing could become profitable without sound financial structure. I sat and calculate my living expenses and the tuition to determine what other avenues I would need to explore in order to earn cash. I knew in my heart that it would only be a matter of time before I made it to the floor and began getting paid for doing hair, which meant more money in my pocket. I was no stranger to the world of cosmetology. Now I would receive the formal training to do so, as a licensed stylist. I dreamed big and although my short-term goal was to get to the bottom floor to begin building a paying clientele, my long-term goal was much heftier. I was preparing to take Hollywood by storm.

Some people say that they don't know where life will lead them, and while I agree that we are not in control, I do believe in maintaining a vision of what we want to happen in hopes that the universe will conspire with me all the way through to manifestation. The remainder of the week, I plotted and planned and by that Friday, I had a strategy in place to prosper. I had figured out how to make the check that I was receiving from the insurance claim that I had filed for my mental health sabbatical, fund my dream. I had one year to make it work and come hell or high water, I knew that I would. After getting all of my paperwork submitted and the money paid for my first round of classes, I spent the weekend preparing to chase destiny.

To say that beauty school was evolutionary is an understatement. For me, it was a time to blossom, right where I had been planted. My first day of school was the first day of the rest of my life in so many ways. I began to pick up on the new rules and requirements with ease.

When you arrived each day, you had to punch in on a time clock before each class, punch out before your lunch break, and punch out before leaving. This helped everyone take responsibility for setting their schedules and maintaining timeliness throughout their daily routines. In addition to punching in and out, we were also responsible for using a chart to track everything that we learned.

I was enrolled as a freshman, and it took about eight weeks to complete the first semester of classes. Theory, was among the first classes and after reading the course descriptions, I recognized that it would provide us with an overview of the basics of hair. I had anticipated it to be far more lecture than practical. As I entered the classroom on the first day, I sat in anticipation for what would be. I chose a seat that was in the first row. I'm not sure how everyone else felt, but I wanted to soak up everything that I possibly could. I was preparing to leave no stone unturned on the road towards earning my license. As the start time approached, more students filled the room. Our class must have had at least fifty students and reflected and the diversity of Los Angeles. There were Armenians, Russians, Asians, Mexicans, and Americans like me and for many England was a second language.

No sooner had I noticed and digested the environment, when the mood of the room changed as a petite, and if I had to guess,

Jewish, lady marched into the room. I had arrived at that conclusion as all of the other little Jewish ladies in the classroom were acting as if Michael Jackson had just moonwalked across the front of the classroom. Lord! Honey, that little lady walked through that room like she was all of that and a bag of chips. Her long black duster appeared to fly in the momentum of her stride. She wore a pair of black, circular metal frames and her hair was pulled up in a chignon.

A few students began to stand up and yell out "Ms. Carol… Ms. Carol, can you give me a formula for my hair color?"

Without hesitation or even looking, she replied with a throaty voice: "Do a little of 26 D and 20 volume." She turned to reply to another person, you should try 27 G with a little 84 D." And to another, "For you, I would only recommend a half portion."

Baby, I learned quickly that Ms. Carol was a legend up in there. Do you hear me? If Marinello had a star, she was it. And as much swag as Ms. Carol exemplified effortlessly in that moment, I would learn over time that she had the knowledge to back it all up. She had earned every ounce of respect that she was paid. It wouldn't be long before I too would yell her name to request advice on formulas to mix and colors to use to achieve desired results for clients. Most importantly, Ms. Carol was very nice. I mean very nice. She was proof that you didn't have to be a bitch to be the best. I also recognized an apparent theme of teaching others to make the industry better overall. These were things that stuck with me over the years and continue to remain in my disposition as I became part of an industry that often touted attitudes and diva behavior. Ms. Carol was strict and no nonsense, and thus, our educational environment was extremely conducive to learning and evolving.

I was just as interested in the theory as I was in the act of doing hair itself. Under the steady hand and tutelage of my father, his extensive knowledge of chemistry proved to be a game changer for me. My comprehension of the concepts that they taught us was deeply rooted. Furthermore, prior to my time in corporate America, I had ambitions of becoming a doctor. I welcomed the scientific playground. We learned about hair and the cuticle, carbon, oxygen, the cortex, and Medusa, the diameter and density of hair, as well as the art of coloring and the use of peroxide. We even studied the muscle tissues of the head, face, and fingers. I enrolled in school for a full cosmetology license, so we were taught skills that would enable us to become hair stylists, makeup artist, nail technicians, and even estheticians. From my point of view, with a skill set such as this, there would be no limits to what I could accomplish in the industry.

As we delved deeper into the concepts of hair, I began to learn about relaxers and why overlapping that type of product on the hair could cause damage. This was a moment of clarity for me. Back in San Antonio, I had spent many days simply applying the relaxer to the entire head of my pseudo clients. I was not knowledgeable of what is referred to as "the line of demarcation," which is the line where the new growth and processed hair meet. Hair that was already processed did not need to be processed again, only the new growth. This was key to the overall health of the hair. When you know better, you have an obligation to do better. Our instructors also taught us how to wrap hair. This is when you comb or brush the hair in a circular pattern around the head to straighten it after it has been washed, straightened, or curled. The wrap helps the hair to achieve a sleeker look. I knew how to wrap hair from my previous experience and in many ways, I was ahead of the game, but the practical knowledge was a welcomed addition to my repertoire.

Time seemed to fly by at lightning speed. I was proud that I was following through on all of the things that Mr. Michaels had requested of me. My personal life had taken a complete backseat to my goals, and for me, it was empowering in so many ways. I recognized that the achievement of my goals also meant an unprecedented level of discipline. Even within the school, I stayed out of the social my classmates made. I went to class and came home to study.

Before we could graduate to stylist and work on the bottom floor, we were required to complete a designated number of hours doing, pedicures, manicures, roller sets, colors, and relaxers.

For every student at Marinello, a major milestone was when you began your last 400 hours of the curriculum. This meant that you would be solely on the bottom floor working with clients. By the time my milestone arrived, I had already established a rotating door of clients who came to my home to have their hair services done. It was an extra source of income for me, but also another opportunity to hone my craft. Now that I think about it, it was kind of funny that I was styling hair to fund my education to style hair. Even so, I was booming.

After being officially informed by Ms. Carol that I would now be permitted to practice with real clients, I could hardly contain my excitement. On the bottom floor, I received my own station to work at. This was really happening. I was really progressing towards being in business for myself. And even though I knew the road ahead would be long, I was one step closer to my dream of working as a hair stylist in Beverly Hills. I had never lost sight of my goal. I intended to chase everything that I thought God had reserved for me. I had left the circus of Corporate America because they refused to let me in, only to enter a gate that led, not only acceptance, but excellence. I had found my calling, just as my mother had advised. I guess the saying, "Mama knows best" is true after all.

On the bottom floor, the clients would pay for their services at the front after we finished. There was also a supervisor to assist us if we had questions or required guidance. On many days, while standing there at my station, I envisioned myself standing in the middle of my own salon. I could count on one hand how many times I requested the supervisor. I was like Edward Scissorhands. I really began to come into my own. My techniques had flair, and even back then I loved for my clients to look slightly edgy. If a lady smiled when I turned her around to see the finished product, I knew that I had made the difference.

Although I believed in myself and my ability, recognition from some significant people helped to solidify what I had believed about myself. One day as I was working on a client, Ms. Carol came by and said, "You cut very well. I can tell you will be good." It's amazing how society claims that words have no merit, but if we were truthful, we'd have to admit that when spoken, they play a great part in who we become and often what we believe to be our truths. Ms. Carol's words stuck to my soul, as did those of many others.

I'll never forget the day that I was finishing up a haircut for a client, who had become a regular, when I noticed that there was a black lady, who was receiving services from one of my classmates, who was of another ethnicity. My cohort was doing a good job, but for some reason I could tell that the client sitting in her chair was watching me. I assumed it was because I too was black, and she was interested in the techniques and products that I was using in comparison. I couldn't have been more wrong. When her hair was finished, she stood up and began to walk towards my station. I smiled cordially and then directed my full attention back to my client. Soon after, I felt a warm hand in the crevice of my elbow and forearm. As I turned toward the woman, she looked me in my eyes and said, "You're really good at what you do." I nodded in appreciation and as I was preparing to speak, she cut me off. "I just want to give you some advice." She leaned in closer so as not to allow the other students to hear and said, "Make sure that you do not date any of your clients. Keep it professional. If you don't, it will change the dynamics of your work and get messy." She squeezed my arm in confirmation and our eyes connected once again. Then, as any aunt would have done, she patted my arm as if she had given me a million dollars and walked towards the front counter to pay for her services. She never looked back, but she didn't have to. I knew that she had shared her words of wisdom from the most sincere place. Over the years, I've learned that what she said was worth more than a million dollars. Her words were invaluable. To this day, maintaining a working environment with a theme of pristine ethics is of the utmost importance to me. It became my personal rule that I would not sleep with any of my clients. And while no one besides the good Lord is perfect, I can say with certainty that I haven't.

With my moral compass intact and a work ethic like no other, I focused even more on honing my craft. I watched as my cohorts styled their client's hair. A technique that everyone was working to perfect was round brushing the hair. Prior to that time, it was what mostly whites were doing. What I knew was that whatever techniques the whites were using, I wanted to experiment with them on African American hair. A round brushing technique left the door wide open for me to do so. Round brushing was an innovative spin on drying the hair. With the use of a blow dryer and a round brush, you would wrap the hair around the brush and apply the heat from the blow dryer simultaneously. This technique would ensure that the hair was smooth at the roots while drying it and sealing the follicle. It was all in the flick of the wrist. Baby, I had that technique on lock, and nobody else was doing that for black women but Elgin Charles. I began to round brush all of my clients and before I knew it, my clientele was massive. Even today, I still got it!

There was nothing that I could not do behind that chair. I had clients lined up at Marinello, ready, willing, and excited for me to put my hands in their tresses. I was doing updos, relaxers, Jheri curls, pin curls, roller sets, and absolutely slaying the round brushing technique.

I comfortably settled into who I was becoming and discovered a lane that I could drive in with faith. I even let my guard down a little and began to socialize with my cohorts, many of whom proved to be pretty amazing. Sometimes, we would hang out in the back of the school and smoke a little weed together. There was one Mexican girl in particular, named Ruiz, who had the best shit. I mean, the best. It was so good. It tasted amazing and even smelled great. We would get so lit back there and then turn right back around and do some of the best hair for our clients. That was my only little vice and it kept me in a winning state of mind. It was actually around the same time that Sade came out with the song, "Smooth Operator." Lord, I would be so high and that song would come on and it was simply life changing. You couldn't tell me that I was not a smooth operator when it came to my client's tresses. I felt confident in my ability to transform anyone. The harder I worked, the more my name garnered attention, and word began to spread that I was the go-to at Marinello. I can honestly say that I took no credit for my gift; I only took credit for the fact that I was finally obedient when led to run towards purpose. And I haven't looked back since.

The closer we got to graduation, the more I found myself awake at night, lying in my bed, staring up at the ceiling. During those times, it always seemed like I could listen to God speak to me without interruption. It dawned on me that everyone who had started at the same time that I did, had not remained enrolled in the program. I, however, was certain of my destination, and I couldn't afford to stop. Period!

I knew that my time was coming and that I would need to brand myself in a way that would keep the clients coming my way. I also needed to remain connected to the people that I came across while out and about. I don't believe that people realized how important socialization was to a stylist. There is always someone in search of a good stylist. Thankfully, I was an outgoing people person and found it easy to meet new people, which only helped my case. I began to consider getting business cards and in preparation for doing so, I sat one evening in my apartment and wrote my name in different variations. Charles Williams. Elgin Williams. Charles Elgin. Although all of these were my actual names, the pairings didn't give me the essence of luxury that I was looking for. I wanted my name to be unforgettable and none of these had me experiencing an "aha" moment. Finally, after pondering additional options, I turned my name around and wrote the words ELGIN CHARLES, in that order. It had a ring to it. I wrote it down in block letters and other various designs, one of them being cursive. I loved it. It was in alignment with the brand that I wanted to create. It gave me the whole Vidal Sassoon vibe, but it was my own. The next day, I went to a printing shop and sat down with a manager to design my business card. I decided to refer to myself as a Glamour Consultant, instead of a hair stylist. My title needed to encompass all of my strengths. The card also included my phone number and listed that I had graduated from Marinello Schools of Beauty. After the manager completed the sample design, I was so happy and proud to see my name in print. That was the establishment of the Elgin Charles brand and yet another beacon of hope for me because it made the career that I had once dreamed of real. Over time I knew that I would see the success that my heart longed for. I was also confident in who God had created me to be and the skill set that was given unto me. Although I wanted to be the black Vidal Sassoon, I had never actually taken the time to learn his story or his blueprint. This meant that I was charting my own path, and while I was inspired by the greats, it was a path that I had deemed appropriate for me. What others were doing was of no concern to me. I simply wanted to be the best.

Prior to graduation, I recall stopping by Mr. Michaels' office. I peered into the door without placing my entire body in the frame. I wanted to be sure that he didn't have anyone else in, as I had not formally made an appointment. He looked up with his long wispy false lashes and flung his blonde hair ferociously to the other side.

"Charlie, come in, darling. How can we help you?"

It was kind of funny because there was only him in the office, but he often referred to himself as "we." I guess he was powerful enough with what he did to be considered to have the force of two, but I digress.

"Well, Mr. Michaels, I know that it's almost time for graduation and I have kept up my end of the bargain. I did exactly what you asked of me and what I promised to do that time I sat in here making the decision to enroll."

"Yes, you truly have, Charlie. We are very proud of you and quite impressed actually," he replied.

"So, does that mean that you will place me as a stylist in a Beverly Hills salon like we discussed?" I inquired.

"Just relax. I assure you that we are working on it." He paused for a brief moment, took a deep breath and then said, "You know what? I just thought of something. There is an opening that you would be absolutely phenomenal for. It is not the spot that I am waiting on for you, but I know that you would grow from being there—even if only for a short while."

I sat up in the chair with anticipation. I was eager to hear what he would say.

"I want you to assist a stylist by the name of Rover Lee. He is getting so much attention, because he round brushes, just like you. You would be a dynamic pairing."

"Where is he?" I asked in anticipation.

"Inglewood."

"What?" In my mind, I was really questioning how my request had gone from Hollywood to Inglewood. What I also knew was that humility was a virtue. Even though I had realized some level of success in the hair industry and proven that I could make a life for myself outside of corporate America, I also knew that I had a long way to go and plenty more to learn to be the force that I wanted to become. "Cool, no problem."

"The location is off of Market Street. It's called The Blue Horizon Salon. I'm going to contact them to get you all set up. We have no question whatsoever that you will be a star. Let's keep your momentum going."

Even though, I had not discovered the love that I had come to LA, so desperately in search of, it was my love affair with hair that had given me a reason to wake up in the morning. Romantically, I had lost, but professionally, I stood to gain the world and more. The rays of purpose were shining down on me and I could feel the warmth, illuminating my path. Hair gave me hope for what could be and while styling my clients, I could see the transfer of hope in their eyes. Hope was what I had of value to offer, which made me the richest man in the world because it was all that I needed to step boldly into the next chapter of my career as a bona fide hair stylist. I was laser focused on seeing my name in lights in Beverly Hills and I now realized that I had one chance to get it right. My personal life would be forced to take a backseat to my purpose. God had brought me a mighty long way, and even I knew that He was not through with me yet.

CHAPTER 9

Faith and Follicles

There is power in not simply living but discovering something worth living for."

—Elgin Charles

I PREPARED FOR MY GRADUATION from Marinello with ambitious eyes. My father and my little sister Crystal came to LA for the graduation ceremony. I could see in their eyes that they were truly proud of me. The looks on their faces gave me exactly what I needed to run even faster towards my dreams.

My new assignment and location was confirmed by Mr. Michaels and I was now scheduled to report for work the Tuesday following the ceremony. I learned that many salons did not open on Mondays and this gave me the notion to open up my home and use it as a salon on that day. I saw it as an advantage. I was managing my money like it was a science. Having watched my father strategically manage our finances had taught me more about making sound financial decisions than I had realized.

I used the weekend to drive around the area near my new place of work. As I drove towards Inglewood, the scenery shift was something that could not be denied. It was still amazing to me to see how different classes of people lived and how resources were allocated throughout the various neighborhoods. The closer I got, the more I could feel a culture that I had not necessarily been exposed to on a consistent basis since moving to LA. There was a richness that had nothing to do with money. It could be found in the food and in the music that you heard playing loudly. The wealth was vested in a people who used their hands and exactly what was in front of them to create some of life's most unforgettable moments. These were my people and it felt good to be amongst them.

While driving, I passed by a salon named Simply Raw and I was amazed. The ladies were lined up to get in there, like nobody's business. That was the first time that I had ever seen anyone lined up to get inside of a salon. It represented the power of the industry and the business that could be garnered from being excellent.

My appreciation for my heritage and the creativity that we embodied was heightened. I realized along the way, just how influential the African American culture was on the entire industry. No one was acknowledging it per say, but we were setting trends on Crenshaw that would somehow be remixed and found on Rodeo Drive. I would now have the advantage of seeing the entire industry with from a bird's eye view. As I continued to drive, I eventually, stumbled upon Market Street. There were so many salons up and down that street that I could hardly believe my eyes. Word at Marinello was that they were doing some serious hair. From haircutting, to updos, and everything in between, Market Street was becoming more and more recognized, especially in the African American community. Mr. Michaels was right. This was right where I belonged, even if only for a short period of time. After locating the salon, I stopped my car just out front and took a second to gather my thoughts and take it all in. I looked down and just to the right of the console was one of the business cards that I had made. It was almost surreal to believe that just under a year ago, I had walked away from a promising career that was structured, and by society's standards "a good job," to become a hair stylist. I couldn't have been prouder of myself in that moment. I had done it. I had managed to escape San Antonio. I had managed to discover something that I was not only passionate about, but that could also be profitable. I had evolved and I was amidst further evolution. I knew that whatever I brought to this experience, I would also be sure to bring an open mind. Doing so meant opening myself up to a new realm of possibilities. And although I didn't know what to expect when I returned, I knew that I was in the right place and it was time to show exactly what I was capable of.

When I arrived in Inglewood on that Tuesday, to officially report to work at The Blue Horizon Salon, I was directed to my assignment, which was to assist a stylist by the name of Robert Lee. His reputation preceded him. He was absolutely killing the roller brushing technique on women of color. And, honey, let me tell you, when they left his chair, he had done a new thing for every one of them. Watching him work was a pleasure and it drove home the fact that I was doing the right thing by perfecting my ability to roller brush hair.

The clients were literally lined up out of the door, waiting to get in. As I entered into the salon, I could feel the intensity from the moment that I hit the door. It was just what I knew and what I loved about the fast pace of our industry. When I met Robert Lee, he was very laid back and clearly focused. He extended his hand to shake mine and gave a few simple directions. I was right there with him, following. It wasn't that he wasn't welcoming, he was just caught in the middle of the action. Even though I had arrived early, before the salon was open, he must have agreed to take a client before hours. I understood. I stood for a moment, observing and getting my bearings. I watched him work briefly before grabbing an apron and going back over to his booth. "What do you need me to do," I asked.

"Well, man, the main thing is keeping the flow of the traffic in here. If you could shampoo and then blow dry anyone who may be ready before I'm finished with the client that I'm working on, that would be a game changer," he said, with hope that I was what Mr. Michaels from Marinello had sold.

I learned quickly that he had thirty-minute appointments. That was fast as hell, but I was ready for the challenge. Out of the gates, I intended to shine. My first client ended up being one that I would need to complete almost the full process on. I walked over to the appointment desk to request the information of who the first client was once the doors officially opened for the day. The receptionist pointed to the lady and I walked over to her and reached out for her hand to assist her up from the couch. It was little things like that which helped the ladies bear witness to how I thought they should be treated at a salon. So often, salons can make women feel like they are being done a favor and that was so not the case. It just takes a person who is more concerned with the care of the client. After I scrubbed her scalp for dear life, she was already floating on cloud nine. Who wouldn't be? I guided her over to the chair that Robert had designated for me to work at.

"Get the roots as straight as you can," he said.

I heard him loud and clear. He didn't know that I played no games when it came to straightening the hair. That was the secret weapon that catapulted me to success at Marinello. Water is like a relaxer on hair and for African American hair, water straightens it out and makes it pliable, which allows it to be easily styled. It is from that state that you can smooth it and achieve any desired style.

I had my own tools, so I knew what my blow dryer and brush was capable of doing. I had purchased them both while in school with the money from doing hair in my home. Quiet and unassuming, I went to work! I knew that Robert would be the next person to add his finishing touches to the hair. I timed it perfectly. I finished with the initial work on her just as another client was leaving his chair. I left some frizz on the ends just before he began to work on the client. His initial reaction to my work was one of disappointment and shock and it was written all over his face. But as he began to blow out the ends and finalize the drying process, he saw how impeccably straight the roots were. He glanced up at me and gave a nod of approval, and it was at that moment that I knew in my heart I had impressed him. He had a small smile in the corner of his mouth and I could sense that if he had been able to give me a high five, he would have. I was what he needed in order for him to maintain that thirty-minute appointment status that he had managed to acquire a name for. I was in there!

And with a mutual respect, we shut that salon down. Tag team was the name of the game. We had so many women coming in and out of the chairs that after the day ended, we each sat in the chairs that we had invited so many clients in and out of to take a rest. Shortly afterwards, I gathered my items and told everyone that I would see them the next day. Just as I made it to the door, Robert yelled out, "Hey, Elgin?" I thought that I had forgotten something. As I turned around, he put his hand in the air and said, "Good job, man."

I smiled and nodded my head. "Thanks. Thank you. See you guys tomorrow."

The late night air of Los Angeles rewarded me with a cool breeze as I walked to my car to journey home. The drive allowed me to reflect on my day and I came to the conclusion that even though I was biding my time until Mr. Michaels found me a placement in Beverly Hills, I was happy in my temporary home.

As the days went by, I learned more about the culture of the salon and the stylists that work in it. Much like Marinello and everywhere else, there was a social scene that you could either indulge in or gracefully opt out of. Some of the stylists would run in the back in between clients and snort cocaine. The music was always playing and it afforded a party atmosphere. I couldn't afford to indulge. I had already tried that shit with Joe and it didn't work out for me then, so I simply assumed that it wouldn't work out for me now. Don't get it twisted though, I was not without flaws. I smoked more than my fair share of weed out back of Marinello. At this new salon, however, I wasn't comfortable enough to indulge. I also knew that Mr. Michaels would be receiving reports on my progress, and I wanted to ensure that nothing blocked me from the placement that I had asked for over a year ago.

I stayed focused and fixated on the work, improving in every way possible. I never questioned for one moment that the phone call would come for me to work in Beverly Hills. It was my destiny and I had spoken it into existence that day in Mr. Michael's office. After two short weeks, my faith took flight and I would enter into a season of perpetual blessings. Today, I recognize that there can be no triumph in the absence of trials. I would come face to face with destiny and dance with some of the most daunting moments of my entire life. As they say, everything is according to God's plans, not ours.

——WOKE——

JUST AS HE HAD promised, Mr. Michaels called to tell me that a stylist by the name of Blaze was ready for an assistant in West Hollywood. One would assume that I would have been floored because my dream was actually coming true, but I can honestly say that the call didn't take my breath away. It did, however, ignite my fire. I was more driven than ever to learn it all and to run as fast as I could towards one day owning a salon of my own. I took on the eye of the tiger in my preparation for West Hollywood.

It is my belief that when you have prepared to run a race, the opportunity to perform at the highest level isn't the prize. The prize is to compete at that level and win. Although open minded and more than willing to learn, I was laser focused on becoming the best.

The night before I was to report to the salon where I would meet Blaze, I conducted my normal ritual of driving by the business. Preparation was key and I wanted to know exactly where I would need to report to the next day. That morning, I had my normal cup of coffee and a bagel, just in case I didn't get to take a lunch until much later, which was beyond common in our industry. I drove my same little light blue Mercury that I had driven to Los Angeles. I'll never forget when my father took me to purchase it off the lot.

"I'm going to get you a brand-new car. I want you to be able to get from point 'A' to point 'B,' without any problems. This will be your baby and your full responsibility, including insurance."

My payments were $135 per month. It felt like it would take me forever to pay it off, but I remained vigilant and although it wasn't fast, I was so thankful it was new and dependable. I never had to worry about the transmission failing or anything else for that matter. Driving up the hill to Melrose Place, however, proved that I needed to be on the right-hand side—the slow lane—but I didn't care. I drove my little, albeit tortoise-like, blue car with pride.

Melrose Place is very different than any street in Hollywood. Back then, it was almost two blocks long. Between Melrose Avenue and La Cienega Boulevard, it splits off and leads you into the coveted Melrose Place. That street was nothing but commercial property and tons of expensive antique shops. There was a skin care studio called Giovanni's and adjacent to it was the Adrian Houghton Hair Salon. That was my new home and where I was to meet Blaze, who worked directly under Adrian Houghton.

I always said that becoming a stylist in Beverly Hills was my opportunity to see, "how the other half lived." During those years, it was new territory for me. I was being introduced to the lifestyles of the rich and famous, but I personally was green, naive, and country as hell. I didn't have the money that I was in the midst of, but I made up for it with my intelligence and the confidence in my ability to slay hair. Most importantly, I had the will to learn anything that I did not know. Pressed down and shaken together, the cocktail of all of these elements, equaled ambition. I could always hear my father's words: "You are a leader. I raised you to find a way to will what you want for yourself in this world." He would always tell me that I would open doors that no one else had opened. We can pretend that the words of those who love us aren't piercing, but who are we fooling? It seemed that the older I got, the more influential the words of Momma and Daddy were in my heart. It was on the momentum of those words that I stepped into The Adrian Houghton Hair Salon, ready to seize the day.

The salon was appointed with big, beautiful, brown doors with large window panes in front. When you opened the door, you could see all the way to the back. The receptionist's desk was large and opulent, and almost resembled a dining room table. There were two telephones placed upon it and two stations for receptionists to work in tandem. There were sofas placed down the middle of the salon from one end to the next. The stylist stations aligning the walls while the shampoo stations were at the rear of the salon. Overall, it was spacious, but the back area, where the staff workspace was located, felt compact.

When I arrived, the stylists were preparing for a full day of work. Everyone was so busy and, in their zones, that it was hard for them to even notice a new face in the building. I stood out because I was black, but otherwise I would have blended in with the rest of the boys.

I knew that I would no longer be surrounded by people who were learning their craft. Everyone in the room was a master stylist and they were known to be the best talent the city had to offer— perhaps even the world. In no way was I intimidated. I felt confident that I had not only earned the right to be there but that God had ordained it. Standing in the midst of purpose does not allow you to fall into the depths of life's puddles; it empowers you to thrive and walk boldly into destiny and that's exactly what I did.

Adrian Houghton was at the height of his career. He had all of the top stylist working for him in Beverly Hills. Hue York, Bruce Johnson, the only black guy in the salon, and then there was Blaze. When I met Blaze, the stylist who I would be assisting, we instantly hit it off. Blaze was a fierce Gemini. He was an older, blonde, white boy, who was bald at the top and wore a tapered ponytail in the back. He also rocked a great mustache and had beautiful, pearly white teeth. His signature thing was always his socks. He had a fancy pair to go with every outfit.

Blaze and I worked well together and through the years proved to be impactful on each other's careers. We even decided to become roommates in 1987, when he bought his first home in the Hollywood Hills. I remember rocking out to "BAD" by Michael Jackson when we lived together.

It took me some time to learn all of the other stylists, but eventually I would watch and learn their styles and the techniques that made them legendary. Hue York was the creator of Farrah Fawcett's signature style. Watching him was quite the show. He would have the comb and scissors and he would sweep the hair in an upwards motion and cut off pieces as they flowed back down. He was very unorthodox and he created absolute art through his styling methodologies. And just as grand as his cutting methods were, so was his lifestyle. He drove a huge Rolls Royce and parked it just outside of the salon, almost at the front door. The front door space was of course reserved for Adrian Houghton. All of the hairdressers in the salon lived lives of opulence and grandeur. At times, it was hard to tell who the real celebrities were, until the client sat in the chair.

It was at Adrian Houghton's that I was first turned on to hair extensions. After being introduced to a fierce stylist by the name of Allison Greenpalm, there was no turning back. Allison was tall and wore long braids all the way down to her ass. She had designed her own line of hair extensions, called Hair Addictions, which was monumental at the time. She was the go to for braids and extensions and had serviced celebrities like Janet Jackson, The Pointer Sisters, and Natalie Cole. You name the star and she was most likely providing them with a service.

She unselfishly taught me and is the reason that I am able to create everything that I can today. With her imparted knowledge, I was able to use my imagination and I soared. She showed me how to tie a knot and how to do a stitch. When I saw the methods, it all made perfect sense. Her faith in me grew and she began sending me clients to style after she was finished with extensions. Allison was married and eventually moved with her family to Washington. She transferred all of her clients in Los Angeles to me while they continued to buy hair from her. She had managed to corner a niche part of the market.

Around the time that I was honing my skill at extensions, Adrian became sick and eventually, he could no longer work. He sold the salon to Robert E Dell. At that point, Hue York left and opened his own salon in West Hollywood on Sunset Plaza.

I continued assisting Blaze for six months, but I was getting antsy. My insurance money was running low and I was only making $135 per week. I needed to carve out another space for myself to generate more income. I wanted to have my own station and I knew that I was ready. My prayers were answered and I was given a space on the floor and for the next eighteen months I honed my skills as a full fledged stylist.

By 1986, things had begun to change rapidly. Adrian Houghton had gone from a thriving business owner to a frail, wheelchair bound man. It appeared that everyone was dropping like flies. If you were a gay man, the prospect of death was prevalent. It was unnerving and a testament to what could happen and it frightened me to no end. Trust me, if you were gay during that era, you were afraid. Point-blank, period.

Blaze negotiated a deal for himself at Char Salon in Beverly Hills. With him gone, I decided to take the opportunity to make a change myself and accepted a position at Sunset Plaza. After only a week, Blaze got in touch and informed me that there was a position for a commissioned stylist open at Char and he asked if I wanted to be considered. I jumped at the opportunity and just like that, I had taken another step towards my dream of having my own salon in Beverly Hills.

Moving to Char Salon was like every other move. My first goal was to ensure that my existing clientele knew where to find me and then I would get settled in so that I could build an even larger base of clients.

As with every salon, there were stars and characters that you came to know and love. At Char Salon, the standouts were Blaze, and Maurice Azoulay, a French Moroccan who ended up buying out the salons. There was also a gentleman by the name of Day Lee. He was from Georgia, but had come to Beverly Hills via Paris, France. He would use words like, "Darling," and he kissed on each cheek to greet his clients. As a hair stylist, when you go to Paris and showcase your work, you are likely to be jaded by the whole experience. It is simply mind blowing that a career using your hands and creativity can open such doors. Day Lee had had just enough of Paris that it returned with him to the United States and although he was black, his clientele was largely white.

My station was positioned next to his, so I saw how hard he worked and how incredible he was at doing hair. And just as much as he liked to work, he also liked to party. It amazed me how hard everyone partied and how easily we would all wake up to seize the day. It was like the night had never happened. In truth, it was more of a lifestyle. After so many hours serving others, you need some time to just do whatever the hell you wanted to do for yourself. It was simply a way to decompress.

I was always there bright and early at 9 a.m. There were times that Day Lee had partied a little too hard and he wouldn't make it in on time. On those mornings, the clients he wasn't there to greet ended up in my chair. The fact that he didn't care, tickled me on many occasions.

The element of comedy was not hard to find in the salon setting. And some moments that come to memory were not funny at the time, but they are sure as hell funny now. There was one instance in which Stevie Wonder came in to have his hair done. Stevie wore braids and over time, braids require maintenance to prevent the hair from looking like dreadlocks. In many ways the art of doing hair is subjective. Every stylist has their individual approach to a client's needs. On this day, Day Lee's strategy was to use a relaxer on the hair while it was braided, in an effort to release the entangled hair. When he applied the relaxer to Stevie's hair and allowed him to sit a while, I noticed Stevie motioning for Day Lee to take him to the bowl. He needed that shit rinsed out immediately because it was burning like hell. In my mind, it was a good thing that Stevie did not bear witness to how badly Day Lee had burned his scalp visually, but I know that he felt the burn physically. The hysteria in all of this was that Stevie's hair was still matted. The relaxer could not accomplish what Day Lee intended for it to do. I felt bad for Day Lee and even worse for Stevie. Needless to say, I didn't see Stevie sit in Day Lee's chair again after that day.

My skills were getting better by the day. I was mastering everything that I put my hands on. I was hungry and eager to be the best. I had the ability to take an average looking woman and make her beautiful according to Hollywood's standards with a whip of my wand. And by wand, I mean any tool that I used to style the hair. I just had an eye for transformation. More importantly, I saw something beautiful in everyone. I still do today. The quirks and things that we often take for granted are the things that make us unique. Playing to those can often lead to beautiful places. I also recognized early on that women loved to be made beautiful by men. There was a different kind of connection that was experienced between client and stylist. I still don't know what that magic is, but I do know that women loved to be told that they were beautiful by men and being a stylist thrust me directly into that space.

By the time I transitioned to Char Salon, I was Elgin Charles, honey! The makings of my brand would remain to be seen. I had so many ideas about how I would build an empire that would withstand the test of time. Although I recognized that I was still in the dues paying stages, I knew without question that I had been ordained to do this work: to cultivate self-esteem and build both inner and outer beauty as a stylist. For many in the profession, it was a job that paid the bills. For me, it was a ministry and a labor of love.

Although I didn't know it, working there would prove to be a spiritually awakening experience for me. While working on a client, a lady by the name of Annie Williams entered through the front entrance. I had seen her from time to time but hadn't had the opportunity to get to know who she truly was.

After speaking with a few of the stylists, she stopped by my station. "Hey Elgin. How's everything going for you here?" she inquired.

"Everything is going well," I replied graciously.

"I'm glad to hear that. Listen, the Holy Spirit told me to invite you to church. Do you think you might be interested in joining us?"

"Sure, I would love to attend," I said, with a slight sense of relief. The truth was I had spent every minute I wasn't in the salon, crying and asking the Lord to forgive me. I was desperate for a reprieve that only forgiveness could yield.

I must have spent forever laying out my clothes in preparation to attend church. Even though I had quite the collection of nice suits from my corporate days, this was a reentry into the church for me. I hadn't been since moving to Los Angeles. And even though I had been raised in the church and it was a place of refuge for me, I felt that this time was special. Once I made a final decision I got myself ready. I was clean as hell.

When I arrived, I walked in and immediately acclimated to the teachings of Dr. Frederick K.C. Price. He was the Pastor, but his leadership could be felt through the church and I admired that. That day, his sermon was centered around the concept of the connection between the spirit, soul, and body.

I appreciated that the environment was one of learning and not the dog and pony show that you would sometimes see in churches. It is my belief that all of that whoopin and hollerin does not amount to anything if the people leave the church and still don't know how to live their lives according to God's word. I knew that I was in the right place because I have always had a thirst for knowledge, and information proved to be the anchor of Dr. Price's church. It became apparent that he not only wanted for his members to be well versed in the word and his teaching, but also strategies from which to apply the word to our everyday lives.

It's crazy how you can go to a place and you feel like the message is tailored to you. On that day, I was almost certain that a little angel was perched upon my shoulder, tapping me and saying, "Make sure you get that part, ok?" During that service, Dr. Price explained the doctrine in a clear and concise way.

"We are all spirits with souls. The spirits and souls that we possess, all live in a body. Your spirit is the God in you. It is your likeness of God. It is your divine connection to God. Your spirit is the key that unlocks the God in you. Your soul is comprised of your thoughts and reflects your intellect, emotions, and everything else that goes on in your head. Now, you must understand that the spirit cannot exist in the absence of the soul. It just isn't possible. To understand just how deeply these two facets are connected, imagine water without wet. It is not conceivable. You cannot have a spirit without a soul. Our physical bodies are made from dust and when we depart this life, they shall return to dust."

The plain yet profound teachings of Dr. Price kept me engaged and I knew without question that I would return. I wanted more. Aside from my blossoming career, this was the first time in a very long time, I felt like I had something that I could hold on to and begin to move past the perils of the great loss that I had experienced. His teachings eventually led me towards an awakening that I can't quite say that I knew existed, or at least it hadn't been a byproduct of my reality. For my entire life, I had been raised to know the word of God, but I was impacted differently now.

Dr. Price preached ideologies that empowered anyone willing to listen. Studying under his tutelage also meant a commitment to the elevation of my entire being: mind, body, and soul. He didn't shout from the rooftops, as many pastors have been known to do; he was a professor and whenever I entered into the doors of his church, it was as if school was in session.

"The physical body is made from dust, and to dust we shall all return," he would often say. Dr. Price urged that we all had access to the presence of the Holy Spirit, if only we accepted Christ into our lives. He further explained that it was not possible for us to accept the Holy Spirit and not have Christ and vice versa. One could not be present without the other. To that same end, the acceptance of the Holy Spirit also meant that we became living, breathing vessels with the power of Christ. The power of Christ is unprecedented, all powerful, and without flaw. Based on these principles, the acceptance of Christ or the act of being born again, gives us all access to the ability to control our flesh. The flesh had been my struggle. It is every person's struggle.

Do you understand the power associated with the ability to control your flesh? In my opinion, it is an undisputed fact that controlling the flesh is the most powerful act that we can ever engage in. Far too often, our flesh makes us succumb to acts and circumstances that are not healthy for us, or that do not prove or lead to pros-perity in our lives. On a deeper level of intensity, my flesh is what had given me the urges to lie with men and to lie with women. I knew what the Bible said about men lying with men, but my flesh had won the battle when I came to LA. It was a tremendous part of the reason that I had come to begin with.

It had long since been my desire to get away from San Antonio and the judgement that I would have been forced to endure, should anyone have found out that my flesh desired men. LA had allowed me to explore in peace. Even so, I always felt con-victed. No matter how deep into the relationships I had gotten, or how in love I felt that I was, I felt guilty before, during, and after. Death was all around me and the closer it came to me, the more I worked to muffle its ability to speak over my life. I wanted nothing to do with who I had been. I wanted nothing to do with the life that I had once driven across the country in pursuit of. In those moments, I wanted simplicity, sin free, holy, and pure from anything that could resolve my hopes and dreams of death. I felt like there was more that God wanted me to do and I wanted so desperately to fulfill my purpose.

I never once let on just how much turmoil I was experiencing at the hands of my carnal decisions. No one would have ever known that I was walking in heaven while at work and at church and returning home to the agony of a personal hell in my mind.

Dr. Price's teachings were impactful because I was now old enough to understand how to apply his words and biblical references to my life in present day. To know that I had the power to control my flesh was to know that I could escape the curiosity that had burdened my soul and led me to unknown destinations of love with men. All my life, I, like everyone else, have lived in search of love. I will never convict myself for living in search of love. The difference between my awakening through Dr. Price's teachings was that the love I sought was not from man, it was now my greatest desire to be loved by God.

Upon accepting ownership of the responsibility to conquer my flesh, I decided to set my past on fire. I wanted it to suffocate by slow death. I imagined small flickers of my past, lit and burning, slowly and intensely. I decided once and for all to cast my past into a sea of forgetfulness. Ashes to ashes, dust to dust.

I knew how weak my spirit was. It was simply human nature. I now had the ammunition to defeat sin. Dr. Price was teaching me weekly how to pray, how to remain steadfast in the Lord, and how to become more holy through worship. I felt like I had been washed, cleansed, and made anew. I was ready to begin life again, but this time in even more abundance than what I had experienced. I now recognized that I had a right to every resource that existed because of my relationship with the Creator of everything that existed.

I became a student of the Bible and increased my prayer life and time spent amidst God's glory on a daily basis. I began to confess with my tongue about the things that had tormented me from my past. I had every intent to escape the bondage that I had been born into and that which I had created for myself. After understanding fully, the power of acceptance, I began to ignite a ritual that was centered around the digestion of God's word. Doing so, helped me to confess. Dr. Price would always say, "Show thyself approved." I understood that to mean that God would hear from me when I had demonstrated that I was working in diligence to be in His presence, study His word, and seek His forgiveness for my sins and transgressions. All I knew was that whatever God had, I wanted more.

Everyone around me was just as into God's word as I was. We were all on fire. It amazed me that I had gone from sitting in a classroom surrounded by people who wanted to become hair stylists, to sitting in a classroom surrounded by people who wanted to become leaders of God's word.

I was listening so hard for a word from God on the direction that I should take next that I made the decision to submit myself fully in hopes of being accepted into ministry school. If I had thought that submitting my application for beauty school was the right thing to do, I was even more sure now. I also knew that there was so much I wanted from God. I would do hair from the early hours of the morning and into the night, just before it was time for ministry school. Every moment that was not spent working with my clients, was spent working for God. Working at Char Salon was very conducive to my spiritual goals and helped me to cope in silence. It was driven by God and he was always invited in.

When you are trying to walk in purpose, the people and the environment to which you submit yourself are critical as to whether or not you sink or swim. Without being in God's presence constantly, I could have found myself treading deadly waters, but through God, I had every intention of swimming. The waters of spiritual enlightenment that I now treaded, gave me strength to remain steadfast on my goals and to feed my ambitious soul.

I began believing God for a salon of my own. I wanted to go deeper in what I asked for and in my faith. I was eager to know what God had in store for me. My prayers became more strategic. Instead of praying generically, I learned through Dr. Shaw, and repeated practice, how to summon the presence of God and how to ask for the desires of my heart. I had never really done that. I had been told by my father on so many occasions that "it would be my turn next" when it came to almost everything. I had always felt up until this point that I was standing in some sort of imaginary line of life, waiting for a turn that might not ever come. The subconscious will take you to places that aren't always conducive to your forward progress. If you allow them to consume you, somehow, they will. But GOD! I had been positioned to align with the power of God. And although I had big dreams, I knew that I would work harder than anyone around me to achieve them because I now owned a more concentrated level of certainty. With God, there was no "waiting for my turn." With God, my turn was when He said it was and had little or nothing to do with someone being in front of me or having been born before me. With God, it was His timing according to the plan that he had for my life. That gave me another sense of hope from which to channel my faith.

Annie Williams, who was a fellow stylist at Char Salon, noticed my spiritual ascension. She told me that she and a lady by the name of Stella Davis spearheaded an organization for professionals in the cosmetology industry who were on fire for God. Annie explained the organization as more of a prayer meeting format, and my goodness, did she undercut the power of what she was accomplishing. I later learned that what Annie and Stella had initiated was the Christian Cosmetology International Association (CCIA). Stella had already been enrolled in ministry school and now I was also, which made the organization a perfect fit for my continued growth and development. Both of my worlds had now been married into a union that could have only been ordained by God.

I found comfort in the fact that both Stella and Dr. Price were teaching the same doctrine. Stella was extremely organized as both a professional and minister. Her total devotion and commitment to both entities, demonstrated that it could be done. Stella went on to receive her Doctorate in Ministry and I was in awe of their work ethics. I was on Holy ground and in good company, which became one of the most impactful blessings of my life and career.

When I attended the meetings hosted by Stella and Annie, there was a prayer request box and we were all encouraged to submit our requests to God. It was there that I learned about the concept of intercession. We learned the importance of praying over things in the spirit. Simply put, when summoning God, you have to let go of yourself and get in His presence. I also learned about speaking in tongues. In my carnal mind, I could not understand it for the life of me. Where did this mysterious language come from? If I didn't know what to say, how would I ever learn to speak this way? For some of my fellow professionals in the meetings, it seemed to come as second nature, but this wasn't the case for me. I was given directives, to just keep practicing and working to get into the presence of God, whatever that meant for me. Lord, that was one for me that I just couldn't seem to crack the code on. I had to wonder, if God would still listen because I needed to just talk with Him using the words I did every day, honey. LORD! Honey, I just kept trying.

By this time, I was waking up every morning to pray for thirty minutes. I would also engage in prayer after ministry school, which lasted for an hour. In the meantime, I just kept on attempting to speak in tongues, while sincerely praying to God for healing from anything that was not of His commandments, including my flesh and the desires of my heart. After becoming a regular at the meetings, I stepped out in even bolder faith and put in a prayer request for my own salon. The scripture that I held close to my heart was Mark 11:24, "Therefore I say to you, whatever things you ask when you pray, believe that you receive them, and you will have them." This verse became the theme of my life. I knew that the God I served held the keys to every door that existed. Through him, I could not fail. I recognized with my whole heart that regardless of what language I cried out in, God was always there and He was always faithful and always listening. What a mighty God we serve!

CHAPTER 10

Unforgettable

"Comfort zones breed mediocrity. I've never desired to live there."

—Elgin Charles

THE CLOSER I GOT TO GOD, the more distant I became from the personal life that I had once known. It was no longer a part of who God wanted me to be. Acquiring the power to silence my internal need for anything other than the word of God had set me free. Freedom from bondage is liberating. I had discovered my emancipation in an unexpected place.

I had drudged through blood, sweat, and tears to build my career and I had toiled twice as hard to keep my personal life separate from anything that did not mirror an image of perfection. From my work ethic to my commitment to being a better human and growing in grace, I was sowing seeds of prosperity on fertile ground. I wore an invisible white crown and I had done all that I could to scour any evidence of a scarlet letter.

Even back then, I was wise enough to know that my personal conquests could have destroyed my professional feats. This wasn't a war that I was willing to wage. There I stood in the middle of the holy ground of salvation, waving a white flag of surrender. And although I knew that I didn't have the power to reason with God, I was extending an olive branch; it was all that I had. I wanted God to free me from the demons that had once consumed my spirit, my time, and my thoughts. I wanted God to grant me abundance within the freedom of the ties of my hidden sexuality that had bound me. Forever. And let me say, there are times when forever is simply a moment in time.

Since God had granted me permission to dream, I began setting my sights on the ultimate goal: a salon of my own. My appeal to God for the salon now made it into the prayer request box at the Ministry on a weekly basis. Not only was God showing me that He had aligned prosperity for me, He was also showing me that He would surround me with the people that I needed in order to reach the mighty goals he had placed within my spirit.

While I continued my spiritual journey, my career blossomed. As God would have it, Hollywood royalty graced my presence in the form of a Queen crowned Natalie Cole. She was the heir to the throne of the legendary singer known to the world as Nat King Cole. The Nat King Cole brand was synonymous with success. As an American jazz pianist and vocalist, he broke barriers for black musicians that no one had ever dreamed possible. With over one hundred recorded songs, he solidified a space in music that had not been filled. His music was timeless and the smoothness of his voice was simply unforgettable. His daughter Natalie had not only acquired his musicality, but charted a lane of her own in the music and entertainment industry. There was not much that she couldn't do. From singing to acting to dancing, her talent preceded her.

Natalie had enlisted me to be her stylist and the keeper of her coif. At the time she had a recurring role on a show called *Big*

Breaks, and I would travel back and forth from the salon to her set to get her ready. It was a hectic time, but I loved every minute of it. The show itself was absolutely amazing and to see everything from behind the scenes was eye opening. On a day that I will never forget, Whitney Houston was a guest on the show. I was suddenly amidst the bright lights that they speak of in Hollywood! That day, I had to rush from set to the home of an acclaimed writer by the name of Ollie Stevenson, who was also a beloved client. As I was traveling down Wilshire Boulevard, the Holy Spirit told me to look over to the left. I'll never forget the address, 8601. There was a huge "For Lease" sign in the window and at that moment, I asked God to bless me with that building for my salon. I kept driving and praying, until I reached Ollie's home.

Once there, I could not contain my excitement. I was believing God for something greater than I had ever realized in his name. With this same positive energy, I gave Ollie a fabulous color, consisting of golden hues that eventually became her signature look. Ollie was a Sagittarius and if they like you, there is nothing that they won't do for you. Amidst our conversation, I told Ollie about the building space on Wilshire and divulged to her my heart's desire. Before I knew it, she had called and made an appointment with the leasing agent for me to see the space on the following day.

When I arrived at the appointed time, my heart was pounding. I was so in sync with God that I knew that He would provide. The blessing in obedience is that God will show you new things and grant you the desires of your heart. There it was, 8601 Wilshire Blvd. The space that I was eyeing was on the sixth floor. I met the leasing agent out front and we shook hands. As we took the elevator up my excitement almost overwhelmed me. The little country boy from San Antonio was viewing a property where he hoped to open doors to his own salon in Los Angeles, California. Wow! The leasing agent explained that the space had been previously a skin care boutique and suite. I had my eyes opened for one thing: water. I knew that if I could visualize where the shampoo stations would be, then it was game over. As we turned the corner, I saw a sink and it was perfect. I could already imagine three shampoo bowls in that same space.

There was no question that I liked the space, now I just had to handle the business aspect of things so everything could be squared away. We began talking about pricing and I told him how much I was already paying in commission at my current location. I knew immediately that I could make it work. The leasing agent showed me favor and believe it or not, I signed the lease that day.

I had never stopped working out of my condo, making extra money at every turn. I was notorious for saving money. Watching my father oversee his finances and my time in corporate America had made me an astute businessman. By this time, I had already made the decision to leave Char Salon. I knew that if I had stayed, I would become comfortable and not push to do exactly what I was doing. I put them on notice that I was believing God for a salon of my own and well, there I was, signing the lease for my own place. I began saving like crazy. Even though I had signed the lease, I now needed to come up with money that I didn't have, at least in liquid form. In my possession, I had $10,000. I was now in need of money for the deposits and furniture to get the salon ready for clients. My credit was not established enough, as I had never really had any lines of credit in my name up to that point. After paying cash for the deposit and first month's rent, I went to visit a furniture store that specialized in beauty supplies. I was hoping to strike a deal. They gave me salon loaner furniture as I waited for what I had ordered to be ready.

In addition to servicing my clients out of my condo, I also began going into the salon daily to set up. Once I got all of the utilities up and running, I began seeing my clients in the salon. I saved every penny that I earned. There was nothing more that I wanted to do than to invest in my business. Where you sow seeds, they shall grow. Talk about working your fingers to the bone. I was the lone ranger. I was running my business as well as working in it. I was the receptionist, lead stylist, janitor, accountant, landlord and any other job that needed to be done. I had never worked so hard in my life. My hands, my feet, and my back would be killing me after the long hours, but every day I woke up with joy in my soul. I was now working for myself and no one could take it away from me. God had shined his rays of love upon my life and for that I was humbled, grateful, and blessed.

After roughly two weeks of toil, the phone began ringing. The calls were from prospective new clients, but also, to my surprise, from stylists who wanted to come and work at my salon. God was preparing to enlarge my territory. Maynard was first stylist and he brought another stylist named Donna Taylor with him. Donna eventually left and went to work with a stylist by the name of Myeisha. Not long after, there was an unfortunate fire that burned down Char Salon and from there I gained both Stella and Devvie, two stylists who had worked together and were hoping to join my team. They knew that I had opened the salon because of my prayers. I welcomed them to the team with open arms. The salon was building so fast that at times my head was spinning.

Even though we were building fast, I still had the deadline coming up to pay off the $10,000 for the furniture that was now installed in the salon. During a routine styling, I mentioned to Natalie Cole that I was working tirelessly to make the money to pay for my furniture.

"Well, how much is it?" she inquired.

"Ten thousand dollars," I replied.

"That's all? I'll loan it to you, Elgin. Now let's be clear, you will have to pay me back in ninety days. Do you think that you can do that?"

"Oh, yes. Yes, absolutely. I know that I can," I replied with anxiousness and excitement.

With a significantly increased timeline, my number one goal was to make sure I paid Nathalie all of her money. It was my priority before all else.

This era was special for me as it also marked the time that she prepared to release the remake of her father's timeless classic, "Unforgettable." Even today, the sweet melody of the song keeps me grounded and helps me to remember the humble beginnings of a dream come true. During this time, Nathalie wanted to change her look. She was tired of wearing wigs and wanted something classic but also edgy. My imagination took me to a place of doing something drastic and groundbreaking for her. I'll never forget the day that she came into the salon and I convinced her to cut her hair. The short and sassy coif ushered her into a new period in her career as she paid homage to her father. Additionally, it was also the day that I gave her a check for the $10,000 that she had loaned me. In my mind, that moment in time was monumental. I had managed to transform an industry vet and realize a dream all at once. God was showing up and showing out, just for me. And although I felt far from worthy, I knew without question that I would run as far and as fast as He would allow me to, in His blessings.

That evening, I sat in my salon, gazing out of the large window that overlooked Wilshire Boulevard. My feet and hands were worn, but my eyes were set on what the future had in store. As I got up and walked toward the window, I actually took the time to notice the stars. They were shimmering and putting on a show for me. I remember smiling and thinking to myself that God had shown me favor. The mere fact that He saw fit for a little boy from San Antonio, Texas to come all the way to Los Angeles, California to make a name for himself in an industry that was never even intentional, placed me at a loss for words. That night, I held my head high.

As I prepared to turn down the lights and exit the building, I noticed the name just outside of the door, "ELGIN CHARLES." My heart was so full that I could feel the emotion welling up inside my soul. I owned every bit of it of what God had done for me. I owned my part in the professional work that I had done and I owned my part in the spiritual work that I had done to get to that very moment. When you work hard for things, no one can ever take them away from you. You've earned them. I had earned that moment and every other monumental moment that was to come.

——THE REAR VIEW MIRROR——

BY THE TIME I MADE it home, I was almost prancing. I was so astounded by the world and everything around me. I took the time to delight in what felt like success. I basked in it; even if only for a moment. Life is peculiar that way. We live for moments that take our breath away, forgetting that we too will experience moments that leave us out without the ability to breathe. And just when you think that you have your whole life ahead of you, a slight echo of your past has the power to whisper your name, even if for only a moment of remembrance. The truth is that no matter who we become, there will always be parts of us that are who we have always been. No matter how hard we try to escape, traces of the residue of who we used to be exist.

In the thick of standing tall, amidst my first major success as Elgin Charles, I was brought back to my knees without notice. Just as I was preparing to undress from the day, the phone rang. I considered not answering it, with the thought that it was a client calling after hours to schedule an appointment. By the time I made it to the phone, it was on its last attempt at a ring.

"Hello, this is El…" I was abruptly interrupted, by a woman's voice.

"Charlie, I think you should come now. He's not well."

And even though she never mentioned her name, I knew her voice. My hand began trembling and my voice was rapidly filled with anxiousness. "Wha… what do you mean?" I said in disbelief.

"Come now, Charlie, before it's too late." It was Cory's sister and I knew exactly what she meant. She hung up the phone in haste, but I was paralyzed, fixated on her words. It was as if I had been caught in the storm of everything that she hadn't said. One of my greatest fears had become a nightmare that I would not be able to wake up from.

I immediately buttoned my shirt back up, tucked it into my pants, and grabbed my keys before heading to the door. That night, Cory told me the truth that I had been in search of. And as he spoke, I sat in dismay. The room was a blur and there was an imaginary divider between us. He was so close but yet so far. I held his hand, but it was as if we were in two different worlds. "I was diagnosed with full blown AIDS and they have given me a very limited amount of time to live."

The words spewed out like fire. He had mustered up every bit of strength that he could just to tell me that. It was beyond obvious that his days were numbered. The tears that began to stream down my face were acidic. I couldn't stop them from coming as I dropped my head. My journey of life had somehow circled me back to the distant land of desperation that I had once believed to be a place of the past. What was I to say? What would happen to Cory? What would happen to me? Was I next? I couldn't even mourn in the moment as the need for self-preservation soaked up all signs of life from my body. The pain of his words pierced my ears and for a moment, I felt as though I had slipped out of consciousness. There was nothing that I could do to help Cory and the ever growing notion that there would be nothing that I could do to help myself was enough to say, "The hell with it all. What the hell had I done to deserve this ending?"

As Cory stared at me with an indescribable meekness in his eyes, I felt insurmountably sorry. In a last ditch effort to maintain face, I mumbled "You know that God has the final say in everything." I meant it because I knew it to be true, but in bearing witness to what the vicious disease had made of Cory, I had very little weight to add to that truth. I remember looking up at the ceiling and the fan spinning until my eyes crossed before I jumped up and said "Listen. I refuse to sit here and take up your energy when I know that you should be resting. I'm going to let you get some shut eye and I will come back to see you again soon. All my love to you." I reached down to kiss the hand that I was holding and let it go just before the tears released from the corner of my eyes.

As I was walking out, his sister tried to say something, but I could not afford to stay there a minute longer. I didn't want to cause a scene and so I moved as fast as I could to get to my car. When I got there, I sat there for what must have been hours, crying tears of pain. Everything that I thought I knew had been snatched away from me. Every milestone that I had surpassed had not been compromised by uncertainty. I had loved with my whole heart, without reservation and just like history repeating itself, I had lost. As much as I valued standing on the truth, I knew that my promise to see Cory again after visiting him at his sister's house was a lie. I knew that would be the last time that I would see him alive. God had spoken and it was so.

——•OVERPRICED•——

I'VE HEARD IT SAID that a man who lives fully, is prepared to die. In my case, at the time, this was the biggest lie ever told. I knew for a fact that Cory would have given anything to have the breath of life. There was so much more that he had left to do. Death was most certainly not a part of either of our plans. The truth is that the thought of Cory's death became an open invitation to the dance floor to tango with my own mortality. Besides Joe, Cory was the absolute closest person to me. The notion of his exodus consumed me. At work, I spent the days pushing myself through moments of despair. I didn't have the strength to reflect upon the times we shared and the seven years of life that we had created together; it would have been too painful to do so. I also didn't have the strength to return to his sister's house because I didn't want to remember him like that. He was no longer the vibrant hunk that I had fallen so deeply in love with. He had been reduced to a fragile package of skin and bones. My heart broke for him.

There are times when confirmation of what you already know becomes startling. This was one of those times. Two weeks after my visit to Cory, his sister called me again; this time to speak the words that set my eardrums ablaze. "Charlie, I'm afraid that Cory has passed away. Know that he always loved you. Take good care of yourself, ok?"

I held the phone in silence and she hung up. My response was warranted. The thoughts that raced through my mind devoured my heart. I asked myself all kinds of questions—some that mattered and some that didn't—regardless, I could not bring him back. Dead? How can I undo a thing I've done? How can I turn back the hands of time? How can I make the noise that has overtaken my thoughts stop?

The news of his death had shaken my soul. The crazy, tingling feeling that I experienced was actually fire, and I had to sit within and let it burn. Shit took my breath away. Had I been so blind that I fought loving him the way that he needed me to love him in his last days? Had I not given him what he deserved? SHIT! I was scared out of my mind. I knew that loving him, also meant compromising life as I knew it. I had to let that shit burn.

I remember throwing the phone against the wall and rushing down the steps of my apartment building. My feet moved so fast that I could have fallen. The fire shot up in my bones and I had to let it burn. I ran to my car. I needed to drive. I needed to do anything that emulated escape at that moment. I needed to be rescued from the hell that I had been invited into. I was engulfed in flames and left only to feel the fire. What happened next became a blur. I have blocked it out in an attempt to not be completely consumed with the sadness that accompanied the memories.

That night, when I returned to my apartment, I fell to my knees. I had been crying so much that my eyes were swollen. My faith was shaken. The shackles of my past had returned and the price that I had paid for freedom was inflated to a price that was unattainable. I began to question the status of my health. If Joe had died from AIDS and Cory had died from AIDS and all of my coworkers at the salon had died from AIDS, what would become of me? Even though Joe and Cory had been the only two fallen soldiers that I was intimate with, we had all engaged in the same acts of love making. We had all been careless one too many times with the expression of free love and the quest to quench our curiosities. The cost of mortality was overpriced.

From that point forward, every day that passed, led me to believe that it would only be a matter of time before I too would receive a note of death. I can recall one night in my apartment, falling to my knees and asking God to heal me. I wasn't even sure of if I needed to be healed, but the uncertainty warranted the ask. I was empty and I longed for the weight that I carried from the deaths of my friends and those even closer to me, like Cory and Joe, to be lifted from me. I wanted the weight of living my life, amidst what had now transpired into uncertainty, to be removed. I wanted to be free. It was in that moment, in deep thought that I realized that I had never truly been free and I was once again overcome with emotion. I had never been free as a child because I was burdened with the weight of my mother's legacy. I had never been free as a teen because I was burdened with the weight of heartbreak. I had never been free as a young adult, because I was burdened with the weight of a hidden identity. There I stood, with one foot on the left of adolescence and one foot on the right of adulthood and for the first time in my existence, I realized that I was broken.

A month after Cory's death, I mustered up the strength to go to the doctor to get tested for HIV. I think that I went to put myself out of misery. I was so numb that I just wanted them to tell me something, one way or another. Back then, it took three days to receive the test results. I had gone in to the doctor on a Tuesday and on that day, they informed me that my results would not be available until the following Monday. I must admit that the days awaiting the results were some of the worst of my life. I was desperate for an escape from the thoughts of my mind, but I had to sit with them. I had to take ownership for all that had happened. In times of peril, we can choose to point the finger, or we can look in the mirror and analyze the reflection. Self-reflection is always the action of choice for me. In this spirit, I began to consider what my truth may have become and what I had done to walk in this existence. Not knowing was just as agonizing as knowing, but it was my cross to bear. If I were HIV positive, what would I tell my parents? What would I tell my siblings? Would I never realize the dreams that I could taste with my tongue? I had so many questions and so few answers.

The following Monday, I received the call to come back in for my results and all I could do was breathe and even that was difficult. By this point, I honestly just wanted to be put out of my misery. As I sat in the waiting room, waiting for my name to be called, I had an uneasy feeling in my stomach. For some reason, everyone in the lobby with me looked like they were awaiting death sentences. Looking back, I'm sure it was paranoia that had taken up residence in my heart and mind. When my name was called, the walk down the cold, brightly lit hallway with chalk white walls was terrorizing.

"You will be in room number three, please," said the nurse.

I was reading too deeply into everything. I thought that somehow meant that I would be the third to die. First Joe, then Cory, then me. I was absolutely out of my mind.

The nurse came in after me and she actually had a copy of the results in her hand. "Hello, Mr. Charles. I'm Rachel, the Nurse Practitioner. I understand that you have returned to obtain the results of your last test. I have the results from the lab right here."

I closed my eyes as I prepared for the worst.

"Your results have returned negative. Are there any questions that the doctor, or I, can answer for you at this time?"

I let out a huge sigh of relief. I was negative. Wait, she said I was negative? I could hardly believe my ears. "So… So, I'm free to go?" I asked in desperation.

"Yes, unless there is something more that we can assist you with."

"I think that will be all. Thank you so much," I said humbly.

She smiled and said, "You take care of yourself, Mr. Charles." Her white coat faded into the frame of the door, as I sat there in a daze.

In complete transparence, I wasn't completely sure that the negative test results that I had received were fully accurate and that scared the shit out of me. I had heard horror stories of how people had taken HIV tests and received negative results, only to find out months or even years later that it had just been too early for the disease to have been detected in their system. What if I would become one of those people? Can you imagine? I was so young and my life hadn't yet fully unfolded. Hell, my suitcase of adulthood hadn't even been completely unpacked. I was mortified. Imagine spending your days walking around, aimlessly, going through the motions of what appears to be a normal routine, haunted by the fact that death could call your name at any moment. Imagine knowing that you are destined for something more than what you have in front of you, but you have to accept that your one shot could potentially be a blank. Imagine being handed a death sentence, simply because you had chosen to explore a part of you that you had been forced to deny all your life. I mean, where does the script of life denote such irony? My thoughts became the residence of terror. The threat of destruction on many nights became the reason I cried myself to sleep. And like most, when you feel you have nothing, you recognize that everything that you are so desperately in search of, can be discovered in the word of God. I began to arm myself with it.

The realization that two of the loves of my life, Joe and Cory, had passed away from HIV, would prove to be the reason that I spent many days with a cloud of repressed feelings looming over my head. I felt immobile, out of touch, and numb in so many ways. They say hindsight is 20/20, but I was confused about everything. How had HIV claimed the lives of men that I had loved and so many that I had worked so closely with? How was it possible that I was still standing? The prospect of death was all around me. Why had God spared me? I'm certain that there was some part of me that felt guilty for getting to live. I had done the same things that the men in my life had done. From the drugs to the reckless acts of sexual exploits, their sins were not greater than mine, but the punishment didn't seem befitting.

During the passing months after Cory's death, I began to plead with God on a regular basis. I cried more during this period of my life than all the years that I had lived in total. I was afraid of what could be. Could I too be HIV positive? I knew that I had taken the test and that my results were negative, but I couldn't help but wonder if it would just one day magically appear and claim my life too. The only reason that I could figure that I was still in the land of the living was that there was a higher calling on my life. I knew that I woke up every morning with breath in my lungs and blood running through my veins for a reason.

On a daily basis, I would cry out and ask God, "Why?" Why had He spared me? I also asked Him why He had taken the lives of those who I had grown to love. It's a painful experience when the wrath of God takes over your life. I do believe that His wrath comes to kill and destroy everything that is not of Him to make anew.

No one at work knew of the attack that my soul had been, and continued to be, under. I showed up every day with what appeared to be vigor and I ran my business with passion. They were both masks for the anxiousness that fear invites in. My professional life was on fire, but my personal life was suffocating from the flames. Somewhere along the way, I realized that the only way for me to survive was to save myself. If God was willing to spare me, I had to be willing to do the work to prove my faith worthy of such salvation. Looking back, I'm not quite sure how, but I was still standing. My head was bloody, but unbowed.

CHAPTER 11

BONE STRAIGHT

"Sometimes, simple things have the power to resemble the complexities of our lives."

—Elgin Charles

THE PIECES OF THE PUZZLE that were slowly being assembled in my life, led me to one conclusion: If I did what was righteous, maybe God would spare me for good. I needed to be free once and for all from any notion of death. I needed to believe that the results I had received were what God had preordained for my life, and I desperately needed to denounce the guilt for my life having been spared. I began going to the church, without ceasing. In a single act of solitude, I made the decision to leave behind the remnants of the sexuality that I had discovered through my exploration. Not only was I making a decision to rid myself of the gay conquests that I believed had been displeasing to God, but I also vowed to be celibate. From that moment on, I knew that if I was to reopen Pandora's box regarding my sexuality, it would only be for a woman who I would call my wife. This was my sacred vow made from my heart to God's ears.

As my hard work persisted and flourished, opportunities continued to come in. I was introduced to a lady by the name of Liz, who was looking for someone to help her build her territory for the Elasta Hair Care Products. The hair care industry was bustling, and many of the product lines were taking measures into their own hands by creating their sales teams and sending them out to sell to individual salons. They were hiring reps they felt could enhance the brand, and the messaging provided to salons, to increase sales. Liz was very methodical and taught her team intricately to ensure that the quality of knowledge they had was impeccable. She set up demos and educational opportunities in almost every salon on every corner that she could find. She was notorious for saturating the industry, and her strategy worked. As a rep, we would go in and demonstrate relaxers and hair colors. When I began, Elasta had a full line of products that they wanted us to promote. I was so young and so eager to attain success that I took it as an opportunity to learn everything that I possibly could. I studied the manual that they had given us from cover to cover. It became my Bible for their line. They had broken down the products from sulfates to pH's and it even included a glossary. The science geek in me was in absolute heaven! Terms like hydrolize, quarternized, and collagen protein were music to my ears.

I even took time to study carbon chain chemistry. Collagen, I learned, was made from intestinal tissue and because of its soft consistency it made hair silky. Soft hair realizes more movement and it feels better to the touch.

I knew it all and much like my days at Marinello, I ate up every ounce of knowledge that I could squeeze into my brain. My thirst for knowledge led to God granting me a position as an Educational Director. Educational Directors travel the world for the company they work for, and I was looking forward to seeing something that I had never seen before. I had heard the stories of how other directors had traveled to London, Barbados, and St. Croix. God had ordained that I would be next.

—◄COUNTERCLOCKWISE►—

THEY SAY THAT TIME heals all wounds, but the scars on my heart, from the life I had known, were ever present; such that they had become permanent. The funny thing about life is that the clock just keeps ticking. Time waits for no man. And if in the event he decides not to live life, the hands on the clock do not cease to turn. Before I knew it, four years had passed by.

It was only by the grace of God that I persevered, finished ministry school, and continued to kill the game as a hair stylist. Looking back, I'm not even sure how I managed to keep my head above water, but some way, somehow, I did. My dad and sister came to LA to celebrate this milestone with me. With a deeper understanding of God's word, my ministry became my life, and God continued to open doors to His kingdom for me.

I was making even more money, which afforded me access to the opulence of Los Angeles. I relocated to a beautifully appointed home on an exclusive golf course named Mountain Gate Country Club in Bel Air. That same course was home to players like Johnny Mathis, Samuel L. Jackson, Magic Johnson, and Sugar Ray Leonard. You name a celebrity, they had played on that course at least once. Living there gave me the luxury of putting a few rounds with them as well. Life was good and God continued to provide. I was paying my tithes consistently, praying multiple times daily, and abstaining from anything that had to do with sex. I had not had sex in over four years and after all that I had been through, that was just fine with me. God saw fit for me to live, work, and thrive in excellence.

My salon was now positioned in the prestigious Beverly Hills zip code. 90211, honey! Say it with me. 90211! I had become the first and only black owned hair salon in Beverly Hills with that zip code. Talented stylists were coming out of the woodworks to work for me and the honor was all mine. The salon was buzzing. We began receiving features in beauty industry magazines, especially those that focused on hair and salons. We began making photo shoots a part of our regular routine in order to keep the people talking. We created videos of our work and collaboratively, we became industry trailblazers. It was my pleasure to work with so many talented stylists, who were just as passionate as I was about making people look and feel their best. It was game over, when I received my first feature in *Shop Talk*, which was a major publication with tremendous reach. The salon was now home to celebrity regulars like Billy D. Williams, Denise Williams, Suzette Charles, Roxie Roker, Marla Gibbs, Khandi Alexander, Teena Marie, Robin Givens, Jo Marie *(Family Matters)*, Monique, Holly Robinson, Nicole Murphy, and Wendy Williams who was a radio host at the time.

I kept praying consistently and asking God to increase His blessings. Those prayers were heard, and, boy, did God move. Due to the increase in volume, I was forced to expand the salon and its ability to accommodate more clientele. We went from the first space that I had rented upstairs, to renting out the entire top half of the building. We were now consuming a total of 3,000 square feet.

I was now able to recognize that God had isolated me, so that I could listen only to Him and humble myself to His calling over my life. Even though my career was progressing at lightning speed, my personal life was almost non-existent. Admittedly, there were times that the hustle and bustle of the salon left me unfulfilled, and the spiritual walk I was on felt more like it was set to autopilot. In truth, I had moments of loneliness. In those moments, confined with my thoughts, I longed for companionship. I'm almost certain that something inside of me was fearful of asking God for companionship because I had been burned. Hell, I wasn't even sure if I could trust myself. I just knew that someone like me, whose heart longed to love, was never meant to be alone. I would one day muster up the strength to ask God about someone to love, but not until I could feel worthy of doing so, whatever that meant.

One of my assignments, as the Educational Coordinator for Elasta Products, was to oversee an ad campaign for a new relaxer and hair care line. As the creative director, I was responsible for wrangling models and conducting a photo shoot to feature the products. I was also tasked with selecting one model from the group of models, who would be featured as the official face of the ad. During the casting, I met so many beautiful young ladies, but one in particular made her presence both felt and known.

Tristan Henderson was a tall, slender, chocolate dream. The melanin in her skin made her stand out among the fairer skinned models that had been cast. She was a sight for sore eyes. I must say that I took time to indulge when I looked at her. I had imposed a lock upon my wandering eyes for so long, and it felt good to really see the beauty of a woman. Even though I noticed her, I held true to the advice that the client back at Marinello had given me about not crossing the line of professionalism. My only plan was to look. I mean, come on, God, you gave me eyes to see! What I didn't know was that Tristan had a set of intentions all her own that would prove to be a little too much for me to handle.

She hit on me each day that we were on set and a friendship developed in a short amount of time. It always seemed to happen that way. Friendship had always been the beginning of something for me. And I mean this in the most humble way possible, but women have always found a way to seek me out. Regardless of Tristian's advances, I had every intention of remaining steadfast on my continued path of celibacy. Now, here is the unfiltered truth, I was horny as hell after not engaging in any sexual acts for four years. I was vulnerable and somewhere along the way, Tristan piqued my interest.

After a brief two-week courtship, we began officially dating. She was five years younger than I, and I couldn't help but feel like she was a little too young for my taste, but I just loved the sight of her. She was well cultured, as she had lived in Milan, Italy, and she was proficient in Italian. She had dated a doctor while living there but assured me that she had broken it off when she moved back to the states.

Over time, we learned that our circles were more closely knit than we had first imagined. I would do beauty shows at the Mark Hotel and Tristan and her friend Melissa would be booked as models at the same venue. She knew without question that I was in ministry, but because Tristan was a Leo, I would venture that she had never planned to take "no" for an answer from me for any reason at all.

Just around the time that I was to review the models' work and make the final selections for the official face of the campaign, Tristan made a surprise visit to the salon after hours. She knew when clients were there because she and I had spent time there before, simply getting to know each other. On this evening, she came up to my personal office in the salon. She began to kiss me on my neck and I must admit, she strong armed me. I fought her off because I was not prepared to open that part of me back up again for anyone, at least not at that time.

I once again found myself in mortal combat with my flesh. Prayerfully, I thanked God for the ability to resist. God continued to bless me, and this time, I set my sights on a new home for myself. I acquired a condo off of Curson and Olympic. It was the model unit and I was feeling beyond blessed. It was sexy as hell and the decor was laid from head to toe in white. The realtor told me that I would need to pay $35,000 to make it my own. It looked like something that would have been featured in a home magazine, highlighting Miami Beach. The way that the palm trees blew, they appeared to be fanning the condo. You had to put on your shades to drive up to that spot. As cool as a cucumber, I invited Tristan to visit after I had officially received my keys. I wanted someone to see what I had managed to do for myself.

When she came over, I met her at the door and everything about it was sexy. The sun was going down and the lights were dim. We were on the couch when she began to crawl towards me. The thought of her coming closer overtook both my mind and body. With the exception of the night that she had surprised me in the office, this was the first time that I had been touched by a woman in a very long time. She liked the side of my neck, sending a wave of chills down my spine. I no longer had the power to resist her. I had been so strong, but I was now searching for the truth in my weakness. She began to touch me, intimately, and I couldn't resist the warmth of her hands. In what seemed to be an instant, I climaxed. I couldn't believe it. I was in a state of shock. I knew immediately that the shock waves that she had managed to send across my body would need to be replenished. She looked up at me and our eyes connected. She smiled, cunningly. We sat together for much longer that evening, until I told her that it was getting late and escorted her to the front entrance. After she left, I locked up behind her and exhaled as I fell into the door. It was on, now.

The next time I saw Tristan, my flesh was roused to the point of no return. She had captured me. That night, we felt the heat together. I was encapsulated by the ecstasy that had brought me to my knees and afterwards, we laid in my bed, simply holding each other, even if only for a night.

The next morning, after it was all said and done, I felt terrible. I had relaxed my morals in exchange for the satisfaction of my loins. Tristan, on the other hand, was noticeably chipper. We sat and had breakfast together, but I knew almost immediately that what we had shared would not be inclusive of longevity. The only way that had managed to bring my flesh under control was through prayer, but I had lost it.

Before our little tryst, I had also noticed that Tristan had an on and off personality that was sometimes a little hard to read. She always seemed to be on the verge of a breakdown. I attributed much of it to her busy schedule as a model, but now I was starting to believe that she was just a little crazy. A week or so later, I was scheduled to teach a course for Elasta in Palm Springs. While there, a mutual friend, who was the creative director for a photo shoot, mentioned that she had an anxiety attack on the set. I was concerned about her and when I returned to LA, I invited her over to hang out. Through conversation, she expressed that she had been through a lot with the doctor that she was dating back in Milan. I could easily gather that she was not over him and eventually, she confessed that she had never really split up with him. She wasn't able to take my disinterest, so she'd lied. I wasn't angry with her, but I did feel misled. Had I attempted to give her my heart, she might have returned it to me in pieces. This was another example of how walking outside of the will of God, doesn't end well. We agreed that we were better as friends. About a year later, I heard that she had moved back to Milan and married the doctor. Together, they had two children.

When it was all said and done, I realized that Tristan had only really wanted to woo me for the cover. Once again, vulnerable Elgin had let his heart fly freely, but this time, I hadn't fallen in love; it was pure lust. I would be forced to deal with the burden of my sins and to seek the repentance that I so desperately needed.

After Tristan, I repented and promised myself that I would ask God to send me a mate. I didn't want to do it without His help, and I knew that if I attempted to do it alone, I would end up creating a mess, as I had done before. I was now looking for love, but not just anywhere and with anyone. I was looking for a love that only God could send, and when He did, I would be ready, willing, and able to walk side by side with whoever He had hand-picked just for me.

——Two Steps Forward.—— Two Steps Back.

PLAIN AND SIMPLE, I began believing in God for a mate. I wasn't sure if it was because I worked around women all day, or if I was now giving off a new vibe, but it seemed like women were coming out of the woodworks. From the day that I set foot back into the salon, after the relief that I had experienced, it was as if I had increased levels of pheromones. Lord knows, I was living for Jesus, but the swag was just different. I was feeling myself. We all deserve to walk in the fullness of the confidence that we have earned. This joy that I had, the world didn't give it and the world couldn't take it away. In the same spirit, I was alarmed at how many women thought they were in line to become my wife. I became a serial dater and although I was not reaching the pinnacle of rhapsody with every lady whom I encountered, I was living my life like it was golden. The ladies were on rotation and I was waiting to hear from God that one of them was to be the Mrs.

Both Dawn Joi from Chicago, and Denise from Georgia, became regular acquaintances. Dawn Joi would even rearrange her plans to be in the same places that I was. It was cute. Denise had gone off the deep end and fallen in love. There was also Debbie Pierre. She was a very elegant lady, who showed significant interest in me, but I knew better than to waste her time, as she was not whom God had sent for me. For me, I was in waiting. I learned to be more careful with the hearts of women. I hadn't realized before how easily women fall in love. It was as if good conversation and a hint of consistency was the equation for love. For me, it was so much more practical than that. I believe this to be the case for every man.

I'm not sure how, but I could feel myself getting closer to the woman that God had created just for me. The thought of finding someone that I could love for a lifetime no longer scared me. My strength to resist the urges and temptation that I had once felt for the same sex had taken a backseat to my desire to build a traditional family. I was in pursuit of my own version of the great American dream. I had made so much money; I was constructing an empire. I didn't want to arrive alone at the top of the mountain that I had fought tooth and nail to climb.

Prior to my move from Mountain Gate, I was introduced to a lovely soul by the name of Sia. We were introduced by a mutual friend named Farrah McKinsey. From the moment I laid eyes on her, I was entranced. She was so beautiful. She was of a fairer complexion with very heavy eyebrows and a lion's mane of curly hair. She gave me Sade vibes, sans the red lipstick, had she pulled her hair back into a sleek ponytail. She was so graceful and maintained a look of effortless beauty. To see her hair blow in the wind was a blessing.

Not only was Sia beautiful, but she was also well established. Sia was the daughter of one of the most prevalent black legends in the entertainment industry. He had appeared in countless groundbreaking movie roles and had gained access to a seat at the dinner table of Hollywood that most had only dreamed of. His long standing reputation preceded him for breaking barriers for black actors. I had to admit that he had raised one hell of a daughter. She was genuinely kind in a society filled with vultures. She and I hit it off so well that it was almost scary. Her moral compass and values were intact. Although reserved, she had a personality that warranted fun. We connected spiritually as she was even more grounded than I was. She attended a church called Oasis that was not far from the salon. I attended Crenshaw Christian Center. I was truly beginning to see her as First Lady material. If I did decide to pursue a hierarchy in the ministry, I would need a lady worthy of the throne. Although I could not predict the future, I was almost certain that Sia would be a part of it. If anything more gratifying than spending time with Sia was to occur, I knew for sure that it would blindside me.

—— $2+2=7$ ——

WITH LOVE ON THE HORIZON, my willingness to open my heart didn't add up to the arithmetic of my tattered past, nor should it have. I didn't care that I was willing to humble myself for love. I didn't care that I was now allowing myself to care. I didn't care that I was smitten when in the presence of Sia. I was ready to take the fall.

I continued working to grow the salon. It seemed that every time I achieved a new level, I dreamed bigger. This is the chemistry that makes ambition possible. The salon continued to become the home of black women all over Los Angeles and an even bigger stomping ground for celebrities. The talent of my staff was so plentiful that the celebrity sightings were no longer startling, they were the norm.

I did take note of a familiar face that asked to use a dryer on my side. The stylist who she had been receiving services from was awaiting a dryer to open up on the main side. I had established a semi private suite to style my clients and my side had additional dryers that were open. Her voice was beyond recognizable, as it had a distinct high pitch, and I was startled when I heard her speak.

"Hi. Can I use this dryer?" She had made the decision to take matters into her own hands and was not shy in any way.

I understood, as I knew that many celebrities schedules were convoluted and their time to receive certain services was scarce. The name Elgin Charles had far surpassed me. It was now a brand, and my goal became to protect it at all costs, which was why I became so cognizant of delivering amazing customer service. "Sure. Let me make sure that it's warm for you," I replied. I recognized her from a popular sitcom called 227. Her name was Jackée Harry and she was in high demand in Hollywood. The thing that stood out most about her was that she was just as beautiful in person as she was on TV. That was not always the case. Some celebrities had to wear an incredible amount of makeup just to look like the people they portrayed on the big and little screens. Even amidst getting her hair done, Ms. Harry was a natural beauty with lovely features.

With the dryer now ready, I turned to her and said, "It's ready. I can seat you now." As she came over, we noticed each other. This wasn't the type of notice that you take when simply realizing that another person is in your presence. It was as if she noticed me as a man and I noticed her as a woman. There was something there, but neither of us allowed it to transcend past the formalities of the dryer scenario. "Let me know if I can help you with anything else," I said carefully.

As I walked away, I could feel her eyes on me, but for some reason I didn't look back. After Jackée finished drying, her stylists came over to meet her. I could have continued to work with my head down, but it would have been a missed opportunity to speak to her yet again. I looked up, smiled, and said "Have a blessed day."

She stopped in the center of the aisle and turned around just enough to look over her shoulder and said, "You do the same, honey." She then strutted off, remaining true to every bit of what she embodied on the TV screen.

Sia and I continued seeing each other and I admit she had truly piqued my interest. I knew without question that our bond would continue to develop and grow. While at the salon, on a cool October day, an actress and regular client by the name of Joe Marie, was raving about her Halloween party. She had everyone excited from the way in which she described what she had planned. As a courtesy, she extended an invitation, not just to me, but also to some of my staff members. I was actually looking forward to it. With my days of intense partying behind me, I always welcomed good, wholesome fun!

When the evening of the party rolled around, we arrived in style. I was driving my S class Mercedes Benz and had decided to dress as Tiger Woods in a golf outfit. Sia determined that she had no interest in attending, so there I was alone with my beloved staff. When I say that everyone had outdone themselves, it is truly an understatement. Joe Marie certainly knew how to throw a party. The energy in the atmosphere was electric. People were eating and drinking and having an amazing time. The few staff members that had arrived with me were so elated that they took off to indulge in the night.

I was standing near the wraparound bar when I noticed someone dressed as Marilyn Monroe arrive at the party. She captured the attention of everyone. When she made her entrance, time stood still. She had gone all out with a blonde wig and the signature white dress. In this case, she had her back completely out and she looked sexy as hell. As she got closer, I could see the fire red hue of the lipstick that she rocked to complete the look. She was bad and her skin was glistening. I raised my eyebrows and turned back around towards the bar. Eventually, I sat on a bar stool and really got into the music. Although the dance floor had been my second home, I resolved that night to keep it calm and not turn Joe Marie's party all the way out. I knew if I got on that floor, I had the power to do so.

A few minutes later, I felt someone tap me on my shoulder. I turned around in response, thinking that it was someone from our group, but it wasn't; it was the lady dressed as Marilyn Monroe. Now, standing before me, and in my personal space, I could recognize every feature. To my surprise, it was Jackée.

"Can I speak to you for a minute?" she requested.

She didn't even really wait for me to respond before she was motioning for me to follow her. Of course, I did. She had that effect on everyone. There was an aura about her that was somewhat irresistible. She led me to a balcony around the back of the building with a breathtaking view of the city. I remember taking a moment to admire her because it seemed as if the city was illuminated just for her. She had the "it factor" that Hollywood either crowned you with, or denied you access to.

"Are you dating anyone?" she inquired.

I knew that my response to that question needed to be one that would not close off any door or opportunities of a future friendship between us. Although Sia and I had been hanging out on a level that far surpassed friends, we had not yet spoken the words that rendered exclusivity.

"No. I... I mean... I do date. But right now, I'm not dating anyone exclusively."

She looked up at me with engaging eyes as if to insinuate that I was potentially being untruthful and raised her eyebrows. She then shrugged her shoulders and served up a hearty laugh. She looked back at me and shook her head and said, "Men!"

Even though she hadn't spoken many words, her personality shined through. If I had read between the lines, I would have imagined that she was thinking that even if I was lying, if she wanted to begin something with me, she had the power to do so regardless of who was in the picture.

Entangled in her presence, I too began to laugh and we immediately hit it off. We stood there talking for at least an hour, which was a long time considering that there was a whole party going on that neither of us found more important than the time we shared in that moment.

After realizing that we both needed to get back to the night that we had originally set out to have, I took a risk by saying, "Let me take your number." She smiled at me and I continued, "It will be a few weeks before I call because I need to pray on it."

With a look of confusion, she said "What? Two weeks?" She chuckled again and I am almost certain that in that moment, she didn't believe me. "Oh, darling. Call me." She walked off and all I know was that she was a view to remember. I would never forget how fierce she looked in her costume.

Unbeknownst to her, I was serious about waiting a couple of weeks to call. I wanted to pray about her because it seemed as though God had sent me two women, and I was a little thrown off. Out of respect and consideration for both Sia and Jackée, I turned to God to ask for His assistance through prayer. God for his assistance. Jackée retreated to the bar to smoke a cigarette. With much to consider, I returned to the bar and remained in a pensive state for the remainder of the night.

The next morning, I recall waking up and simply talking to God as I did every day. I asked Him about Jackée and if she was who I should pursue. I kept coming up short with the response. What I did know was that she was different from Sia in many ways. She had more experience and possibly even more hurt or loss from navigating the world. I wasn't sure. Sometimes when you are not certain, that means that it's best to simply be still. I remained more focused on work and less focused on finding an answer, even though I was beyond ready.

Roughly two weeks after the Halloween party, I was invited to attend a fundraising event at the exclusive Los Angeles Country Club, off Rosmoore. This time, I was accompanied by Sia and Faith, who had introduced us. While there, I recall sitting at a table near the bar, which had a clear view of the entryway. I have always lived for a good, grand entrance. That evening, my eyes widened as I noticed a bit of a frenzy near the door. People were lined up to hug and greet someone who was arriving. As the fog of people cleared, Jackée appeared. She had stolen the show and she was bad. I was sitting next to Sia, who had looked up to notice the commotion, but had looked back down immediately. Hollywood and the social status were nothing new to her, as she had witnessed it all her life. Her father was of the elite and this was everyday life for her.

I on the other hand was captivated by everything. The glitz and the glamour were attractive to me. So was Jackée. She hadn't noticed me there with Sia initially, and I was ok with that. I hadn't called yet, and I wasn't sure of how she would receive me. During the event, they hosted an auction to raise money for the cause. Jackée donated $1,000. She was a boss and I liked it. Just after the bidding, I glanced over to where she was sitting and she waved at me—almost like a princess wave—and revealed a smile that was captivating. She had seen me there with Sia the whole time; I just hadn't noticed. There was something about her that I was attracted to and it made me want to learn more about who she was and what she was about.

I recall glancing over at Sia and glancing back at Jackée and thinking to myself that I would use the number that she had given me after all.

I began talking to Jackée on the phone regularly. We would laugh about something or nothing for hours. Through our exchange, God revealed that we had more in common than I could have imagined. I learned that she had also decided to go celibate, and that she had been so for two years and counting. She had been looking for love but hadn't discovered it and her heart's desire was to be married. It was peculiar that were both in the same place in our lives. Eventually, I invited her on a date, and we hit it off instantaneously. Our conversations shifted from sparse engagement to the everyday.

One night during conversation, I mentioned that through work, I had been presented with an opportunity to go to London to do a hair show.

"Well, what if I come along with you and we go to Paris first? It will be fun!" Jackée said.

The company that I was traveling for bought coach tickets for me. When I shared this information with her, she didn't even bat an eye. She purchased a ticket and flew coach right beside me. Jackée was very humble and that only intrigued me further. She was the epitome of Hollywood and that entitled her to the spoils that her celebrity status had to offer, yet she was down-to-earth enough to do whatever it was that I was doing. We could spend time together, with no regard for what bells and whistles were present. That was dope!

I had prayed for more favor from the Lord; that he would send me a helpmate and a lady that I could share my life and world with. I wasn't completely sure, but on a plane to London—in coach— it was quite possible that I had found her.

—TOUCHÉ—

PRIOR TO FULFILLING MY contractual agreement with Elasta Products, to demonstrate new techniques at an international hair event in London, Jackée suggested that we make a pit stop in Paris. We frolicked in the streets like two love birds. The aura of romance couldn't be denied. Between us, there was passion and a unique presence of kindred souls that was hard to deny. Being with her made me forget about everyone else. We were in a whirlwind and I loved the breeze from her love and affection. I had searched for so long to feel that way.

Caught up in the rapture of love, right there in Paris, Jackée suggested that we get married upon our returned to LA. It was the perfect way to encapsulate the moments that we never wanted to do without. Sealed with a kiss, we determined that two would become one.

I went to the hair expo in high spirits. My life was unfolding in a beautifully unexpected way. I could not believe that after what felt like a lifelong search, I had finally discovered love. I was winning at life.

As I stood on the stage, I was in my element and people crowded around to view the demo. The contacts and the support from attendees was unbelievable. I was living my dreams out loud as an internationally recognized stylist. It was surreal.

After my demo was over, I retreated backstage to take a short break. As I set my bag of supplies down, I felt ill. It came out of nowhere. It was as if an elephant was sitting on my chest. Was I having a heart attack? I had to remain seated. People passed by and asked if I was ok. With my head collapsed in my hands, I motioned that I was. In almost an instant, the feeling of sickness was gone. I knew that I had been running nonstop and that often, the stress of the climb towards excellence can lead to fatigue. I got to my feet and reminded myself that I had very little time for that. I needed to be great. The world was calling.

When we returned to the States, life was as it should be. Jackée and I were on the fast track and my thoughts about growing my brand were running rampant.

One afternoon, while reviewing some business documents involving the salon, the office phone rang and I got up to answer it.

"Hello?"

I heard a familiar voice on the other end of the phone say, "Charlie?" It was Holly. I awaited her next words. "They found Momma on the side of the railroad tracks."

"What? Holly, please. Please don't do this right now." I was overwhelmed by the truth of her words. "What happened to Momma? Holly, what happened?"

She began to wail on the other end of the phone and the sound of her anguish somehow made it all real. "I had to identify the body, Charlie. She was so badly decomposed that her fingers had fallen off." Holly broke down, crying hysterically.

I could no longer hear what Holly was saying, I was instantly engulfed in a sea of sorrow. The tears drowned every attempted breath. I was being strangled by devastation. I couldn't relinquish the weight of the pain upon my chest. I still needed her. I still needed her to touch my face. I still needed to smell the scent of her sweet skin. I still needed to hear her voice. I still needed her to reassure me that I was ok.

My eyes were foggy and the haze of the tears clouded my vision. I dropped the phone and slumped against the wall. I never had a chance to comfort Holly. At that moment, I had nothing inside of me. My cup was empty. For the second time in my life, my heart was broken. My deepest scars were revealed and I was left to suffer somberly.

I had been terrorized by the grim reaper. I had been robbed of my most valuable treasures. I was bound in hurt and sorrow and abandonment. The chains of uncertainty were wrapped around my neck.

I tried to stand and I could hardly gain my balance. I managed to crawl to the couch and pull myself up towards the seat. I laid my head against the soft cushion, but my face felt so numb that it hurt. I attempted to stand again, but I couldn't maintain my stance. I threw my hands up in the air and a burning pain shot through my body. Nothing—no one—could give me comfort. Who could I run to?

All I could manage was to curl up in a fetal position on the floor. In that moment, I needed to die. I was desperate to rid myself of the hurt. The memory of my happiest moments had been snatched out of the frame of my mind. I needed salvation. I stretched my arms out towards heaven and I screamed as much as my body would allow. The agony found no rescue. The burning sensation inside of my soul refused to flee. "Dear God. Please help me." It was my humble plea.

In a matter of hours, I would learn the tragic details surrounding Momma's death. She had been the victim of a brutal carjacking. After a dispute with some degenerates, she had been beaten and tormented. She had died by the same sword that she had lived by. All of the things that she had done had caught up with her.

That night I hung my head as another piece of me died. It would never be resuscitated. There was nothing that could heal me. I knew that this agony was mine to claim. I was now the owner of a heart that wouldn't heal. I was left to pick up the pieces, as I had always done.

I sought empathy and shelter in the one place that I had entrusted my heart. To my despair, my wife-to-be came up remarkably short. Amidst the deepest, most unimaginable grief that I had ever experienced, I was met with words that pierced my soul.

"Stop all that crying and act like a man."

I was too hollow to hurt. I was too ashamed to feel. The harsh reality was that the very essence of who I was, was invisible to the women whom I wanted to see me most. I had nothing left to give. And for a moment in time, my heart stopped beating.

When we returned home to bury Momma, I was dazed. All I knew was that I would take responsibility for every detail in order to give Momma the honor that she deserved. She was the very essence of me. I was left to figure out once more who I was and how to get lost in the right direction. I was left with her words: "If you live by the sword, you die by the sword." And in the doom, my heart was forever pierced.

——◄AMAZING GRACE►——

GENERATIONAL CURSES LOOM over our heads like gray clouds, and their spells of doom and terror can only be cast out when we pick up the sword of righteousness, to slay and destroy them. Not one family is exempt from becoming a soldier in the army for redemption to save lineage to come. These cycles are less often broken, as they appear familiar. From our ways of life, to our train of thought, we must take notice of what holds us captive and the things that have held those we love captive. We must learn to recognize the signs of distress and be willing to become the vessels of relief.

Had I predicted the directions that my life would take, I would never have gotten as close to the plans that God saw fit for me. He would soon open up the windows of heaven and pour me out a blessing that would save me from myself. And in the majestic plans of God, He would use the priceless gift of an increase in family to do so.

Stephanie, my cousin, who was more like my sister growing up, always had my heart. She was close in age to me and we were practically raised together. When she became a woman, she would bring forth life with her body. Her children were special to me in so many ways. Although Stephanie never wished to leave San Antonio, and I had established a new path of my own in Los Angeles, we never allowed the distance to keep our hearts from connecting. Although the miles were far apart, the love remained intact.

One of Stephanie's daughters would be named Karisha. Karisha was biracial and had been bound in that she never knew her father. Despite the unanswered questions of her identity, she was an exquisite soul whose wit was undeniable. Her being raised on the east side of San Antonio, a place in which the air seemed to consume hope and opportunity, left her with very little access to abundance. As she evolved into a young woman, she bore three children, two girls and one boy, whose name was Frank. Frank was forced to bear extenuating circumstances before ever being granted a fair chance at life. At the tender age of eighteen months he was still too young to understand the magnitude of the loss of his mother, whose untimely demise occurred after being gunned down by a boyfriend.

In a matter of months, Frank's father, known in the streets of San Antonio as BAE BAE would also succumb to gang violence, taking his last breath after being shot several times in cold blood. And thus, by the age of two, Frank had suffered the loss of both parents.

Frank had been separated from his siblings and placed in the care of his great-grandparents (his father's mother and her husband) in order to increase his level of stability. Ms. Bertha and Paw Paw did what they could, to provide a foundation from which Frank could discover any sign of normalcy. It was known by the family that Ms. Bertha and Paw Paw received a check for their guardianship over Frank. When life wages war on the young, only God can save them from destruction. Frank would eventually need something to believe in and something to restore his hope and faith in what could be. How could a child be expected to dream and hasten toward anything other than what he had been exposed to?

At a time when I had lost the very essence of my existence, my pain would cause me to cross paths with Frank's young soul as he was bearing witness to a similar trauma. After returning home to San Antonio to bury Momma, I sat at Holly's house in a trance. There were kids everywhere, which was not unusual. The life in the house was a reminder that there was something to live for. Of the many kids running around, Frank was one of them. There must have been something about me that his soul connected with. In an instant, he ran towards me and stood there, staring into my eyes as if he saw something familiar. Maybe his heart recognized the pain in mine. I saw the fire in his pupils and I recognized it. He came closer and eventually reached out his arms for me to pick him up. There he sat, perched on my knee and I could feel the pain from my spirit being lifted. He was healing me from my hurt with his presence. God had sent me an angel to console my breaking heart in the wake of my mother's death.

The scenery outside had shifted from day to night and the conversations and reminiscing that we engaged in, went on for hours, but Frank never left my lap. Out of all the adults in the house, Frank had attached himself to me. As things were wrapping up, I began to gather my belongings in preparation to leave. I sat Frank down and told him to run and play, but he just stood there and his face revealed a numbness to disappointment. It was almost as if he accepted it as truth. And just as I prepared to leave, hand in hand with Jackée, I heard a voice from behind me. "You should take him with you. He needs you, Charlie. And from the way it looks, you just might need him too."

Stephanie and Jackée had taken notice of the unspoken bond between Frank and I, and they were not prepared to let it go. As I stood there, holding Frank's hand, he too had already made the decision that his future was wherever I was. It still amazes me that at such a young age, he saw a future with me. He saw me as someone who could save him. It was a complete shock to Jackée. She had been an innocent bystander, and now, she was being asked to act as an accomplice. I knew that it was a lot to ask, but I also knew that there was no mistake in what Frank was feeling. It is my belief that God had sent him to save me, and I him. I could not bear the thought of leaving without him.

In a matter of minutes, my divine purpose had shifted. God had allowed the departure of my mother from this life, to serve as the open door for the arrival of my wife and my son. With them in my heart, I would instantly be made whole. And even though it sounds so poetic, it was anything but easy to introduce the burden of parenthood to my wife to be and my growing career. I wasn't sure how it would all work, I was just certain that I wanted to give it all I had. I knew that I couldn't, under any circumstances, fail Frank.

"We'll take him back to LA with us," I said, as Jackée stood firmly by my side and my decision. I will never be able to repay her for the void that was filled in my heart, as she accepted our made to order family.

Stephanie insisted that I follow her to Ms. Bertha's house to collect some of Frank's belongings. When we arrived, I parked across the street and Stephanie went inside. She returned with as many pieces of clothing that she could stuff into his small, blue duffle bag and placed it beside him in the backseat of the car. Jackée and I had arrived in San Antonio as a party of two to pay our respects and say our final goodbyes to my mother. That night, as we drove back to the hotel, we had a plus one: Frank DeVanique Brown. The following morning, we woke up and caught a plane back to Los Angeles with Frank in tow. The road ahead would prove to be rocky, but if God is for you, then I ask, who shall be against you?

—This Is Us—

WHEN WE RETURNED to LA, there was tension between Jackée and I. The truth is that Frank, who we affectionately began calling DeVanique, had bonded with me. In all fairness, Jackée had accepted a proposal from a man who had no children and no additional commitments—other than building an empire—and although she knew the immense amount of work that it would take to realize, she had been there and done that and bought the t-shirt. However, no one had forewarned her, or even stopped to ask her, whether or not she was prepared to become a mother in a matter of minutes. I can't imagine how hard this must have been for her. In complete transparency, the weight of the charge that I had been given to oversee was heavier than anything that I had ever felt, and I was determined to get it right. There was also a part of me that felt that God had demonstrated that DeVanique's life was my redemption.

I immediately went in search of a nanny that could potentially help me and worked hard to do everything possible to keep Jackée happy. I was spread so thin, and honestly, it felt like the only thing that I was excelling at was growing the business. The salon continued to bear fruit. I felt like it was God's way of encouraging me to keep moving forward. It was hard amidst the deadlock of battle that Jackée and I found ourselves in. DeVanique didn't attach himself to her. I would imagine that it was far more challenging for her to fall in love with him amidst this tug of war. He hadn't yet learned to recognize her heart, and the unspoken scars of detachment from his parents were ever present.

It seemed like it took an eternity for me to try to find a system that would allow me to manage everything that was being thrown at me in my personal and professional life. We were outgrowing the salon and I was tiring of the lack of support from the management of the building. Since we were located on the top floor, the windows did not open. With the amount of chemicals and fumes that circulate in a salon, it is necessary to have open windows. My repeated attempts to have the management deliver a solution became a series of unfulfilled promises. Additionally, the location had grown to be a little sketchy. We even had a client leave late one night and a strange man got on the elevator with her. Luckily, she escaped unscathed.

These impactful situations were a part of the stresses of being a business owner and I needed to find a resolution. To make matters worse, the tension between Jackée and I had become so tumultuous that she moved out of our shared home. It hurt my heart to consider the prospect of losing her before we had even walked down the aisle. In many ways, I empathize with her position, but I truly felt like I was left with few options when it came to agreeing to care for DeVanique. I was determined to allow her the time that she felt she needed, but I couldn't let her go. I had been believing God for a wife for so long and when Jackée finally came along, I knew that she was who He had sent.

The only glimmer of light was that DeVanique was settling into his new environment, and I was finding a way to make sense of it all. However, life is a phenom: Just as you settle into an act of playing the cards that you have been dealt, a wild card is resurrected and added to your hand.

One evening, after a long day of standing on my feet at work, I received a phone call from Stephanie. She stated that the word around San Antonio was that I had kidnapped DeVanique. The true trajectory of the events that had taken place had been altered. Not long after our phone conversation, I received a formal notice for a court hearing that would take place in San Antonio. My heart ached for DeVanique and I worried that the ruling would not be in my favor and it would mean another transition for him.

In true Queen fashion, Jackée was by my side after I shared the news with her. Together, hand in hand, we returned to San Antonio for the hearing, as a party of three. The emotional distress of it all was almost too much for Jackée. Even though she and DeVanique had not bonded in spirit, her maternal instincts had come full circle, and she too wanted the absolute best for him. Her willingness to open her heart, made me love her even more.

During the hearing, an outburst of tears from Jackée led the Judge to ask if she was a family member of DeVanique's. Because we had nothing other than our good intentions to prove her relation to him, she was asked to remove herself from the courtroom. The entire scene brought tears to my eyes. There we were, trying to give a child a better quality of life and we were the ones being questioned about our intentions. After bringing the courtroom back to order, the Judge asked me why I had kidnapped DeVanique.

"I didn't kidnap him. I just wanted to give him a place to stay," I replied, with a slight tremble in my voice. I knew that Ms. Bertha had the legal rights. It had just been my assumption that everyone wanted the best possible life for him. I hadn't stopped to realize that the prospect of a check would also mean that his life was for ransom. As I sat in the courtroom, it hit me like a ton of bricks that I had no rights. I had been so wrapped up in becoming his savior that I had disregarded the law. There was also a part of me that believed that no one, including Ms. Bertha and Paw Paw could do for him what Jackée and I were capable of doing.

With tears in my eyes, I spoke to the Judge once more. "If Ms. Bertha has guardianship, that's fine. I know that he has bonded with me and I know that I can give him what he needs to live a full life, but I do respect the law."

Even though he could not have known what the proceedings on that day meant, DeVanique's heart always had a way of speaking to him. I'll never forget how he looked up at me that day. It was almost as if I noticed the presence of his numbness to disappointment again.

Jackée and I had entered the courtroom as parents and we left after being released of our duties. Before leaving, I remember kissing DeVanique on the cheek while Ms. Bertha held him in her arms. I whispered to her before stepping away. "Don't worry. As soon as he gets older, he will come to me."

I didn't stick around to see the response in the courtroom. I bolted through the doors in search of Jackée, who was seated just outside the room. Stronger than ever and hand in hand, we returned to Los Angeles. The pain of losing DeVanique brought us together and the passion kept us united.

CHAPTER 12

90210

"Time inevitably moves forward, people are called to do the same."

— Elgin Charles

ALTHOUGH WE HAD created many memories, and the foundation of my success was built at the salon on Wilshire, it was no longer sufficient. Not only had we exceeded the space, but the management continued to render far less than stellar service, and our requests went unnoticed.

I eventually learned that the building owner was going through hard times financially. He wasn't fixing the building like he was supposed to and my business was not the only one that was suffering. The building was over twelve stories high, and over the years it had become raggedy as hell due to lack of maintenance. He didn't have the money to invest in proper upkeep, yet he expected everyone to remain loyal and pay. I was completely fed up and began believing God for a new location that would allow The Elgin Charles Salon to grow and prosper.

I began praying and asking God to give me the resources to find a new space that would foster continued growth and success. Just as I had done before, I stepped out on faith and began searching for a new place. I carried a scripture with me at all times; they had become the words that I lived by and I never once questioned if God would send me what or who I needed to usher in a new era for the Elgin Charles brand.

I have always believed that if we take the first step, God will show us his power. I began to speak of my intention to find a location in the Beverly Hills area. I had driven by a commercial space that had a "for lease sign" in the window. When I contacted the listing agent, she informed me that she had a salon off Santa Monica that would soon be coming available and we arranged an appointment for me to view it. When we arrived, I was in awe. The salon was simply beautiful. Although, it did not have as much square footage as the salon on Wilshire, the setup would allow for increased efficiency for my stylists to service their clients. I knew almost immediately, that I wanted to put a bid on it.

The Asian gentleman who owned the building, informed me that he was having a hard time maintaining the place. After I explained to him what I would do with the space, he said, "Man, you have to take over this salon. You're going to be so famous. You're going to be so famous if you come over here. You will have people coming by just to see you. It will be really good for your career."

He was so adamant and intentional with his words that they stuck with me. God kept his words at the forefront of my mind and my heart. His words were a sweet melody to my ears and spoke to what I had dreamed of for my future and my career.

"I'll take it," I said.

He instructed me that before I could lease the building, I would need to write a letter stating why I thought I could move in and make the space work as a successful business venture. I briefly questioned why he had asked me to write the letter and wondered if it was because I was black. There was no one that looked like me opening a hair salon in Beverly Hills. I would become the first. I was so excited that I put the negative thoughts aside and wrote the letter with haste.

> *To Whom It May Concern,*
>
> *Sound management of a business is not something that you do, it is who you are. For me, business and the hair and beauty industry have become a way of life. Although, I have served clients as a hair stylist for as long as I can remember, I have been an official stylist for nine years, achieving great success in the city of Los Angeles. I opened my first salon on Wilshire Boulevard in a high rise on the 6th floor. Even without a large sign on the building, to give identity to the salon from the street, I have still managed to establish a massive clientele. The drive, determination, and will to win are essential attributes that force me to be driven towards success for my business and my clients. The Elgin Charles brand has become synonymous with excellence, and I am confident that any location we assume ownership of will become groundbreaking. Your current asking price is equivalent to that which I currently pay. The difference that I believe to be critical is location and efficiency. Should you decide to do business with me, you will make history.*
>
> *Regards,*
> *Elgin|Charles*

About a week after I submitted the letter, I was given the authority to assume ownership of the lease on the building. I was also informed that the salon would come fully equipped with furniture. God had made His presence felt. He once again demonstrated that His plans were always greater for me than what I could have ever imagined for myself.

The acquisition of the property ushered in a new era. The move would prove to be monumental in more ways than one. The Elgin Charles Hair Salon would now be positioned in the heart of Beverly Hills. No person of color had ever done that before. At the time, I realized the importance of the move, but never fathomed the magnitude of what it meant for people who looked like me. Only time would tell how many more doors of opportunity I would be empowered to open, simply from obedience to God's plan and a desire to achieve widespread success that would prove to be larger than life.

After receiving confirmation that we would be relocating, my next task was to inform the stylists. To my surprise, I was met with great apprehension. Looking back, I now understand that God had not given the stylists my vision, or the blueprint for what He would call me to do; He had only given that information to me. They were apprehensive because there was no one who looked like us in Beverly Hills.

My excitement and sense of purpose would not allow me to become entangled in the web of resistance. I had to move forward with certainty and anyone outside of that plan would have to be a casualty of the divine purpose that I had been called to fulfill. As I saw it, we could not allow fear to have a say in the abundance that God had for us all. As the leader, I also knew that if I showed any signs of uncertainty, it would be recognized by the team that I had assembled and I did not want that for them. I wanted to inspire them to chase their dreams as relentlessly as I had. As I stood in the center of the salon, I remember saying with the fullness of conviction, "You can either come, or find another salon to work at."

At some point, Barry, who was the owner of the building on Wilshire, got wind that I was moving, and he too displayed a great deal of resistance. For months on end, I had complained to him and requested maintenance, and the adoption of measures to ensure the safety of my staff and the clients in the salon, but it was to no avail. He had never made good on his promises to open the windows or to increase security for the building. My conscious would have never allowed me to be at peace had something worse happened to the client who was almost attacked in the elevator. I will never forget how frightened she was when she ran back into the salon screaming and yelling. I remember running into the hallways in search of the attacker, but he was nowhere to be found. Enough was enough. I was going to do what was best for my clientele and the business, which meant getting the hell up out of that building that was suffocating the life out of all of us. For me, the packing and moving process was the easiest part. I knew that we were moving on to greener pastures. I began carting things from one salon to the next, which made my departure official.

As I was returning to finalize the transitional process, I discovered that Barry had changed the locks on the doors to the location on Wilshire. I could not understand what would lead him to do such a thing, but I couldn't say that I was surprised. He had not intended to allow me to depart without a fight. I called him and all I could hear him yelling into the phone was "You're leaving. If you're leaving, you can't take anything that is attached to the wall with you." Of course, the only things left were the stations, which were attached to the walls.

Fed up with his antics, words of anger flew from my mouth before I knew it. "Guess what Barry, if it makes you happy, you can keep all that shit."

I prepared to hang up the phone with the intent to sever my business relationship with him. I knew that I was going into a salon that was fully furnished. As I was placing the receiver down, he was still yelling in anger.

"I'm taking you to court," he screeched.

Those words caught my attention. I lifted the phone back up to my ear and said, "You do whatever you feel is best." I made sure that I hung it up completely after those words.

Barry followed through on his promise to take me to court, but nothing that he attempted prevailed. It was revealed that I was not the only tenant who had been victimized by his lack of attention to the building. A gentleman, who had run a business next door to me on the same floor, had a case that was already established against Barry. And because of the additional complaints, everything that he had attempted to initiate against me was severed. That was the way God worked. Like I always say, never plan to dig a ditch for a child of God, unless you plan to dig one for yourself right next to it.

—◆A Fresh Cut◆—

ONE NIGHT, JACKÉE and I were sitting and talking as we always did and we began to solidify plans to be married.

"Now, you know at some point, you're going to have to—"

I cut her off before she could even finish. "Of course, I'm going to formally propose. I wouldn't have it any other way. You deserve the best."

The pressure was on. I knew that I couldn't pick out just any old ring. When she lifted that hand to show off her ring, it would say more about me than her. I was nervous as hell while strategizing the purchase of the type of ring that I knew she deserved.

Aside from building family, I was adamant about building my business in Beverly Hills. There was an unspoken weight upon my shoulders, that was rooted in the desire to succeed. I knew that if I could establish a track record of success in Beverly Hills, that I would pioneer a new horizon for black and brown people like myself, who never believed it was possible to open businesses in the prestigious compartment of the city of Los Angeles. Moreover, I also knew that I needed to be the breadwinner for my growing family. Jackée has charted her own path to success and was continuing to make history in Hollywood. Prior to our deciding to create a life together, she became accustomed to a certain lifestyle and I wanted to give her nothing less once we were married. I knew that I had to run as fast and as hard as I could toward the destiny that God had opened the door to.

I find great favor in the fact that God will use your past to allow you to experience full circle moments in your present. The days of decorating my childhood home in San Antonio proved to be helpful as I was now tasked with appointing the salon in Beverly Hills. This was no small feat. I knew that to have a salon in Beverly Hills, also meant looking the part. Before moving all of my new stylists in, I spent a great deal of time pacing the length of the salon floor. I envisioned the blueprint for how I would organize the flow of traffic to increase the productivity of the stylists and comfort of the clients that we would serve. I imagined with my heart and my mind the decor, and how I would ensure that it mirrored the luxury that Beverly Hills was known for. I wanted for anyone who set foot in the salon to get a glimpse of the magic that had orchestrated my life. I envisioned each of our clients getting the Elgin Charles experience.

In good faith, Jackée demonstrated a belief in me that would prove to be crucial to our efforts to become a team by investing seed capital in the amount of fifty thousand dollars. Although I was initially against it, she insisted that I take it to execute the plans for expansion into the new salon and our future together. I knew without question that this level of encouragement was a sign that she believed in me and my talents. It was especially pivotal because she had initially questioned why I was opening a new salon in the middle of our courtship and just before our marriage. I don't believe that she thought it to be a wise decision at the time, but she undeniably got behind me and backed me wholeheartedly. I had built my business prior to meeting Jackée and I had every intention of building it even more aggressively as we approached marriage. I now had to show everyone who had invested in me that it was not in vain. I had a point to prove to God, Jackée, and most importantly, myself.

With the new seed money, I had more stations installed, increased the cabinet space, added lockers for the staff, selected new paint for the walls, and even began having fresh flowers delivered weekly. It was so Beverly Hills. By the time we officially opened for business, we were bustling. The stylists were throwing down and we were lighting the beauty industry up. I had never really noticed before, but I was now aware of the fact that the salon had become a point of interest for tourists. People started passing by just to witness the salon. It was still unbelievable that there was a business of color, thriving in Beverly Hills. As we worked, we would notice people walking through the doors of the salon and taking pictures, just to say that they had seen it. I didn't mind one bit because I recognized what our presence meant for so many.

After two months of being open, we began the planning process to host a grand opening, purposed with a message to let the world know that the Elgin Charles Hair Salon had arrived! I enlisted a well-known publicist by the name of Kenneth Reynolds to oversee the event. I wanted to make a big deal of it all because it simply was. Reynolds' claim to fame was his work with the voice, Whitney Houston; he was a friend to all of the black starlets in Hollywood and had a gleaming recommendation from my wife-to-be. On the day of the grand opening, we had tons of press and media arrive along with photographers and videographers, who provided coverage of the event and all of the amazing guests who attended. It was a lavish, beautiful party. Celebrities from all walks of life attended, and it meant so much to me because it was a full circle moment. I felt like I had arrived. My biggest dream was accomplished and I knew that from that moment on, the sky was the limit. I had both the girl and the business of my dreams. The funny thing about dreams is that just as hard as you work to realize them, you have to work twice as hard to maintain them.

Solidifying the love that I shared with Jackée was one of the scariest moments of my life. I longed for her to find me worthy. After all, she deserved the best. My heart had created a space for her that I never knew existed. She filled my soul. I wanted the ring that I got for her to resemble, not only how I felt, but also the value of her love. A Saturday afternoon would prove to be the one of the few times that I could pull myself away from my hectic schedule to begin the ring shopping process.

Saturday mornings had become quite the cheddar. A line would for and wrap around the corner of the salon, with clients waiting to be Elginized. Oh, what a feeling. Even so, I knew that on this day, I would need to make Jackée's ring my priority.

I discussed the sentiments of my heart with one of my clients who was a regular on Saturday mornings. She encouraged me to see her jeweler. I knew that she was a class act and that whoever she recommended would likely have pieces that fit the bill. After I left the salon, she escorted me to Fadul. He worked in a jewelry store named The Mark. I was in prayer because I wanted so desperately for God to lead me to what was right for Jackée. I couldn't help but wonder if my pockets could accommodate what my heart believed that she deserved. I would venture to say that this is a concern for all men, tasked with the purpose of the ultimate display of their love.

As we entered the jewelry store, we took time to peruse all of the different selections. Little sweat beads had taken up residence on my forehead; I was so nervous. After taking the time to pace the floor, my eyes were drawn to one ring in particular. It was a beautiful, eternity band. I asked Fadul to allow me a closer look. Taking it out of the display, he explained that the way it had been created, made it unique. It had gold all around it and the marquis cut diamonds were laced throughout so that they appeared to never end. It was a sight for sore eyes. Never had I seen a piece of jewelry with this much personality. I just knew that I had to get it for her. Through a discreet exchange, Fadul cut me a deal that would flush my pockets for $50,000. I could only be thankful because he had given it to me for a steal.

Leaving the store with that ring was the final piece that I needed to complete the pledge of my love for Jackée in the way that she so deserved.

I wanted the proposal to be simple and to keep the focus on us. One night after dinner, I got down on one knee and proclaimed my love for Jackée Harry. It was such a proud moment for me. I had found someone whom I could confide in and who accepted all of me for who I had been and who I aspired to be. That was the love that I had asked God so desperately for. When I unveiled the ring, she got up, yelling with excitement and I knew that I had done a good job. We had discovered what God had intended for us and we were both deserving.

After the grand opening, my focus shifted right back to running the business. I was dead set on growth and development. In full leadership mode, I oversaw that all of the stylists got down to work. To my delight, we encountered very few issues outside of the normal trial and errors that accompany the execution of the day to day operations of a salon of our capacity. Over time, I worked to mold and cultivate an internal culture within the salon that we could all be proud of. I set rules that we maintain the highest level of professionalism, like no smoking outside of the front of the building. My vision was to ensure that if and when someone passed by, they only saw excellence. Eventually, the business that we were garnering, demonstrated that we are on fertile ground.

When we first arrived at the new salon, the surrounding area was nearly barren. With the exception of the Bank of America building, positioned across the street, and a Johnny Rockets restaurant, no other businesses really existed. There had been another salon owned by Jose Eber, but it had caught fire and the lot was now empty.

I can say with certainty that we breathed a great deal of life onto that block. The absence of other businesses did not affect the massive presence that we represented. After about four years, we would recognize a resurgence of business.

One particular day, a group of white men came into my salon and asked to speak with me. They were with Vidal Sassoon and needless to say, I was blown away. I had always wanted to be the black Vidal Sassoon. The day they visited, the shop was buzzing like crazy, and I had to make a concerted effort to tear myself away to have a moment with them. I was unsure of what they wanted, but I was determined to find out through the conversation. They began asking me a series of question about how I liked the area and how business had been. I didn't know for certain at the time, but my thought was that they were prospecting.

My suspicion was later confirmed when the building adjacent to us began undergoing renovations. The city came in and began making repairs and the next thing I knew, Vidal Sassoon had set up a salon in that building. Meeting him personally was like a dream come true. The thought that I was running a salon in such close proximity to someone whom I had idolized in my respective industry was surreal. He was very kind, and on a regular basis, he could be seen with his wife or walking his two dogs. He always smiled and listened when people spoke to him. He was a man of few words, but I'll never forget the day that I proudly proclaimed that he was my mentor face to face. He was very gracious and told me that he was proud of what I was doing.

Although I was never trained by his school, I was a student of his infamous angle cutting techniques. I basked in his systems and I saw his styles and how they took on so many different shapes. During those times, I worked hard to take the inspiration that I garnered in other places, and created my own lane of creativity and execution. I remained a student of the industry and coined the term "unit." A unit was a hair piece that was custom made for a client. This hair piece could be attached as a wig or a partial wig. Today, the term "unit" has been established as a household term in the hair industry. Blazing new trails and setting trends was the ultimate sense of fulfillment for me.

The presence of other salons was never a threat because we had managed to carve out a niche market. My clientele of black and brown women, was running the salon. There was simply no one else who provided the services that we provided in Beverly Hills. There were no other black salons.

With the growth of business, came the growth of a business owner. I was now charting new territory financially. I was forced to tighten my accounting practices and procedures, increase my paper trail for transactions made, and master the art of balancing my books. My experience in corporate America had schooled me well, and skills that I had garnered in the past were, once again, making their presence known.

I am a strong proponent of knowing how to execute on every level in your business. Even if you hire others to do a job, you should maintain a general understanding of what needs to be done to remain afloat and set plans for success and upward mobility. I honored the fact that God had given me authority and command. When it comes to your books, you have to count every cent daily and set financial goals accordingly. Although challenging, and filled with moments of intense growth, I was journeying through some of the most rewarding years of my life.

——For Better Days——

IN DECEMBER OF 1996, Jackée and I wed in what Jet Magazine referred to as a "Lavish Hollywood Ceremony." Jackée had spent a great deal of her time being attentive to the intricate details of the wedding day. She created what would be categorized in history as a fairytale wedding. She left no stone unturned. From purchasing tickets for flights, to chartering buses for family members to be brought to the ceremony. The day had all of the makings of a royal wedding. I might have attempted once to give my two cents about the plans for the special day, but I was politely asked to stay out of the process. I took my cue and resolved to be told where to show up and where to stand. I wanted her to be happy and to experience what she had always dreamed of. Just before the wedding, I can recall being confronted by one of her sisters, but I was up for it. I had found my bride and I was not going to allow anyone or anything to stand in the way of what I knew God had blessed me with. I also recognized that our courtship had been short, so it was only natural that there would be questions. It was she and I against the world, and we were preparing for the fullness of the bliss that we had both envisioned for our marriage.

Aside from the presence of our families, the ceremony was a star-studded event to say the least. Jackée had spared no expense when it came to taking advantage of her status as Hollywood royalty. You name the celebrity and I would likely be able to confirm that Jackée had invited them to share in our special day. From Denzel and Pauletta Washington to Janet Jackson, Angela Bassett and Courtney Vance, who had just begun dating, as well as Star Jones. I also invited all the staff from the salon. They were so much a part of who I was, I could not have envisioned the day without their presence.

The sentiment in the room was love. I can't remember seeing a face that wasn't smiling. The music was beyond phenomenal, which took me to another place. One of the highlights of the night was when my cousin Buggy and I took over the dance floor. It was like old times when we used to dance in Texas. I can't recall the song, but I remember that Jackée had gotten up to go around and greet guests, and it was right then that the music called my name. When I connected eyes with Buggy, it was all she wrote. We fell right back into our old groove and the crowd was there for it all. Guests began encircling us and we were lost in the moment. Jackée ran over to see what all of the commotion was about, and there I was in my element. I could see her massive smile and it warmed my heart. For the first time, I had found a Queen who would allow me to be me. She was a bright star, but she didn't force me to dim mine. That night, I knew that what we had was something beyond special. What we shared would withstand the test of time. As I returned back to my seat, I looked up towards the heavens and thanked God for what He had done in my life. I was preparing to walk the straight and narrow line that He had prepared for me and it wasn't forced. I was so ready to become all that she needed me to be and all that God had planned for me.

The honeymoon was beautiful, colorful, and interesting. Aside from the romantic moments that we shared, I had my fair share of what I refer to as "man" moments. One morning, I woke up early to exercise, as I often did. It was quite possible that the testosterone was too potent to keep me from thinking straight. When I returned to the hotel room, Jackée was standing in the center of the room, wearing a massive red chiffon petticoat, red slippers, embellished with fur, and red teddy underneath it all. She was a sight of opulence, but at the time, I didn't have the romantic intellect to appreciate it. Without hesitation, I burst into a series of uncompromised laughter—at least in my mind I did. I saw so much red and chiffon, that I was dazed and confused, and my survival instincts must have hidden the roaring laughter behind my smile. Regardless, she was furious by my unwarranted reaction. After recognizing her displeasure, I began to repair the broken moment. She didn't give me a second. Let's just say that I had to spend a great deal of time working to reinstate the romance that I had allowed to slip through my fingers. I did a lot of making up to get things back right. Bless her heart.

When I returned from our whirlwind of romance, I re-focused my efforts on creating a better quality of life for myself and ensuring that I lived up to what Jackée needed me to be.

I loved to shower Jackée with gifts. I would buy her jewelry, and exotic trinkets. I spoiled her with Elsa Peretti, Tiffany & Co., Cartier, you name it. I also gave her an allowance of $5,000 each month. I wanted her to have the very best of what I could offer.

If I hadn't been relentless before, I was now. It was more important than ever to be innovative when creating new avenues and revenue streams from my business. I began meditating daily to allow God to speak to me about new and original ways that I could take the brand that I had constructed to higher heights. I saw this as a critical time to further carve out a niche in the industry.

During this era, I ran even farther up with the term "ELGINIZED." It was a word that I used to describe my processes and methodologies. I began working on a subsidiary product line that used patented formulas that I knew had the power to transform hair. I had managed to watch in awe at the transformative elements of an avocado and oil mixture that I had been using on my clients for years. It was a no brainer to use this same formula as the basis for the product line. My goal for women of color was to restore the moisture that was lost from overprocessing and from the use of products that were created to strip the hair. Too many coifs had fallen victim to these elements. There was also an upward swing of interest in creating niche product lines and many of the bigger companies began following the trend. This was even more motivating for me because I knew that I was on the ground daily, working with the specific clients that I was seeking to serve.

One name that changed the trajectory of what would happen in our industry was Paul Mitchell. He came out, guns blazing, and demonstrated that product lines could be offered in a variety of retail locations. The bigger companies began buying the smaller lines. This made it challenging for smaller companies to compete. I was journeying an uphill battle, but I was never afraid. I had a mark of my own to make.

To make the impact that I so desired, I would need to establish an infrastructure that could sustain continued growth. I wanted to ensure that those who I enlisted to help me grow the company were people whom I could trust. I tapped my brother Edgar to oversee the construction of a sales team. He was in his element, and his charisma would prove to be beneficial in instructing the team on how to sell the products. Edgar had a hunger for success that was crucial.

During this same era, weave hit the scene like a force of nature, and the hair and beauty shows provided the largest stages to display your skills. The new equation for success became, develop your product line, establish yourself as an expert by teaching a new technique or simply showing your creativity on the stage at a hair show, win popularity from increased exposure, and finally, sell your products like wildfire.

I became a household name at the hair shows. My ability to rock the crowd was second nature to me. The lights were the lights, no matter the stage, and I was drawn to them. From demonstrating my cutting edge techniques, to how I had mastered the art of weaving, and the creation of what many now refer to as "units," I was the epitome of a trendsetter. At the shows, people were coming to me and wanting to take pictures. I was making money like crazy on my new products and reinvesting everything back into the business.

The growth of the first extended venture, prompted me to create a relaxer. Relaxers were all the craze. There was not a woman of color who did not want one. The relaxer had the power to make kinky or curly hair straight and sealed the follicle with a coating that gave it a sheen that women of color longed for. Some felt like relaxed hair was more manageable. What we would eventually learn was that women of color were born with hair that had the ability to do amazing things, but the industry had not caught up to the culture. The first batch of relaxer from the Elgin Charles product line, costed me $11,000 to create. I had studied the formulas and worked with a chemistry lab to design a product that would maintain the health of the hair and be most beneficial to my clientele. When the truck arrived with the relaxer, it was massive. It took ten staff members to unload the truck and my entire office was filled with small cases of relaxer. Needless to say, I had built an empire. Wisdom dictates that the more earning potential we are granted access to, the more vultures swarm.

——BULLSEYE——

AS MUCH AS I WANTED to pretend that everything was well on the homefront, there were undeniable patterns of tension that prevailed within our home. Although I had forgiven, I had not forgotten how distraught I had felt after the death of my mother. I looked to Jackée for comfort, but I'd been met with words that demasculinized me. That same sentiment became a common thread. I had always been a calm being by nature, but there were times that I felt provoked to act in ways that were not in alignment with who I was and who I wanted to be.

With the highs and lows of my wife's career, also came the highs and lows of her disposition towards me. On the other hand, nothing had changed for me. My responsibility was to ensure and keep the financial stability of our home intact. I was working astronomical hours, but there would be times when Jackée would remain at home all day. I never knew what I might return home to, but I always hoped that love was the most abundant sentiment.

One night when I got home, Jackée told me that she had prepared a meal, consisting of fried shrimp and a few other side dishes. As I sat down to the plate, I recall the shrimp batter being stuck to the shrimp. Either the shrimp had not cooked for the right amount of time or the oil that she had used for the preparation had not been hot enough. Either way, the shrimp was underdone. In a desperate attempt to appease her, I tried to take a bite of the shrimp. I had never been a person who enjoyed seafood, but raw seafood was on a level that I couldn't reach. Jackée noticed that I was not satisfied with the meal and an argument ensued.

"Oh, so you can't eat the meal that I took time to prepare for you?"

"I want to eat it. I just can't, if it isn't cooked," I replied.

She became belligerent and continued to poke at me verbally. After the frustration mounted within my soul, it turned into anger. I snatched a handful of raw, unfried, battered, slimy shrimp and threw them at the wall. It was out of character for me and we both paused in silence. I stared Jackée directly in her eyes and she stood there, looking at me in shock. After a pause that must have lasted for a full minute, she burst into laughter. At first, my hurt feelings would not allow me to join her in the discovery of humor, but eventually, we both slid to the floor in repetitious laughter as the remnants of the raw shrimp slid down the wall. Although funny in the moment, the unnecessary bouts of drama were at times too much for me to bear. I had such a great deal of stress on me from everything that was mounting at the salon and the responsibility to create a home for my wife. I wanted to return home to a sanctuary of peace and one where I would be catered to instead of mocked.

Not only did I feel like a target in my own home, but in many ways, I felt the presence of a bullseye on my back when outside of the home and in the business as well. People were trying to sell me anything that they could. From pitching opportunities to work with me, to services that others wanted me to acquire, I felt like a target with a dollar sign plastered across my back.

As the owner of a salon, you have to keep your eyes and ears and senses open for your clients, but also for the many gold diggers that come with the territory. Many masked as "helpers," can prove to be detrimental if you don't sit with a watchful eye. I was forced to learn that discernment was the key in business and in life. When God lets you know that someone or something is not right, you must be willing to take heed and to yield to the cautionary senses that we far too often ignore.

——THE NEW NORMAL——

AT THE PINNACLE OF my career, I found myself pouring every ounce of power into my wife and the continued upward mobility of the Elgin Charles brand. Even though I was happy, I felt like I was fighting to keep everything afloat. As a man, it is possible to have the weight of the world on your shoulders. With mounting responsibilities at both home and work, I knew that all of my true strength would come from God. My father had prepared me for such a time as this, and I now empathized with all that he had done to give us the best life that he possibly could. And just when you think that you can't handle another block in the structure of your life, God will bless you once more.

By the time DeVanique was four years of age, he had begun to call me regularly, just as I had predicted. It was my honor to remain in contact with him. As he got older, the calls were more targeted towards his feelings of dismay. He would often complain to me about his Paw Paw and his Auntie and how he would often get into fights with them. He would constantly call me out of the blue. Ms. Berta eventually agreed to allow him to visit Jackée and I during the holidays and summers.

DeVanique's environment in Texas was one where they treated him like a bundle of joy. He could run around and misbehave and it was tolerated. When it was time for preschool, he acted out on a larger scale. Even so, he was excellent at finding friends that had nice families. The Swans were a Caucasian family that had two sons, who were close in age to DeVanique. He bonded with them in Texas and thankfully he knew how to be a good guest. He would clean, wash dishes, and get to know the family.

In addition to the families from school, there was also a coach who took a tremendous interest in DeVanique. The coach was putting forth great effort to mentor him, but DeVanique thought he was weird and insisted on maintaining his distance. I never questioned his intuition, as I knew the importance of it remaining sharp and intact.

We began a pattern of DeVanique coming to visit with us for the holidays. Even though we had maintained such close contact through the phone, he had a negative attitude when he was in our home. I believe that he was nervous and unsure of where he fit in with the busy lifestyles that we maintained. There was also noticeable friction due to the past and the back and forth on whether or not DeVanique would live with us.

Upon one of his visits, a Jewish lady by the name of Sherri Kagan, invited DeVanique to a children's party at her home. He misbehaved and due to his behavior, I was both embarrassed and hurt. For the life of me, I couldn't understand why he was acting out. I recall having to leave the party to take him home. It frustrated me to no end. What I never wanted was to be an accomplice to DeVanique's downfall in any way. I knew that the repetition of respect and the work ethic that my father had so diligently instilled in me were the reasons behind my success. I wanted the same for DeVanique.

I knew that I had to discipline him because choosing not to, would otherwise make him a victim and product of his environment. I hung on to the hope that had manifested in my heart, for him to break the cycle that had served as an overarching theme within our family. In those moments, the memories of that orphic moment when my daddy whipped me such that the belt broke in half, replayed in my head. I could never forget the impact that it had on my life. I questioned it, recognizing both the error in his ways and his motives for doing so. Never in my wildest dreams did I wish to deny DeVanique the opportunity to learn, grow, and thrive under my tutelage. Although not heavily discussed, DeVanique was with his biological father when he was shot. It was said that he had experienced a repetitious series of bad dreams that tormented him. I was overwhelmed with so many thoughts, but I took the responsibility of caring for him very seriously.

After snapping out of the trance and the thoughts that threatened to outweigh my call to action, I reached for my Gucci belt and I went and got dramatic.

"I can't believe you're doing this. You are over here, being blessed, and acting like that in front of guests?" I was angry and disappointed in him. I lunged toward him as he was jumping over the bed and running for the door. I snapped the belt and it hit the wall. He stopped and when I realized that I had his undivided attention, I said, "You stay in here and don't come out until I come back to get you."

Later, when I went back to his room, he was all apologies. I never had to threaten spankings again. I closed the door to his room and I let out a sigh of relief because I knew that I had reached him. I believe that he needed me to show physical strength.

It seemed the deeper we got into parenting DeVanique, the more my marriage deteriorated. To make matters worse, I received a notice at the salon that I was being tapped by the IRS for an unpaid tax bill nearing one million dollars. They were threatening to place a lien on my business and all of my financial accounts if the bill was not cleared. This added insult to injury because the tax bill was not mine. I did not owe the IRS any money. I was not at all an advocate for taking ownership of such a massive bill that had been created prior to Jackée and my union. As they say, ain't no romance without finance.

In lieu of the financial strain that was placed upon our relationship from her past and the lack of romance in the present, the temperature on our intimacy had turned cold. Additionally, Jackée decided to go back out on the road to generate an income for herself and to further her career. It got to the point that I was no longer even sure if we missed each other. We had drifted so far apart that we were now two ships in passing. We were not getting along and we had both lost our desire to love the way that we once had and our marriage suffered gravely because of it. No matter what happened between us personally, we had always found a way to remain amicable in order to handle any business affairs that needed to be addressed. Jackée owned every part of the IRS debt and demonstrated in more ways than one that she had no intention of sticking me with the full amount. There came a point where we both recognized that the thrill of our marriage was gone. We were prepared to work together to figure out how to get the IRS debt removed from my realm of responsibility. I hold her in the most respectable light for that. She handled her business and never under any circumstance did she place her prior responsibilities upon me.

Together, we devised a plan of action for our impending separation. She suggested that we sell the home we shared in the Hollywood Hills and that we equally split the profits made from the sale. She would use any liquid funding that she acquired to settle her tax debt and I used the money to purchase a home in the lavish Sherman Oaks community.

The Asian woman who owned the home, cried during the sale. I could tell the place was sentimental to her by the way she relayed the memories of the life she had created there. Everything about the house was zen. The landscape brought me the sense of peace that I had been in search of. There was a lovely atrium in the center of the house that further spoke to the calm spirit of the home. Boasting four bedrooms and an open floor plan, the home also revealed a living room, dining room, and family room with a fabulous view of the city. All in all, it was a sight for sore eyes. One thing that I did notice was that there seemed to be an abundance of birds and nests surrounding the homes. It was more than I had ever taken time to notice at any of the other homes that I had acquired.

Even though Jackée and I were not on terms of love, she moved into the Sherman Oaks home with me. We intended to co-parent DeVanique in peace. It was more like living with a good friend, as all romantic ties had fizzled. As the months passed by, DeVanique began spending more and more time with us in Los Angeles. The dynamics were in a constant state of development. The relationship between Jackée and I was forced to thrive amidst all of the moving parts. We didn't agree on everything, but we did agree that we loved and respected one another enough to always have each other's back. We knew that we would be one of those "weird families" that people would question the makeup of, but neither of us cared.

The birds that I had noticed prior to moving in, started coming to the windows of the home on a regular basis. And as weird as it sounds, it was like they were messengers. I knew that some major changes were about to take place in my life, but there was no way for me to predict what they would be. The presence of the birds sparked my intuition. They would tap on the windows, repeatedly, and I would have been annoyed, but it felt like they had a purpose that they were attempting to carry out. To a person who was out of touch with the spirit of discernment, their actions could have been missed, but I recognized their mission loud and clear.

With DeVanique as my focus, I recognized that I needed to do more to be available for him. Jackée and I would learn that he had dyslexia and I felt a need to work harder to make sure that he had both the academic and emotional support that he needed. Even though I was not his legal guardian, I knew that God had brought me into his life for a purpose and that I could not fail him.

While in the salon, I was made aware of a home that had become available in San Antonio. The home was not just any home, it was awe inspiring. The only reason that it was of interest to me was because of its location. With the intent to provide a steady home for DeVanique, I assumed that establishing a residence there would provide a heightened level of security and balance for him. Additionally, I had always recognized the value in building my financial portfolio through real estate investments. Even though I had just purchased the home in Sherman Oaks, I felt that my efforts to give DeVanique a permanent residence would not be in vain. I could hardly believe that I was approved for another loan to purchase an additional home, but I knew that if God had ordained it, so it would be. In good faith, God showed me favor once again and granted me the clearance to purchase the home in San Antonio. Even though I had been the owner of many of homes in Los Angeles, this one was the most meaningful and the most lavish. There was marble and granite everywhere and the ceilings were so high that you could see the clouds. I knew that it would take me forever to furnish the home and quite frankly I was exhausted by the idea of it because I had just gone through the process back in Los Angeles.

I was now living in both cities and the back and forth caused a tremendous amount of wear and tear on me both mentally and physically. With a failed marriage on the horizon, I was ready to do anything to find success within my promise to be a part of DeVanique's life. In 2003, after seven years of matrimony, the union that Jackée and I shared officially ended in divorce.

BY THE WAY
I Don't Want Your Pieces

WHEN I MET YOU, I was believing God for a companion. I was in search of the good thing that the Holy Bible speaks of. I was believing God for a soulmate, and I believed with my heart that I had discovered that sacred being in you. Our meeting was unusual, but our connection was real.

The significance of the numbers 227 were startling. My birthday is February 27th and so much of your legacy was rooted in the numbers 227. We were movements apart, but a force when we were together. We brought smiles to so many faces just by virtue of our union.

Your support, and your strength became my refuge from the world. I longed for it. I never questioned that you were all I needed to get by. Even so, the baggage became too heavy and burdensome at times. You emasculated me in so many ways and it hurt. Maybe I was wrong to think that your strength was enough to overcome the pain from your past. Maybe I was wrong to believe that you would never hurt me. Maybe I was wrong for believing in us.

I was so tired of not measuring up. The preconceived notions of how I should behave in certain situations and the constant antagonizing, filled my mind with thoughts of retaliation. I was in need of protection from the protector of my heart.

At times, I hated you for not loving me. I never received enough love from my mother and I thought that I would discover it in you. To be abused and called weak is what I earned instead. That stuck with me and it cut me so deeply.

You wanted me to need you, but I didn't; I wanted you. I never understood what that meant, but I was willing to go to the ends of the Earth for you. As soon as I allowed myself to need you, you broke my heart and tore it into pieces. And no, I don't profess to be perfect, but I wanted to be for you.

Amidst the chaos, God blessed us with the peace of new life. Sharing the responsibility for another human being is not to be taken lightly. For this reason alone, we will share a bond that can't be broken. His life has served as a beacon of hope that love lives and breathes. It is my desire that you discover it and that it fills your heart where there is a void. This is the same sentiment that I share for myself.

I will always love you. Sometimes life is like simple arithmetic. 2+2=7. There are two sides to every story and seven is the holy number of completion. I know that God has allowed us to complete our season in one another's lives, and I leave you with the words that helped me to heal. Accept yourself. Love yourself. Celebrate yourself. For each of us deserves to know the trueness of love inside of our hearts.

Eternally,
Elgin

CHAPTER 13

A WRECKING BALL

"Through the fire of life, you can find redemption in the flames."

—Elgin Charles

If I was completely honest with myself, I was in a state of uncertainty and turmoil. I needed a reprieve from the life that I had tried so desperately to create. It had crumbled and I was left to sweep up the ashes from the fire that had cleared the land. I didn't have time to focus on the placement of blame. Life had taught me that there was no glory in the blame game. I needed to feel alive again. The failed relationship, my successful business, and the responsibility of becoming a parent to DeVanique had sucked the vibrancy from my ability to dream. I wasn't sure what God was doing in my life and I knew better than to question Him. Instead, I resolved to do whatever the hell I wanted to do. I know that a statement such as this will be scrutinized, but we all go through times where we are determined to be selfish above and beyond the call of duty. I had been made numb and I simply wanted to feel again. I began smoking weed to ease my mind. The smoke became a gateway to many other things. Whether they were right or wrong, I decided to live for the moment. I made a conscious decision to do what felt good. I was no longer interested in building a family in the traditional sense. My attention was drawn instead to building memories that would make me happy. I let go of the old ball and chain and welcomed in the weightlessness of feathers. I was looking for fun and eventually, I would stumble upon it.

—◄Imposters and Tariffs►—

AFTER FALLING OUT OF LOVE, I made a pact with myself that I was no longer going to live for anyone other than myself. I decided to do what made me happy and disregarded any notion of what others might have thought of me. I had tried with every fiber of my soul to walk the straight and narrow line and that hadn't worked out—ever. My heart was distressed, as it had been torn into pieces and drizzled with gasoline. The match had been lit and the flames grew like the wildfires that torment the summers of Los Angeles.

And as painful as all of that was, somehow, someway, I was still in search of love. Even I don't understand how the heart has the capacity to resurrect itself from the dead. I guess I am just one of those people who recites the solemn oath to never love again with fingers crossed behind my back. I will never stop searching for love and it never seems to stop discovering me. My heart was a GPS and I would soon learn that a new love was headed in my direction. This time I would be turned about but on my own terms.

My life began to revolve around a new theme: Out with the old and in with the new. After Jackée had officially moved out of the Sherman Oaks residence, I wanted to refresh everything around me. From my relationships to the decor in the salon, I needed a fresh start in more ways than one. As I always had, I began to discuss my new plans with my clients in passing. One in particular, named

Cheron, took a great deal of interest in the decor conversation. I hadn't previously known that she had expertise in interior decor. I was drawn to her and her to me. Through continued conversation and a little light planning, she helped me to visualize the possibilities of a salon overhaul. We bonded in the name of decor and began talking outside of the salon. From dinner dates to walks in the park, more than a friendship was budding. Through our many discussions, I confided many things, including my pending tax woes that had resulted from the unfairly assigned tax liens.

In the interim of my budding relationship with Cheron, a stylist known in the industry as DaRico relocated from St. Louis to Beverly Hills, to work at the salon. He was uber talented and it was good to have his gifts as a part of the team. DaRico brought with him a vibrant soul named Sean, who worked alongside him. Sean was energetic, charismatic, and possessed a colorful personality. A flamboyant flame from St. Louis, we would all learn over time that Sean was downright fearless. He had been assisting DaRico at their previous salon in their hometown and was another great addition to the Elgin Charles team.

I had gone from spending very little time with my staff outside of the salon, to simply wanting to be in the company of people who knew how to have a good time. I recollect a weekend in which my cousin Buggy came to town to visit. She suggested that I take her out and I obliged. I also extended the invitation to a few stylists from the salon. As the night progressed, everyone had invited themselves back to my house for a nightcap. My house always seemed to be a place that people wanted to hang out for one reason or another, but I was up for it.

Moving forward, I didn't force myself to choose like I had in the past. Instead, I indulged in the company that moved my spirit at that moment. In addition to our personal time spent together, Cheron and I continued working on the revamp of the salon. I also took the time to consult with an attorney, who advised me on a strategy to get the tax lien dropped from my name. Through our confab, it was determined that if I could prove that I was no longer legally married to Jackée, and that I was indeed no longer romantically tied to her in any way, then it was possible to have the debt cleared from my name. I was suggested that I have a letter written by Cheron that stated that we were together. She willingly accepted my request to write the letter, as she knew the grave impact that such a debt would have on my business and personal wealth. Things were moving in the right direction to have the lien removed and the old look and feel of the salon was slowly disappearing.

I moved forward in business with Cheron by signing a contract for fifty thousand dollars that would include the execution of the full plan that we had dreamed of together. As with every well laid project, nothing went according to plan. I began noticing inconsistencies in the contracted work being done. It appeared in many ways that the contractors lacked the extensive direction needed from Cheron to complete the expected renovations with excellence. Furthermore, the budget wasn't being used properly. The items selected for the decor resembled the high end pieces from Home Goods and lacked the quality of what had been discussed. To make matters worse, the entire project was in limbo for a period of almost two weeks when Cheron mysteriously disappeared and couldn't be reached and my salon looked and felt unkempt. I was furious and shocked as I had never seen that side of her, even in all of the time that she had been my client. The consistency that I had known to be her truth was now a lie.

Upon her return, she was met with the repeated calls and messages that I had rendered during her vanishing act. She eventually explained that she'd needed to take a mental hiatus and that she had done so in Paris. What the hell? Plainly stated, her hiatus was a vacation in Paris with my damn coins. I was too through. She halfway completed the renovations and I was left to pick up the pieces as usual. By this point, if there was one thing that I knew how to do well, it was finishing what other people couldn't. I knew how to forge ahead, regardless of how anyone attempted to swindle me.

The good news and the most profound blessing in all of it was that nonsense, was that the tax lien was dismissed from my good name. I couldn't have been more relieved. All in all, I'd say I paid fifty thousand dollars to regain my freedom, and I would do it again. Next time, however, I would just ask for some better adornments for my salon. But, like they said in *Amistad*, "Give us free."

—ZADDY—

I DON'T KNOW HOW OTHER people define a midlife crisis, but by my own terms, I was experiencing one. I had tried everything that I knew to find love and live according to God's word. But to no avail. I was truly at a loss for what I could have done differently. I knew that every relationship would have ups and downs, but I had really devoted my heart to creating something that would last and it hadn't. If I had to pick a phrase to describe my disposition, the most prevalent would have been "fuck it." I began blowing out my hair, smoking weed, and being rebellious. I wasn't angry with God. I continued to love Him and I understood His word. I simply wanted to focus on living in my truth and being myself completely—whatever that meant.

After all that had transpired with Cheron and her trifling ways, I deserted any notion of a relationship with her, under any circumstances. I wanted nothing more to do with her. Even though my time was split between my home in San Antonio and Los Angeles, I desired to see how everything played out. He had been there and watched it all play out, but had remained respectful.

I received notice that a court date had been arranged and set in the city of San Antonio in order to discuss my obtaining full custody of DeVanique. I put things on ice in Los Angeles and returned to my home in San Antonio to prepare accordingly. On my birthday, February 27th, I stood in front of the Judge to state why I had the capacity to be a parent to a child that I had grown to love. He was my own flesh and blood and his spirit had connected with mine. I knew that God had called me to be his guardian angel while on Earth. I had such a good feeling in the courtroom; I knew that something would work in our favor on that day.

As I stood before the Judge, he plainly inquired, "So, you think you can handle this kid?"

I proclaimed from the top of my lungs with the biggest smile on my face, "Yes."

"Are you sure this is what you want to do? Do you have a place of residence in San Antonio?"

"Yes, Your Honor, I do. Not only can I give him stability and what he needs financially, but I will also be able to put him in the right schools and change his life for the better."

Before I knew it, I was granted full guardianship of Frank DeVanique Brown. A major milestone in both of our lives. The smile on his face was a vision that I will never forget. He knew that

I had come to save him and that I had never wavered in my promise to be there for him and protect him. In that moment, he experienced what was good in the world. It was a moment of Agape love.

As much as being granted guardianship of DeVanique was a victory, it was accompanied by real work. There was no way for me to know how to predict what his immediate and long term needs would be, and there was a great deal that I would have to learn along the way. We had to develop our relationship, erase past habits that did not serve him well, and create space in his heart to accept love in the capacity in which I was prepared to give him. Of all of the things that I had experienced, this was indeed the most challenging and the most rewarding. Due to his behavior, he had also been assigned thirty days at a Juvenile Justice Academy. I was now responsible for getting him there safely.

The Academy looked like a small house. Each of the residents, including DeVanique, had to wear a uniform. It was clearly stated that they couldn't miss any days during the thirty day term, or they would be forced to begin again, or worse, face harsher consequences. Prior to the uniform that he was forced to wear, he could be seen flaunting a pair of sagging pants, a big ass t-shirt and a red headband. He had an attitude from hell. He was tough and life had made him so, but he was also angry, and I understood more than he knew just how much.

When we arrived at the Academy, he sat in the car, sulking and he didn't want to go inside. His body language mirrored refusal, but I was not having it. Now, officially responsible for him, I knew the importance of putting my foot down and showing him the power of a strong male presence. "Take your ass in there," I demanded.

Begrudgingly, he listed to me. I wasn't new to him, just officially his father.

"Ok, Dad."

Coincidentally, Buggy transitioned from Kentucky with her three kids, grandbaby, and a dog back to San Antonio. By the time she arrived, they had repossessed her car. I felt responsible in many ways and I offered for them to move into my San Antonio residence. I also purchased her an older car, or as we called it, a hoopty. The small, ugly Camaro costed me $1200, but it was a ride, and I assigned Buggy with the task of ensuring that DeVanique made it to and from his alternative school.

While there one day, I rode with Buggy to pick DeVanique up. We wanted to go to the movies, but DeVanique had other plans.

"I ain't going in there like this. Look how I'm dressed. I can't go in public and have people see me like this." He refused to get out the car because he was embarrassed by the uniform from the Academy.

As I saw it that was of his doing and I got extremely pissed off. His behavior was outright disobedient. I had sacrificed so much of myself, my business, and my finances to provide for him, so what I was not going to do was to take care of a disrespectful kid. That was my promise—over my dead body, so help me God. I got real emotional with him and he recognized that I was in a state of pandemonium. I'm a Pisces and when I get emotional, I water up. I was planning to wear him the fuck out in the parking lot of the theatre.

I could see by the look on his face that he had retreated. I began to speak calmly to him, "If you want me to work with you, you are going to have to work with me. That is the only way that we can discover peace," I warned. "If you are going to disobey me, that's the ultimate disrespect and I will not have it. If you don't get this shit together, I can get the hell out of San Antonio and go back to LA. I need you to understand that this cannot happen anymore. I come from the same place you come from. I lost my momma just like you lost your momma." Tears began to well up in my eyes and I could feel the heat from my soul rising up in my heart. I was hurt and I had no one to comfort me. I wanted more than anything to be there for him, but I could not allow him to hurt me in the process. "I've been through what you have been through. If anyone understands, I do. I can teach you how to navigate this world. You are not alone.

In an instant, he too began to cry. Life had thrown him around carelessly, but I would see to it that it ended right there—that moment—in the car. God had given me a sword and told me to protect it with my life. Frank DeVanique Brown was the name that was engraved on the handle. The assignment to protect his life was, and forever will be, my redemption.

——Pyramids and Ponzi Schemes——

BACK IN LOS ANGELES, I was preparing to make the transition to bring DeVanique there to live with me full time. The home in San Antonio was more of a burden than a lucrative investment. Moreover, I needed to attain more stability in my life and the salon. I was open to the universe and the potential for realignment. At the salon, we would get all types of characters who stopped by for one reason or another. After all, we were in Los Angeles; the entire city was a mixed bag and you never knew what you would get.

A white man in a gray suit, entered through the front doors, one afternoon and began talking with no regard for assistance from a receptionist. He immediately came to where I was standing and began to speak with conviction. "Man, I was drawn here because of the energy. Do you know who you are? I can feel your vibrations, man. You are something really special. There is greatness inside of you, but I don't believe that you are aware of it."

Before I could get a word in, he continued, "I work for Mercedes. I wanted to tell you your consciousness is really high." He pulled out a twenty-dollar bill and proceeded to explain the graphics on it. "You see all of these bricks coming together? This entire section takes up a huge part of the pyramid. This part is the majority of people in the world. There is a space between the next section of the pyramid. The top is separate from the body. In that area, on the top of the pyramid, there is an eye and it says, 'In God We Trust.' You're vibrating right here at the top of the pyramid." He motioned and pointed to what he meant. "Your functioning here, but you see that space? To get to the next place, takes a leap of faith. You're going to have to be willing to take the leap. When you do that, you will have the power of the eye, and you will get to see all that the universe has for you."

When he concluded his sermon, I understood it all to mean that to get to the money, you have to be willing to make the jump. The strangest part of it all was that he came in to give me the message and disappeared immediately after. From that day forward, I never saw or heard from him again.

I was never opposed to the fortune tellers or tarot card readers that frequented the streets of Los Angeles, but I was now aware of how gullible I had been over the years. I was always looking for divine messages from God. As a giver, I was always looking for inspiration that filled me up. In hindsight, I think I obtained a lot that wasn't good for me because of my intense curiosity. I took what he had said for what it was worth and looked to the next phase of my life. His advice in the end would prove to be sound, as I would be introduced to an opportunity that would prompt me to take one of the largest leaps of my life.

—BEVERLY HILLS FABULOUS—

NO MATTER HOW MANY times my personal life seemed to experience the tumultuous turbulence of the sea, I was a skillful sailor of my professional life. I had toiled relentlessly and I always found time to reward myself with the luxury that I had not had access to while growing up. You can't live in Beverly Hills and not desire to experience opulence. I felt that I deserved it. It was a way to repay myself for the work that I had championed. I had never stopped building my wealth, and I had no plans of slowing down. As fate would have it, old doors of faded hopes and dreams of love would close, and new doors of opportunity for prosperity would begin to open.

Clarence Avant's son, Alex, had a childhood friend named Jason Hervey, who was working on a show called *The Wonder Years*. It was extremely popular and had become a recognizable household brand. Together, Alex and Jason had formed a production company which had established lucrative deals with several networks. He had the ability to get through the doors to pitch shows, which was half the battle in Hollywood. He had spoken on several occasions about doing a show that featured an urban hair salon.

Alex said, "Man you need to see my boy, Elgin. He is in Beverly Hills and he would be perfect for it."

I received a call to discuss my interest, but what they didn't know was that I had always wanted to have my own show. This was a part of the grand vision that I had so desperately sought after for the brand that I had orchestrated.

"All I can do is get you in front to the president of the production company. If you can sell it, and get the green light, you will have my full support," Alex proclaimed.

Even though Jackée and I had parted ways, we respected each other as business partners and most importantly, DeVanique's parents. The age of social media was upon us and it would prove to be beneficial to keep those relationships fruitful in more ways than one. One day, while at the salon, I was on MySpace, a platform that connected people for both business and personal exchanges. I received a series of bulletins that I was intrigued by. The content was curated by a gentleman named Christopher Broughton. I learned that he was a thoroughbred in many professional realms and I reached out to him to further engage. As our digital conversations ensued, he informed me that his expertise could be of service in the resurrection of Jackée's career. Over time, we finessed a business idea that led to Christopher taking a four month hiatus from his job in private equity, to focus on her career. I was adamant in doing what I believed to be best for her, which led me to introduce them to each other. At the time, Christopher was relentless in his pursuit of establishing a name for himself in entertainment management. He immediately closed on a Nutraceutical deal for her that commissioned over thirty-five thousand dollars for signing alone. He went on to get her an appearance on ABC family, an appearance in a movie with Christina Milian, and an appearance on *Watch What Happens Live with Andy Cohen*. Through Christopher's hard work and diligence, the episode that Jackée appeared on became one of the most noted episodes. He had managed to book her when the show was just starting. He also garnered appearances on the *Mo'nique Show*, and *Anderson Cooper*. Jackée was popping. I saw that as a win for all of us. What could be more amazing than your family winning? As I saw it there was nothing greater.

After watching Christopher in action, he became a business and creative consultant for my brand. By 2010, I enlisted his assistance as my manager. Sharing a manager meant that both Jackée and I were vested in each other's success. My loyalty would never waver, it was just how I was built. I believed us to be family and I knew that any success that either of us achieved, would also prove to be beneficial for the child that we shared responsibility for.

I leveraged my contacts and the insight of clients, who knew the TV industry much better than I did, to create a concept that would be strong enough to land my own show. I knew that my life was filled with a bevy of interesting elements and people who were interesting enough to create a stir on the small screen. Although this was new territory for me, I was up for the challenge. I had crossed so many barriers and for me, failure was not an option. I was determined to make history yet again. Everything about the action that I was taking was intentional. When I began to pursue a show on television, there was no one of color telling a story like mine. There were no examples of hair stylists, who had created a name for themselves and built a brand to the magnitude that I had built. It was history in the making. I also knew that I needed to facilitate an environment that produced magical moments and magical personalities.

Sean's energy was something that the world had not yet seen, but they needed to. He was quirky and entertaining. Working off him would be easy for me because he kept the drama coming. I was encouraged to bring two personalities with me to the meeting that would give the TV executives a feel for what I had planned. Sean felt confident that a peer, by the name of Katrina, would be the perfect fit. Upon my introduction to her, I had to admit that she was cute. I liked her vibe. Katrina was a Sagittarius. Although, she didn't actually work for me, everyone understood the fact that if I needed to assemble a story that would depict the narrative that I was constructing, I would stop at nothing to do so.

That morning, I stepped into new territory as both the professional and the talent. My first order of business was to report to work at *The Insider*. I serviced my clients and made certain that they had what they needed prior to making their appearances. Afterwards, I switched gears by enlisting the assistance of Rainer, a makeup artist who was uber talented. I told her that I had a meeting with VH1 and that I needed her to get me right. Just like that, I became the client. She beat the hell out of my face and I dressed to kill. I had done my hair the night before and it was laid. My nails were freshly manicured and I opted to wear my $4,000 Prada alligator shoes with the matching belt. My Cartier watch was playing peeka-boo from the sleeve of my suit. I also opted for my big diamond earrings and ring. I wanted to impress the executives and to show them the glory of the opulence that I believed we could bring to the viewers, who would watch our show. I wanted to give them something that they had never seen before.

Sean and Katrina met me in the hallway and from the looks of their attire, they too had taken the meeting seriously. We waited for what felt like forever before being called in for the meeting. We introduced ourselves and immediately afterwards, we were asked a question that would prove to change all of our lives.

"Why would you be good for a show?" The network president wasn't about wasting anyone's time and got straight to the point. Sean and Katrina had a rapport and began to demonstrate through their exchange what would prove to be a humorous and entertaining conversation. The network execs kept looking at them until finally, I redirected the conversation and convinced Sean to start talking directly to them about what elements we could bring to the small screen. At the other end of the table, I cornered another executive with a never-ending list of concepts for the show. I explained my history with TV and what I had accomplished and then gave them the rundown of what was happening in Beverly Hills. The meeting finished with a round of stories explaining what occurred in the salon. Not only were they highly entertaining, but they also explained how the show could reveal the truth about life in a high paced salon. These things weren't prepared, they just happen.

The network president really liked Sean. He was interesting to say the least. Sean always gave the unexpected. The way that he looked on the outside, was not the way that he sounded. He had a very deep voice and it had the ability to capture anyone he was speaking to.

Overall, we felt good about the meeting. There was indeed the presence of a synergy that couldn't be denied. About forty-eight hours later, I got a call that the execs had given us the green light to create a sizzle reel. A sizzle reel is the ultimate sneak peek at what a show's concept will look like. It helps the powers that be understand the direction of the show.

The green light to create the sizzle reel was only half the battle. I knew that the reel had to be one that possessed shock value and displayed the intricacies of the stories and the characters in the salon. I was not afraid to go the distance to push the envelope and to create something that the world had not yet seen. I am still amazed at how we have the ability to draw upon skill sets utilized during previous moments of our lives to propel us forward. I possessed no formal training in the TV production sector, but I had gumption and an uncanny level of determination.

I utilized stylists from the salon, who I believed could bring the heat on the small screen. Energy matches energy and The Elgin Charles Salon was filled with vibrant stylists. One in particular, named Lolita, evolved into one of the main characters. I also decided to feature two assistants, one of whom was Tifphanie Griffith, my head assistant and a native of Pasadena, CA. The other was a gentleman by name of Nakia, who was about Sean's age. He lived in Chicago and would travel back and forth to the salon.

Having the right cast is a huge part of the proper execution of the process and soliciting the right production team is the other. We sat down with a few directors to find the right fit. Once that detail was finalized, we began to plan the intricacies of the show and how they would play out on camera. The creative process led us to establish that the show would dictate an "east side vs. west side" scenario. My side of the salon represented one set of stylists and the other represented a second group of stylists. When the cameras began rolling, the magic unfolded. There was a cohesiveness that we could not have planned. We were depicting all of the things that happened on a normal day in the salon. The beauty of it all was that with the backdrop as Los Angeles, there were no normal days. We were talking shit and doing makeovers. Sean and Lolita were going at it and arguing on a continuous basis. There was more drama than the average viewer could stand. Lolita was hysterical. They were truly best friends and the on-camera chemistry was a riot. Although Sean had brought Katrina to the meeting, over time Lolita stole the show.

I remember pulling Lolita to the side to express words of encouragement. "When you are a star, ain't nothing you can do but shine.

If you let loose and really show the world who you are, there is a possibility that I can get you on the show."

It felt like Sean was trying to block that from happening because it was possible that Lolita was fickle like that. He wanted nothing more than to be the star. Katrina got lost in the show. She was eye candy but did manage to come through in the clutch for some highlights on camera. Discussions of Barack and Michelle Obama, Beyoncé, Oprah, and anyone else that had a name worthy of salon talk made the cut.

My role was to just be Elgin Charles, the ultra-fabulous hair stylist and entrepreneur. I was the star of the show. When I walked into a room, everything stopped. That was what I commanded, whether the cameras were rolling or not.

After we collected all of the footage from the episodes that had been strategically planned out, we went into editing for the sizzle reel. The finished product blew my mind. It was more than what I had dreamed of. There was no way the network could turn us down. I knew without question that we would get the green light to move forward with taping episodes.

The network execs called us and told us that we had the green light for a total of ten episodes. It was a dream materialized. I understood at that moment, the favor of God. This was a dream of mine coming to reality. Once word was out that Elgin Charles had a show on VH1, all of the local celebrities, and all the people in high positions, came out of the woodwork to support me. I even began receiving calls from people that I had known back in San Antonio. I'll never forget the tone of the voice messages that I received and the outpouring of love and encouragement.

An old friend, by the name of Shirley Hazlip called and said, "I hear you got a show. I knew you were going to be something."

I was so happy to hear her sentiments of support. She continued, "Just cause you got the show, don't you start changing and acting like you are better than everybody." Shirley had written a book about her mother, who'd had eight children, five of which resembled and passed for white, while the other three were black. Over time, the world wondered who had lived the better life and they found out that the children who resembled and identified as black had experienced more fruitful times. Her words stayed with me.

I came to realize that there was an assumption that my true nature would change amidst fame and that disheartened me. I knew that Shirley meant me well and wanted to protect me from what she had experienced, but I needed to remain hopeful that people still saw me as they always had. I was just Charlie from San Antonio with Elgin Charles sized dreams.

Sadly, I would learn that Shirley's words held weight in more ways than one. I learned that your greatest levels of support don't always come from where you expect them. To my surprise, I sensed the presence of resentment in my ex-wife. I knew that she was happy for me, but I couldn't help but feel that there was some other sentiment waiting in the wings. I felt like the element of shade was lurking. My thought was that if one of us received an opportunity, it meant that it was a win for both of us. Hollywood is strange in that even those closest to you, are not always the advocates that you would assume them to be. If you are to succeed, you have to push past anything that mirrors doubt or a lack of support. There is no alternative to forward progression.

At the time, reality TV was not garnering the same levels of respect that true sitcoms were, but we were on to something amazing. The concept of scripted reality was gaining momentum, but it hadn't quite arrived. There was an aura of negativity that concluded that real actors didn't want to be a part of it. Jackée had even turned down many opportunities to enter into the new realm of storytelling. For many, being on the cusp of greatness is unchartered territory. I knew then that I was making history and that my efforts would result in a powerful act that would open doors for others to eventually walk through. I was willing to do whatever needed to be done to write my own history, my own way.

R-E-A-L-I-T-Y or Real Tea?

I was happy and anxious for what was coming. Landing my own television show was quite possibly the one thing that I had hoped for in the distance. I'm not sure that I ever believed that it would happen, but there I was, watching it all unfold. I felt such a sense of accomplishment. I sat back and thought of how there had not been one thing that I set out to do that God had not granted me the endurance to achieve. Not one. The fact that I had become a leader and a game changer in an industry that I had come to love with my whole heart was deep. I had waited for this moment my entire life. For the first time, I felt joy deep down on the inside. I had my family intact, and the career of my dreams. How many people can actually say that? I'd venture to say very few. God had granted me the desires of my heart and there was no turning back. The show and the production were coming along strong. We just needed to get ten episodes finished in two weeks

I was insightful enough to recognize in the developmental stages of the show that its purpose was to entertain. I had so many agendas that I desired to push, but to garner the support of viewers, we needed to entertain first. I wanted to get into the character and make things happen on screen with an energy that was infectious.

To get what you are chasing, you have to also be willing to give up a great deal. For me that meant sacrificing the time that I spent alone perfecting formulas and new techniques. The cameras were with me at all times to capture the moments that could not be repeated. I have always been a master of ceremonies of sorts, and I was determined to orchestrate things in the salon that I knew would keep people glued to their televisions. I knew how to spark interest through what was happening with various stylists and even the clientele. There is really never a dull moment in a salon environment and that meant no shortage of content or material.

No matter how much you plan and script, there will always be personalities that shine more on camera than others. I believe that to be the beauty of reality TV. There are unexpected surprises that you can't quite plan. Lolita had done such a phenomenal job on the sizzle reel, that they asked her to be on the show. I enlisted the assistance of an entertainment attorney, by the name of Gary Cohen, to help me in negotiating the contracts for the stylists, who I had selected to be regular personalities on the show. We were booked for a total of ten episodes, which meant that we would need to film a minimum of one episode per week.

The downside to the aggressive schedule was that we needed to shut down the salon during filming. Financially, this would cause me to have to restructure my clients and my business. This was not the ideal climate for my finances, but I had received so much positive feedback about how the increased exposure would positively impact sales and business that I was willing to take the risk. I had transitioned from Elgin Charles, stylist to the stars, to the showrunner in many ways. The showrunner is the one who makes it all happen. There are no real limits on what the showrunner does. One day, you could be producing a segment and the next you could be getting water for a customer who is parched. This was not far-fetched for me because I have always operated under the concept of "by any means necessary." I knew that God had not brought me this far, for me to not do everything within my power to ensure the success of the show. Thankfully, my cousin Marsha, aka Buggy, spent several weeks with me during filming and provided some much needed ancillary support.

I felt in many ways that my brand was on the line, and under no circumstances would I allow it to do anything except prosper. The balance of trying to keep the business afloat and ensure that the show had the attention that it so desperately needed, ran me absolutely ragged. Somehow, someway, I managed to get it done.

After the episodes were completely filmed, we had to begin preparations for the viewing party. Even though people knew that the show was coming, there was a distinct difference between the way that we were treated when the show was just a thought and when the show was actually on air. As we were preparing for the premier, I knew that more needed to be done to adequately prepare for the volume that we would now receive from product orders and increased clientele. I didn't feel that we had adequately thought through the management of inventory, shipping procedures, and customer service. I had so many people around me, but I still felt extremely overwhelmed with the immense responsibility. I needed help and the presence of someone who could track my accounting more strategically on every level. My first thought was to discuss this with the network, as I had been advised that whatever I needed, they would support me.

There was a bit of discussion amongst members of my team who believed that I should not mention my product line to the network because they would try to cut themselves in on the deal. In many instances, when you have a show, you no longer belong to yourself nor does the brand that you created. The average person would be surprised at the amount of creative control that you lose when you are an entity of a network. I always believed that being forthcoming was the best way to do business. I liked to lay everything on the table and I wanted for everyone to be clear. Against my better judgement, I kept quiet about my product line and allowed the show to air accordingly. When the show hit the airwaves, it was just as I had imagined, pandemonium. The age of social media was upon us and Facebook was gaining momentum. This meant that news of the show traveled at lightning speed. My face was now a household name to people that I might not have otherwise encountered. Requests for interviews were coming left and right. As much as I had always wanted to be a star, I learned by experience that being one was not easy. The demands on your personal life, your resources, your family, and everything else that you can think of, drives and you become a passenger in your own journey of life.

I had so many professionals advising me in so many different directions that at times, it was hard to see the forest from the trees. Jason offered me a management deal. Alex had his own commentary that governed what he believed would be best for me. Christopher was advising me to look more closely at the terms that were being presented. It seemed that outside of the show, the bulk of the interest was in solidifying a licensing deal for my product line. Anyone with an ounce of intuition could see how successful that venture would be as soon as the show premiered. There was also a large-scale agency who had connected with Jason and it seemed that they wanted more creative control over my brand. Alex was in the background with a resounding message, proclaiming, "You can't let them control you." It became apparent to me how so many celebrities had fallen victim to ill-advised guidance because it could become plentiful if you dared to step into the spotlight. There was much to learn and I was well aware of the fact that I did not have all of the answers.

By the time, the show was released, life was a whirlwind. My goal became to not get swept away by the storm of it all. I went from being recognizable in Beverly Hills to being recognizable from city to city. Fame was unfolding in ways that I had not previously been exposed to. An appearance on the *Wendy Williams Show* would prove to be one of many baptisms by fire. I had been slated to do a segment, inclusive of a hair demo. I was advised to not talk about the Elgin Charles product line while styling the model's hair. I wanted to trust those closest to me and to believe that everyone had my best interest in mind. While on the show, in front of a live audience, Wendy asked "Do you have any lovers?" What my love interests had to do with hair was beyond me, but it was Wendy so I was willing to play along. "Well, I've had many lovers," I responded with a smirk. I kept twirling the model's hair until I achieved the desired look to show off to the audience. What I knew was hair and how to finesse a conversation. As much as Wendy was Wendy, I was Elgin and I did not come to play. I enjoyed being in front of the audience and showing my talents. It reminded me in many ways of the hair shows that I had taken the stage for in the past.

As they say, hindsight is 20/20. After careful reflection, I recognized that not mentioning my own product line in front of that many viewers was a foolish mistake. The lights of Hollywood bring all things full circle if you watch closely enough. Not only would I have to learn to continue to trust my instincts, but also to prepare myself for private secrets to become public.

What I did know was what I had managed to single handedly build my brand from the ground up. With the grace of God and a few investors, the solid ground that I stood upon was one that I had toiled to create. It was that train of thought that led me to remain one hundred percent in control of my brand. I made a tough, yet strategic, decision to not split my business with anyone. I have never regretted that decision and I advise entrepreneurs to understand the nuances and guiding factors before even considering giving away a part of what has taken blood, sweat, and tears to construct. Jason was not pleased with my decision to reject the deal that had been proposed.

Over time, I felt like I was becoming a target in many ways. Even the original company who had designed my website, schemed to assume control of my domain name. They wanted for their company to maintain control over everything regarding the brand digitally. I had never signed anything giving them rights to do so. There were tons of sales coming in for products. The game of supply and demand was a fun one to play. The brand was growing, and maintaining autonomy was challenging. Christopher stepped in and put a permanent banner on a new website that directed our clients to the correct site to make purchases, which saved the entire operation.

Even though I now had a nationally recognized television show and had been established as the go-to professional and guru in the hair and beauty industry, the spirit of animosity was looming. The characters, whom I had created to be featured on the show, began to take on life sized personalities of their own. Everyone believed themselves to be stars. For the life of me, I couldn't understand why everyone on reality TV believed that life would unfold for them the way that it had for NeNe Leakes. Let's be clear, she changed the game when it came to converting stardom from one level to another, but there can be only one.

It is imperative that we all find a way to carve out success along a path that we have created. I was Elgin Charles and my name held weight because of the work that I had done. No one had given me anything. I had fought tooth and nail to get to where I was. I grew weary of the larger than life attitudes of people who had done very little in the industries they were attempting to become known for. It was foolishness and I wanted no part of it. My only goals with the show had been to increase the platform from which I stood, to let the world know about Elgin Charles, and to create opportunities for others. Period.

I was anti anything that came to steal or destroy my peace. I had too much going on otherwise and needed someone who was willing to protect my peace at all costs.

The undercurrent of tension that I now recognized to be constant, was also something that had played out on the show. On a Monday, I would suffer the blow of another loss. While lying in bed, attempting to overcome the unsettling feeling I had from lack of rest, the phone rang. It was an executive from the network. After realizing who it was, I sat up in the bed, leaning against the headboard.

"Hey Elgin, how are you?"

"I'm very well. How are you?"

Without answering the question, he cut directly to the chase. "We just wanted to call and bring you up to date on the show. We want you to know that we are in it with you for the long haul. The show has garnered some major success. Unfortunately, we are not going to pick it up for the next season. Let's keep in touch and see what happens. Ok?"

With the remnants of slumber in my eyes and the breath stolen from my body, I could hardly comprehend what was being said. I sat up to keep myself from choking. It was taking me a while to digest his words.

"Are you still there, Elgin?"

I was in a state of utter shock and disbelief. Had I heard what I actually thought I heard? Was I just experiencing a nightmare? His words slapped me back into consciousness. "Oh... Ok... Alright... Thanks so much for calling."

I held the phone in my hand and allowed my arm to slide to the side of the bed. I fell back into the pillows and the phone slipped to the floor. There was no one on the other end and in that moment, I was left without answers for my broken heart and my bruised ego. I had realized the highest level of success, but I was forced to acknowledge that I had egg on my face. It felt like I was falling from grace with no parachute.

I'd gone to bed the night before with fireworks exploding in the park of my life, but I'd woken to the presence of dreary rain. How would I face everyone? Who would I tell? What would I do about all of the business ventures that I had placed on ice for the show? How would I explain any of it? None of it made sense, not even to me.

There was so much that I still wanted to say to the world. There was so much that had been promised to me. I felt robbed of my one shot to tell the world my story. I had been advised by my production team that the pilot season was simply to introduce me and to show the vibrancy of my personality. I'd been so vested in the second season. I had dreamed that it would depict my life in its entirety and show the business acumen that I possess. I wanted the world to see me as a father. For the first time in my life, I believed that I could give all of myself, and all that I had worked for would be elevated. I'd been robbed in broad daylight. None of the promises were upheld.

I sat and watched as over fifty crew members worked daily to create a storyline that yielded very little results from the story that I wanted to tell. That show and those people were employed on my back, my work, and my legacy. I had even rented space upstairs, above the salon, to have as a place for the producers to rest as the show was filmed. I had ushered in an opportunity to maintain the attention of 3.5 million people and I was stripped of the chance to say all that I had wanted to say to them.

In a single moment, the momentum of my entire life had changed. It was hard to swallow all the sacrificing I had done for the unfulfilled promise of the renewal of the show. I had made the ultimate sacrifice. I had taken time away from my son, myself, and lost out on tons of money. I had done everything that they told me to do. When they told me to jump, I responded, "How high?" At the time, I'd seen it all as a worthy sacrifice. A way to create something bigger than myself and to make history. Faith in the possibility that the show would get picked back up, allowed me to put one foot on the floor. My mind allowed me to believe in the hope that was embedded in my veins. The prospect of a return, a renewal, an invitation to create something even bigger than what we had originally conceived, allowed me to dream.

After four years, I came to terms with the deafening truth that *Beverly Hills Fabulous* was no longer my reality. As they say, every good and perfect thing must come to an end.

CHAPTER 14

OMEGA

"And one day in your life, you will stumble upon a day that determines who you are."

—Elgin Charles

BEING THE FIRST TO DO anything always comes with a hefty price tag. I had broken boundaries and defied the odds in so many ways, but I felt as though I was staring at a glass ceiling and I wanted nothing more than for it to be shattered.

I had been the first African American proprietor of a salon in Beverly Hills, and the first to step into the limelight on a reality show of the genre that we created. There were no other shows featuring stylists in a scripted reality setting, prior to *Beverly Hills Fabulous.* After the show ended, many other shows began to grow in popularity. Shows like *LA Hair,* and *Jerseylicious,* among others, highlighted what some now refer to as superstar stylists.

Even so, while at the climax of all that I had realized, I felt as though life was pounding me with a series of obstacles, one after another. At the time, I couldn't conclude a reason why or what I had done to deserve such torment. I have learned over the years, that life doesn't always owe you an explanation. There is not always a "why" that will make sense. Sometimes, the plans that God crafts for us are simply about going through the fire and coming out on the other side, having lived to tell the story that someone else might find the blessing in. In those moments, this was my truth.

Moving forward after the demise of the show that I had placed so much stock in, hurt like hell. By 2012, the show had been absent from the network for almost a year. I was no stranger to pain and I knew that I had to find a way, against all odds, to create another opportunity for myself. One fact that always remained true was my ability to bounce back. No matter how hard the blow, I have always found a way to sustain.

The success from the exposure that you gain from being on TV can't be duplicated. We had grown in popularity and posted record numbers with the product line that I had launched. And while many need the success of a show to catapult their business endeavors, the widespread awareness, or dare I say fame, is what manifested for me. The lights had always called my name and I wanted them to shine as brightly as possible on me as well as my staff. It was important that our hard work reached the heights that we had experienced. After being introduced to the process of pitching a show and executing a successful run, I felt that I had what it took to do it again. I allowed myself the opportunity to dream of concepts and dig deep into my cache of stories to devise a new pitch that would not only empower me but also Jackée and DeVanique. Jackée's gigs were not a plentiful as they had once been and DeVanique was in need of open doors to walk through for his future success. I truly felt that creating a new show would be a way to revive, restore, and reintroduce us all. No matter the status of our relationship, I continued to recognize my role as the leader of our family whose job it was to ensure that we all had a way to thrive.

━━◆ON MY OWN◆━━

WE HAD ALL REACHED a crossroads. I was coming down from the high of my show and Jackée had not embarked upon any new roles since *Sister, Sister,* featuring Tia and Tamera Mowry. We now shared Christopher as our manager and he was tasked with negotiating deals on our behalf, as well as discovering new and innovative ventures from which our careers could flourish. We began strategizing a way to incite a resurrection for all of our careers.

We explored in great depth a concept of two exes who lived under one roof to provide guidance, and a consistent base from which to nurture their son. Christopher and I began discussing a plan of action to pitch our concept to the OWN Network, established and created by Media Mogul, Oprah Winfrey.

We presented the concept to Jackée and she loved it. Although we were no longer married, we were playing for the same team in respect to wanting the bests for each other as well as our son.

In later years, Christopher confided in me that that concept was the first time he'd believed that he could bring us together on a project that would be fruitful for all. We also presented the idea to Jackée's agent, who had been in the business for over forty years and maintained an extensive knowledge of what the industry was in need of. He was all in. We knew that we were on the heels of innovation yet again.

We received the green light to create a sizzle reel with Authentic, a production company who had taken off with *Honey Boo Boo.* They loved the concept and wanted to begin immediately with production, to create visuals that would allow the network to determine how many shows they wished to order.

Upon learning the news, I took Jackée and DeVanique out to dinner. I wanted to surprise them. I was so proud of myself, and my mood had been lifted from the haze of clouds that had dampened my spirits with the cancellation of the previous show. I knew now that I had the ability to do anything that I set my mind to, regardless of the obstacles set before me.

Just as we were finishing our meals and prior to reviewing the dessert menu, I removed the production agreement from the inside pocket of my sports coat and set it on the table in front of Jackée. My smile was so wide that it hurt my face. I wanted to be her knight in shining armor and prove that I was still the backbone of the family, regardless of how nontraditional we were. I was astounded by the look on her face. I could confirm a multitude of emotions, but neither happiness nor excitement were present. In fact, I would venture to say that she was angry with both Christopher and myself for championing the deal. I could not have been more distraught, but truthfully, I figured that she would come around. It was no secret that our return to TV would have lasting effects on our careers, hopefully for the better. DeVanique began begging her to do the show. He had even agreed to make appearances in order to earn money for himself. He had begun a boxing career and knew that the show would be a way for him to fund his venture independently, without relying on either of us. I prayed and I knew that God would bring us full circle together like He always did.

The ball continued to roll and the discussions regarding the money for each of us began. As soon as the funds were transferred into an escrow account to initiate the process of filming, things took an unexpected turn.

With the help of Christopher, I had managed to solidify a deal that I thought could take us all to another level financially. Unfortunately, we began to feel the absence of Jackée. It was almost as if she didn't know what was going on. Her agent acted as if the show was all a hoax, even after I had shown him the papers proving it was solid. The most traumatic part of it all was that we never even made it to the point of working on episodic salaries.

All of it had me wondering what in the hell had just happened. I think that I would have understood and respected it more if she had simply told me that she wasn't interested. To be deceived and completely blindsided was disconcerting and exhausting. After it was all said and done, it drove an undeniable wedge between Jackée and Christopher and they resolved to no longer work together, relinquishing all ties.

I was devastated and I felt a sense of betrayal in my heart. It hurt me to know that we could not come together and work toward a common goal after all that we had shared. I was also distressed financially because I had purchased the home in Sherman Oaks for the show. I was counting on the money from the contract to make my investment back. That did not happen. I was now left to foot the bill that would round out to be in excess of $10,000 per month, inclusive of maintenance and upkeep. The lesson that I learned from it all was to never count your dollars before the deal is signed. That knowledge has carried me so much farther in my career and business dealings. Despite it all, I would not allow my heart to be hardened by the actions of anyone. No one would have the ability to change what was in my heart. My intentions had been good, but from that day forward, I recognized that if I ever took a loss, it was simply a test.

——CHESTNUTS ROASTING——

BY 2013, I BEGAN TO accept the fact that the likelihood of my appearing on the small screen would be no longer. It was a hard pill to swallow, but I knew deep in my heart that God had not stopped listening to my prayers. He had by no means left me. The truth is that spiritual warfare is real and anyone that tries to deny its existence is living a lie.

Time waits for no man. I was determined to look in one direction, forward. Whether the show came to fruition or not, I was still waking up in my 7,000 square foot home in the gated community of Sherman Oaks, surrounded by celebrities like James Earl Jones and Glodean White. I was still blessed.

Everything in my home was white. The house itself, the custom hue that draped the walls, the cobblestone leading up the driveway towards the house, it was all white. And what does a man, who has learned from the ups and downs of life do? He looks around his big ass house and decides to throw a muthafucking party! I planned so profusely with Christopher that both of our heads were spinning.

Christopher invited the executives from Discovery, which was the company that owned the Own Network. In addition to heavy hitters from a production standpoint, special invitations were also delivered to much of Hollywood's royalty.

On the day of the party, even I was blown away by the opulence, and I had been privy to the plans. When guests entered the house, they were greeted by waiters and waitresses offering champagne and passed hor d'oeuvres of canapes, petit fours and pâté. There was a coat check and an abundance of staff, ready, willing, and able to enhance the experience for all of the guests. The grand foyer, revealed a huge beveled mirror and an honest glance up led guests to view the massive self-portrait, housed on the lower mezzanine. We made sure that the entire house was draped in Christmas décor. The food and presentation were like nothing I had ever seen. Guests were invited to feast upon traditional Christmas dinner selections. We had everything: Cornish hens, honey ham, turkeys, green bean casseroles, and even a chocolate fountain.

The home was illuminated by ambient lighting, and there were various music selections piped throughout different rooms in the house. Christopher's plan was to create zones so that people could socialize with ease.

I'll never forget what the beautiful actress Vanessa Bell Calloway said, "Well, damn, I need to be doing some parties over here." I couldn't have been more flattered.

The party was the first chance for some of our mutual friends to see that I was fully capable of standing on my own two feet. This was my house and I was not in anyone's shadow.

Closing out the year, Christopher began to strategize ways for me to use the estate as an investment, which had been its original intent. Thinking outside of the box was his expertise. We found ourselves with an offer to be featured on an episode of a show called *New Money*. The premise of the show was to peer into the lives of those who were self-made. I was elated to learn that my show would premiere after the finale of *Keeping Up with the Kardashians*. The viewership was high and the appearance continued to tell the world my story.

Around that same time, I had been contemplating the idea of throwing a bash for DeVanique's twenty-first birthday. Since we had previously discussed him being on the show, which had fallen through, I felt that having the party during the filming of *New Money* was the perfect opportunity to make up for previous disappointments. I also knew that DeVanique deserved to have his mother be part of such a momentous occasion. In unison, as a family, we threw our son a party that he would never forget.

We spared no expense, and it was all captured exclusively for the show. There were ice sculptures of DeVanique, Jackée , and myself at the entrance. The guests were brought in on a party bus and Jackée even purchased a very elegant dress for DeVanique's girlfriend to wear. Everyone was dressed to the nines. I wore a Tom Ford suit paired with Versace shoes. DeVanique wore Giuseppe Zanotti shoes and an Armani suit. The gifts given during the party were the most elaborate. Among them was a Rolex watch, a diamond crucifix necklace, and a Mercedes Sprinter, which was purchased by myself.

And as much as we had planned this moment in time for DeVanique, he didn't know half of the people there because it really turned out to be another big soiree for the adults. We had a custom dance floor juxtaposed to the house and tables arranged in the garden. I'll never forget the smile on his face as his family and so many others wishing him well. Fifty thousand dollars later, all I could say was, "Oh, what a night!" I was thankful that I could give DeVanique the party of a lifetime. He deserved the very best of what I had.

━◄JOY COMETH IN THE MORNING►━

ALTHOUGH IT SOUNDS cliché, as I ushered in a New Year, I also ushered in a new me. The theme of my life fully embraced the notion that every promise made, doesn't work out that way. I recognized that no matter what had transpired, I was still a massive success in all that I had touched. God had allowed me to witness miracles unfold right in front of my very eyes.

Perception is a peculiar thing. The salon was booming and the exchange of money was flowing like a waterfall, but invisible to the naked eye were the tremendous expenses associated with overseeing a business of that caliber. No one would ever understand the tremendous burden that was placed on me to maintain such a venture. I had stylists, administrative staff, accountants, lawyers, sales reps, manufacturers, consultants, and even the stray sales people who frequented the salon, selling their latest products, on my payroll.

If there was one thing that my daddy taught me, it was that a man should have his own money. I've always felt the need to have enough money to not only cover my expenses, but also to ensure that those close to me do not fail or fall financially. I can't recall a time in my life that I didn't have to assist someone else monetarily. In this space, considering all that I was responsible for, I had to ask myself, who had I been doing this all for? Had I dreamt of this life for myself or had I been trying to create something larger than myself for others to enjoy? I can say with certainty, that I just wanted to help somebody along the way. I wanted to be the difference, the reason that someone chose to never give up. I am driven by seeing others happy. It warms my heart to know that I can create an opportunity or a source of income or serve as a resource to others. In doing so, I was forced to step back from it all to examine my motives and all of the happenings that unfolded with the people that I had allowed into my life.

Only a fool would not take the opportunity to recognize the trends in life. For each of us, there lies an undercurrent that runs deep and consistently. In a moment of complete transparency, I might venture to say that throughout my life, I've chosen people who I felt that I could help. In turn, that has meant that my needs have taken a backseat to theirs. Gullible, maybe. What I do know is that if you don't put yourself first, you can't teach anyone else to do so.

I knew then, like I know now that I won't change. I refused to allow the actions of others to harden my heart in any way. I've just made up my mind to be wiser and to live for the essence of making myself happy. For the first time in my life, I made the decision to climb the mountains that I chose to climb. I was determined to live with my mask off.

Sometimes we are so caught up that we forget to breathe. We forget to keep the person in the mirror alive. Today, right now, this very moment, I can assure you that I'm doing me.

I resolve to date who I want to date. I resolve to fall in love with who I want to fall in love with. I resolve to be my own judge and my own jury. I will not allow society, my family, or even my own insecurities stand in the way of what makes me happy. If I find a man that delights me, I will date him. If I find another woman worthy of my heart—which I doubt—then I will date her. I will never stop believing in the power of love. I love being in love and today, I know the type of love that I am worthy of. I won't stop until I get exactly that.

I'm done apologizing for how others may feel when I put myself first. I'm done apologizing for who the world thought I was. I'm done apologizing for what hasn't worked in other people's lives. I'm done apologizing for not solving everyone else's problems. I'm done apologizing for walking in truth. I'm done apologizing for everything and to everyone.

Today, I understand the woes that we face at the hands of societal imposed scrutiny for one reason or another. Yet, I still believe that what the world needs is more love. I still believe that society wants to love. I still believe that humanity wants to love. It brings me great joy to acknowledge that in this day and age, there is an openness that the world is embracing, allowing us to discuss the realities of our sexuality, and to remove the stigma. Today, my truth is indicative of me living my best life, in spite of it all.

I will not dim my light. I refuse to wait in the wings for anyone to give me an opportunity. I resolve to create my own lane as I have always done. I have blazed the trails from which others can follow. And because I am fueled by divine purpose and love, I believe with everything inside of me that my best years are yet to come.

——◆FOOTPRINTS◆——

THE MEMORIES. It's all just memories. The only thing that will outlive us are the memories that we manage to create in those left behind. One of my fondest is my father's last years. He was adamant about coming to visit me in LA. When he arrived, I surprised him with tickets to a football game. DeVanique and I loaded up the car, and Daddy sat in the passenger's seat, with a smile that couldn't be erased. He was filled with such pride and joy from witnessing what I had accomplished with all of his years of teaching, coaching, and guidance. Those moments in the car with the two men that had impacted my life the most were monumental for me.

When we arrived, we were met with extreme crowds. I had never stopped to consider how far away we would have to park. After finally discovering a parking space, we hopped out with excitement and prepared to take our trek. Along the way, DeVanique and I began to notice that Daddy was slowing down.

"You got it, Daddy?'

"Yes, Cha Cha. I'm just a little slower than I used to be, that's all."

As we continued walking, I noticed that his hesitant walk had transitioned into a hard stop. I recognized that he would require assistance. I took two steps to the right and motioned for him to put his arm around my shoulders. I encouraged him to bear all of his weight down on me. I practically carried him the rest of the way. There were moments that I thought I wouldn't make it, but the glimmer in his eyes reminded me of the times that he had cared for us as children, with no help. The thoughts of his sacrifice ran through my mind with each step. He had taken so many steps to ensure my well-being. Fatigue and discomfort be damned; it was my honor to carry him. By the time we made it to the stadium entrance, I was dripping with sweat, but it meant so much to me. I had now carried the same person who had carried me, my entire life. The look on his face as he sat in the stands was priceless. Together, we were witnessing the glory of his work. It was then that I knew that I had made him proud.

On October 1, 2015, the greatest man that I have ever known took the most precious breaths ever. They would prove to be his last. His service was immaculate. Blondie laid Daddy to rest in the most regal way possible. From the twenty-one-gun salute, to the intricacies of the service, Daddy proved to me, yet again, what a life well lived looked like. With pride, dignity, and valor, I aspire to become all that he was. If I can look back over my life and know that I honored Daddy, I will also know that I have honored the wishes of my Heavenly Father.

"Whereas ye know not what *shall be* on the morrow. For what *is* your life? It is even a vapour, that appeareth for a little time, and then vanisheth away." James 4:14 (King James Version)

BY THE WAY

An Open Letter to Hollywood

MY DARLING HOLLYWOOD. I'd be remiss if I didn't begin with a simple, yet profound, fuck you. I'm afraid that there is a thin line between love and hate. My relationship with you has been an intricately designed roller coaster, filled with ups and downs and twists and turns that have introduced me to both love and heartbreak. For as long as I can remember, you've called my name and sparked my interest. You wooed me with your abundance and you've held me captive under your spell. Your flashing lights are addictive. I moved to be near you and to feel your presence in my life on a daily basis.

The largest stage in all the world, rests, rules, and abides in your bosom. I've been around the world and I have never managed to experience a love quite like what I've experienced in your arms. Your influence shot me with an arrow from cupid's bow and I've been smitten at the mere thought of you ever since. I've longed to dance on your largest stages and to be welcomed by your adoring fans. On many occasions, I've held the desire within my heart to simply be recognized by you. I wanted so desperately for you to call my name in the distance. I wanted for you to reach for me, as I extended my hand out towards you. At times, I've felt your fire of rejection. Nothing could stop me from wanting to be with you. And as much as I've loved you, the pain that you've caused, has helped me to discover all of your faults. Not one of us is perfect, but I realize more than ever that our imperfections speak the most profoundly about who we are and what we become.

Anyone, who has had just a taste of your love, can attest to the sweetness of your nectar. Being with you is to be caught up in the rapture of love. You are the ultimate high. But everything that goes up must come down, even in love.

In your euphoria, all people are not treated equally. There is an unspoken pecking order that looms in the darkness. Those not wise enough to prepare for what may be, will become rapidly victimized. You have this way of pretending to care that is rather convincing. Those whom you come into contact with don't often realize until it's too late that they are nothing more than a product. You've created a culture where people no longer engage in meaningful exchanges, and the coveted become commodities and casualties of the fickle preferences of a superficial world.

In your presence, you've allowed the next best thing to overshadow the tremendous value in building a legacy and merit that withstands the test of time. With you, nothing lasts forever. Those who have experienced you have gained power amidst the notion that to be vicious is better than being victorious.

And when I thought all hope was lost from having allowed your pretentious love to slip out of my hands, I realized that I held the key to the most important lesson that you ever taught me: let my light so shine. So many times, in life, we encounter people, places, and things that make us believe that dimming out light is a better way to survive. In spite of it all, I can proudly proclaim that my destiny does not, and has never, rested in your hands. It brings me the greatest joy to know with certainty that I've gleaned some of the best lessons of my life in moments of uncertainty in you. I learned to discover all that I needed within.

I stand in the fullness of self-actualization knowing that whether you are for me or against me, I will make it. My story will be told and my truths will be realized. Whether I am tasked with creating my own stages and garnering my own audience, what God has for me is for me.

I thought that I needed you on my arm to command attention from the world—I didn't. I only needed to recognize who I was. Letting go of your hand allowed me to see myself fully. I am Elgin Charles, and with or without you, I am a star. I've earned the right to be treated accordingly. Much like an abusive mate, you've tried to box me in and shut me out. You attempted to isolate me from so many, but your attempts failed. I'm kicking ass and taking names. I'm here to give the people what they want. I'm on my Cardi B. I'm so inspired as I bask in the glorious truth that I never really needed you. No one actually does. You're just a mirage in the desert. As I prepare to impart all I've learned into the hearts of future generations, I do so in the power of a single sentiment: Power lies not in who celebrates you, but how you celebrate yourself. It is with this sentiment that I will teach the world how to recognize their value and worth, and that it does not rest in what others think of you.

In case you've forgotten, my name is Elgin Charles. The next time you see me, be sure to put some respect on my name.

EPILOGUE

MASK OFF

I STOOD, WITH MY HEAD held high and my hands resting on my hips in awe. Glancing out over the salon, revealed so much that I had never taken the time to process. I was drawn to a phrase: Bound. Broken and Wrapped in Chains. Those three phrases once described the bondage that I had subjected myself to for many years. No longer.

If anyone had told me that the only way that I would ever discover freedom in its truest form was to pack up everything that I had worked for and dreamt about, rearrange it and start anew, I would never have believed it. If left up to me, I would have remained forever enslaved.

Every box in the salon represented a beautiful memory. And while they were all filled with elements that represented various eras of my life, they also served as proof that I wasn't free. Freedom is a phenom. For the first time in forever, I attempted to discover it for myself. Packing the boxes represented my having broken the shackles, and doing so, brought me to my knees. I had been crippled by the weight of the expectations of the world, not realizing that I also had the tools to construct the ultimate base of support.

Wisdom has taught me that the loom of tragedy in inevitable. Every face bears a story that the world knows nothing about. The calamity in my journey was that I held the keys to free myself all along, but I had remained in chains. For some reason, imprisonment felt better. I felt comfort in knowing that I was needed, and that I could make a difference in the lives of others, even if it was at my own expense.

——THE PROCLAMATION——

IN EVERY PERSON'S LIFE, there is an undeniable pattern of threads woven together like a tapestry. With wisdom, we begin to recognize the most prevalent designs and allow them to shape our lives in ways that we could never have fathomed. With acquired wisdom, we learn to shift our sails to gain momentum from the undercurrent that runs deep and consistently in accordance with the work of our souls. Amidst this friction, we can discover the very essence of who we are. Our intrinsic motivations and the drive that we might not otherwise be willing to admit, thrive in this space.

On that day, as I set each box near the door, I proclaimed to let freedom ring. The boxes represented my past and I was preparing to usher in a new era that would prove to be filled with the abundance that God had prepared for me.

——THE NEW ERA OF ELGIN CHARLES——

MANY ARE CALLED, but few are chosen. When I depart this journey, I want my work to speak for itself. It is my greatest hope that I will never cease to create pieces of my legacy for the world to enjoy and that they will never be forgotten.

THE EMPEROR OF HAIR

—The EDUCATOR—

PLANS FOR THE ELGIN CHARLES School of Beauty and Design have been officially placed into motion.

—The CEO—

Elgin Charles Hair Care Product Line

WITH A VIBRANT NEW campaign and my tried and true formulas, you need this in your life. Available at:

WWW.ELGINCHARLES.COM

Elgin Charles Custom Wigs Salon

THIS INNOVATIVE NEW boutique salon will welcome clients, who wish to purchase the most luxurious pieces in an upscale setting. Offering private appointments for those who seek a taste of Hollywood, you will get your wig snatched, literally.

Men's Grooming Line

THE ELGIN CHARLES GROOMING Line will feature custom formulas designed for men, who desire to be well coiffed and well groomed.

EC Lifestyle Apparel

IN COMPILATION WITH this book, my new line of lifestyle apparel, which bears a crown, was created to remind us that we are all regal and that greatness is within us. Get yours at www. elgincharles.com.

—The ARTIST—

Writing

THIS BOOK IS ONE OF MANY. Trust me when I say that there is a lot more where this came from. I have already begun penning the next literary work.

Acting

HOW CAN SOMEONE with so many sides, not have been bitten by the thespian bug? From theatrical productions, to more small screen appearances, I am gearing up for a new season. All that I can say is, "Stay tuned and watch what happens next!"

Reality TV

I'M BAAAAAACK! Let's just say, I'm filming as we speak.

—THE ADVOCATE—

Christian Cosmetology International Association

AS AN ADVOCATE of Christ, it is my hope to bring more cosmetologists to the fold and to demonstrate the value in approaching the profession from a spiritual disposition. There is so much power in doing so. We have healing hands.

The Elgin Charles Foundation

THE ELGIN CHARLES Foundation seeks to provide complimentary wigs to cancer patients and those who suffer from alopecia.

By the time you read this, I will have walked away from the salon as you knew it, with my hair blowing in the wind. So much of what I've accomplished has been for others. On this day, I proclaim that I will resolve to live the rest of my life for me. I will continue to touch lives and to leave a lasting impression in the world. For me, a life lived well is about the impact that you have made and how many hearts that you have touched. May God allow my hands the freedom, liberty, and power to touch the world until I take my last breath. This is my solemn vow. Amen.

BY THE WAY

Watch the Throne

BEING YOUR FATHER, taught me the greatest and most profound lessons and it is my desire to commit them to paper that they may never depart from your heart. It is my solemn prayer that these lessons will embed themselves into your soul and bring you comfort that surpasses all understanding.

I'm not certain that I have ever taken the time to express to you, who I was and all that was inside of me. I knew that my time would be better spent raising you and carving out a lane, that you might realize your own success. I believed that God had called me to shield you from the complexities of my life. I knew that they were not your cross to bear, for you had been given your own. All that I've ever wanted to do was to walk beside you, helping you to carry your cross. Sharing in this load has been my greatest joy. Taking ownership of your life has been the most rewarding thing that I have ever done.

—LOVE LIVES INSIDE OF YOU—

ALONG MY JOURNEY of life, I've searched for a love that I could call my own and one that I could believe in. I've looked high and low for a love that would restore my faith in the good in humanity and one that would accept me for who and what I was. We all desire to be loved and to discover love. I believe this to be human nature. There is, however, great fault in searching aimlessly for love. There is heartbreak that can and will occur in this space. I've learned that love isn't something that we can seek out, it must be found within.

Prior to you, I was in search of the power that I believed love to possess. I never found it, until I found you. When I was ordained by God to love you, it taught me how to be selfless and to give more love than I even believed I possessed.

When you find an innocent spirit, so pure and so full of fire, you realize that you are holding life itself in the palm of your hands. I had been deemed the keeper of your soul. This burden was worth every moment that I had dedicated towards this end. Being responsible for another life, inevitably means that your life and your desires are no longer first. The things that were once important to me, took a hard second to anything that did not involve nurturing you. For you, I was willing to put my life on hold. For you, I was willing to risk my life to save yours. I would have done anything to make sure that you had everything. In return, I experienced the touch of your unconditional love. The bond between parent and child is one that is not easily broken. God sent you to me, after having prepared me to understand your challenges and struggles, even before you would understand them. He allowed me to quiet the raging storms of your life. God instilled in me an empathy for your journey before you had ever even set out on it. Loving you, made me understand God's why.

It is because of you that I now know that love is replenished; the more that you give away in good faith, the more that is returned. This epitomizes the defining factor that love lives, breathes, and thrives inside of you. It can only be found there. The quest to discover love in other places is an empty search. Love lives in you. And when you recognize this truth to be self-evident, God will open the doors to the abundance.

——HEIR TO THE THRONE——

WATCHING YOU LEARN, grow, and wander in the world has demonstrated that the essence of all that I have taught you was not in vain. I see so much of myself inside of you. Your presence has allowed me to see my future. The birth of your son will allow you to bear witness to yours. Together, you are the most precious jewels of my crown. You are the heirs to my throne. The Bible teaches us that parents are supposed to leave their inheritance to their grandchildren and it has become so clear to me that the teachings grant us wisdom to build a legacy. I feel yet another urgency in my heart to ensure that you are prepared to cultivate your son as I have cultivated you.

It is my wish for you to know without question that my heart belongs to each of you. I want for you to know that I love you with the deepness of my heart. Above all, I know that God has equipped you with so much. Never forget that within you lies the power to achieve all the goals that your heart desires. You have that stock in your blood. You are the head and not the tail. You shall be above and never beneath. You are a winner at all times.

In our lives, the greatest work that we will ever engage in, is the establishment of a legacy. There were so many ingredients poured into me by my mother and father that cultivated the success that I've realized in my life. It is my desire to ensure that this same recipe is preserved and sustained and passed down that it might live on forever. You are the heirs to the throne. May you forever reign.

AFTERWORD

A S MANAGER AND CONFIDANT to Elgin Charles, it has been both my mission and my honor to create opportunities for the world to see the man behind the brand. So much was unknown regarding his journey and his legacy, and the spellbinding layers that composed who he was and all that he has evolved into. After coming across the social media pages of acclaimed writer and book publishing expert, Ardre Orie, and her publishing house, 13th & Joan, I was captivated by the passion conveyed for telling the greatest stories of our souls. I knew immediately that there would be immense power in Elgin chronicling his life's story.

There have been many compelling themes that have encompassed Elgin's triumphant life and rise to fame. These themes allowed me to recognize that perhaps his purpose is to speak to the hearts, minds, and spirits of those in a world that is in dire need of the same answers that he sought in his quest to live unapologetically.

Throughout his entire life, the need to please others has prevailed. This is true for many of us. Nestled behind the glamorous exterior was a small voice, crying out in the distance; pleading for self-actualization. Elgin is a radiant being whose light can not, under any circumstances, be dimmed, although many have tried. It was, and still is, my belief that this intricate process of storytelling would unveil the layers and allow him the unprecedented opportunity to think, speak, walk, and embody the fullness of truth.

I have watched him live in captivity, concerned with the notions of what others have professed about him. I have heard people sully his name and besmirch his character. I have looked on while his head was bloodied, but unbowed, by the daggers which society threw. Even with his appearances on television, they tried to create a vision and narrative of what a salon for clients of color would be in Beverly Hills. It stops today. His memoir serves as the end of a slanderous era and the birth of new beginnings. Every preconceived notion, ends. Documenting his truth in this book has resulted in the unequivocal reprieve of his heart. The pages are symbolic of freedom ringing from the mountaintops.

Ever the protector of others, it is carefully chronicled, in these pages, that he has had very few people who have existed or served simply to protect him. I have assumed that role in many ways. I have watched with my eyes and listened with my ears, as he has been victimized through manipulation and the abhorrent behavior of others. The most prolific testament of his character is that never once, in all of the years that we have worked together, has he allowed any of this to harden his heart. He cares about his family, his friends, and his clients and those whom he meets in passing. Above all, faith is the guiding force in his actions and the way that he thinks. The world needs more of him.

In an industry where you have to be cocky, arrogant, and sometimes, even an asshole, to be taken seriously and to earn the respect needed to be well positioned, he is none of those things. In general, he is wired to take an Oprah approach to life. He believes in spirit and in truth and that the ill treatment of others does not grant you access to success. He believes that everyone can and should eat off the fat of the land. This is one of the many secrets to his longevity as The Emperor of Hair. His clients know that he exists to make them look and feel their finest. He genuinely wants the best for all. And because he generously fills the spiritual cups of so many, I recognize that he too has a need for the same acts of benevolence. No one has been there to do that for him. If for no other reason, the etchings of this book, are a testament to the fact that Elgin Charles is not alone.

This book also illuminates the fact that Elgin Charles is a shrewd businessman. He is the first African American proprietor of a salon in Beverly Hills. He has been invited to the largest stages in the world and has maintained the intellectual prowess to see every venture that he began, through to fruition. There is no one that has reached the heights that he has in his industry. With appearances on *Oprah, The View, The Talk,* and *Wendy Williams,* he has managed to generate millions and become the true embodiment of fortitude.

Elgin desperately needed to write this book because there are so many who suffer in isolation and silence; feeling as though their very best is not good enough. There is someone, somewhere, right now, who feels that they can't live their best life for fear of rejection or the backlash they may receive. But none of it matters at the end of the day. We must remember these words, "Judge Ye Not."

I wanted for Elgin to experience the freedom that can only be derived from walking in truth. I wanted for Elgin to create something that would speak of his lineage that one day his grandchild might read and discover a piece of himself. I wanted for Elgin to express his thoughts and deepest sentiments on his eccentricities that he never felt safe sharing. This book is Elgin's moment in which to say to the world, "This is all of me. Take me in the fullness of who I am and what God has created me to be."

The central theme that prevails is the "search for love." The truth is that we are all looking for love and divine connections. The force that is Elgin Charles, exudes love. If we become a bit more empathetic, the world as we know it would be a very different place. That is what he represents. That is what the world will remember him most for. This is the life, love, and legacy of the force that is Elgin Charles!

ABOUT THE AUTHOR

ELGIN CHARLES, known the world over as the "Emperor of Hair," has been the proprietor of his upscale beauty salon in the heart of Beverly Hills for more than twenty-five years. The San Antonio, Texas native can best be described as a scholar and creative genius; due in part to rearing from both his father, a biochemist, and his mother, an award-winning blues singer. Never one to rest on his laurels, Elgin decided to walk away from a highly successful career in finance at Smith Barney in his early twenties, in pursuit of his passion – hair!

His innovative styles and techniques have made him one of the most sought-after celebrity hair stylists in the industry today. His client roster has included: Joan Collins, Diahann Carroll, Drew Barrymore, Serena Williams, Gabrielle Union, Joy Behar, Estelle, Verdine White, Star Jones, Natalie Cole, Tia & Tamera Mowry, Baroness Monica von Neumann, and countless other notables. With a background in biology and chemistry from St. Mary's University, Elgin has developed his own signature line of luxury hair care products that fosters the needs of those with varying styles and types of hair. His principles for attaining one's beauty and life goals can be found in his top-selling book, *Believe It, Conceive It, Achieve It.*

Elgin and his ex-wife, television icon Jackée Harry, have a son together, Frank; a graduate of Beverly Hills High and an aspiring

professional boxer. In addition to family, Elgin, a known philanthropist, is giving of his time and resources to a number of causes;
chiefly, United Way, United Negro College Fund, Women's International Center, and Daughter's Of Power.

Elgin is also a very giving performer, with his talents ventur-
ing far beyond the beauty industry. He has made appearances in
Chris Rock's critically-acclaimed documentary *Good Hair*, the Style
Network's *Split Ends*, countless talk shows, including *Oprah*, *The
View*, *The Talk*, and *Wendy Williams*, and has even starred in his
own top-rated VH1 docuseries, *Beverly Hills Fabulous*.

Although he is already at the top of the hair industry heap, Elgin
continues to expand upon his globally recognized brand. Additional salon locations, a school of cosmetology, and an expanded
product line are all in the works. Elgin Charles is an undeniable
force and an icon in the multi-billion-dollar hair industry. His phi-
losophy is, "It doesn't cost to look beautiful… it pays!"

CONNECT WITH ELGIN CHARLES ON
SOCIAL MEDIA @ELGINCHARLES

WEBSITE: www.elgincharles.com
FACEBOOK: ElginCharlesBeverlyHills
TWITTER: Twitter.com/ElginCharles
INSTAGRAM: Instagram.com/ElginCharles

CPSIA information can be obtained
at www.ICGtesting.com
Printed in the USA
BVHW071315120321
602296BV00003B/200